The International Legal Regime of Areas beyond National Jurisdiction: Current and Future Developments

Nova et Vetera Iuris Gentium

Publications of the Institute of Public International Law of Utrecht University

Series A: Modern International Law

VOLUME 26

The International Legal Regime of Areas beyond National Jurisdiction: Current and Future Developments

Edited by

Alex G. Oude Elferink
and Erik J. Molenaar

MARTINUS
NIJHOFF
PUBLISHERS

LEIDEN • BOSTON
2010

This book is printed on acid-free paper.

Library of Congress Cataloging-in-Publication Data

The international legal regime of areas beyond national jurisdiction : current and future developments / edited by Alex G. Oude Elferink and Erik J. Molenaar.

p. cm. – (Nova et vetera iuris gentium. Series A, Modern international law ; No. 26)
Includes bibliographical references and index.
ISBN 978-90-04-17097-1 (hardback : alk. paper)
1. Marine resources development–Law and legislation. I. Oude Elferink, Alex G., 1962-
II. Molenaar, Erik Jaap.

K3485.I58 2010
346.04'6916415–dc22

2009043641

ISSN 1871-6725
ISBN 978 90 04 17097 1

PRINTED IN THE NETHERLANDS

CONTENTS

PART THREE

ENTITLEMENTS TO MARINE LIVING RESOURCES

PART FOUR

COMPLIANCE WITH INTERNATIONAL REGULATIONS: ADDRESSING ENFORCEMENT GAPS IN THE LEGAL REGIME FOR AREAS BEYOND NATIONAL JURISDICTION

LUNCHEON SPEECH

PREFACE

This book is based on the proceedings of the Fourth J.H.W. Verzijl Memorial Symposium, which was organized by the Institute of Public International Law and the Netherlands Institute for the Law of the Sea (NILOS) of Utrecht University and took place in Utrecht on 21 November 2008. This series of international law symposia is named after professor Jan Verzijl, who held the chair of public international law at Utrecht University between 1918 and 1958, to recognize the important contributions he made to the study and practice of international law.[1]

The Third J.H.W. Verzijl Memorial Symposium, which was held in December 2004, took place 11 years after the previous Verzijl Symposium.[2] The lively debate and stimulating exchanges of views at the Third Symposium confirmed that too much time had passed since the previous Symposium. Having now held the Fourth J.H.W. Verzijl Memorial Symposium we are looking forward to continue to convene the Symposia on a more regular basis. The Fourth Symposium again confirmed the attractiveness of the Symposium's format. Well in advance of the Symposium, four reporters submit a fully developed draft of their presentations, allowing the four commentators and other participants due time to form an opinion. This format of the Symposium was, we feel, appreciated by all participants, who actively took part in the debate that followed after the presentations of the reporters and commentators.

In drawing up the final versions of their reports and commentaries, the contributors to the present proceedings could profit from these discussions. This book contains the texts of the four reports presented at the Symposium (by Tullio Treves, Tullio Scovazzi, Richard Barnes and Rosemary Rayfuse respectively) with such changes as the authors saw fit to make in the light of the debate at the symposium. It also includes the main commentaries of Daniel Owen, Nele Matz-Lück, Andrew Serdy and Rónan Long, comments submitted by participants and the luncheon speech by the Vice-President

[1] For an account of the life and work of professor Verzijl see C.G. Roelofsen *Jan Hendrik Willem Verzijl 1888–1987* (T.M.C. Asser Instituut, The Hague: 1993).

[2] The proceedings of first three Symposia have been published (see A.H.A. Soons (ed.) *International Arbitration: Past and Prospects* (Martinus Nijhoff Publishers, Dordrecht: 1990); H.H.G. Post (ed.) *International Economic Law and Armed Conflict* (Martinus Nijhoff Publishers, Dordrecht: 1994); and A.G. Oude Elferink (ed.) *Stability and Change in the Law of the Sea: The Role of the LOS Convention* (Martinus Nijhoff Publishers, Leiden: 2005).

of the International Tribunal for the Law of the Sea, Helmut Tuerk. These texts are preceded by an introduction that discusses the overall theme of the symposium, the choice of specific topics and its outcomes.

The Symposium would not have been possible without financial support from a number of sources, including the G.J. Wiarda Research Institute of the Faculty of Law of Utrecht University. We also would like to thank the participants to the Symposium for creating the stimulating environment in which the contributions to the present proceedings took their final form. Special thanks are due to Esther van Weele of the Institute of Public International Law/NILOS for her diligent assistance in preparing the manuscript of the texts and the lists included in these proceedings. Finally, our appreciation goes to Peter Buschman, Hans van der Mey, Ingeborg van der Laan, and Anita Roodnat at Martinus Nijhoff Publishers for getting this book ready for submission to its intended audience.

Utrecht, 15 July 2009

Just before this book went to press we were informed of the sad news that Louise de La Fayette passed away after a period of illness. We will remember Louise for her dedication to the law of the sea and her kind personality. She participated actively in the Fourth Verzijl Symposium and her four contributions to this volume bear witness to the broad scope of her interest in, and knowledge, of the oceans and the law of the sea.

Utrecht, 2 December 2009

Alfred H.A. Soons
Chairman of the Fourth J.H.W. Verzijl Memorial Symposium
Professor of public international law
Director, NILOS

Erik J. Molenaar
Senior research associate, NILOS

Alex G. Oude Elferink
Deputy Director, NILOS

ABBREVIATIONS

1994 Agreement	Agreement Relating to the Implementation of Part XI of the United Nations Convention on the Law of the Sea of 10 December 1982
Aarhus Convention	Convention on Access to Information, Public Participation in Decision-making and Access to Justice in Environmental Matters
ABNJ	areas beyond national jurisdiction
AC	Appeal Cases (Law Reports, England and Wales)
ACE	annual catch entitlement
AJIL	American Journal of International Law
ATS	Antarctic Treaty System
CBD	Convention on Biological Diversity
CCAMLR	Convention on the Conservation of Antarctic Marine Living Resources
CCSBT	Commission for the Conservation of Southern Bluefin Tuna
Ch	Chancery Division (Law Reports, England and Wales)
CHM	Common Heritage of Mankind
CLR	Crown Lands Law Reports (Queensland Land Court)
COFI	Committee on Fisheries
Compliance Agreement	Agreement to Promote Compliance with International Conservation and Measures by Fishing Vessels on the High Seas
CRAMRA	Convention on the Regulation of Antarctic Mineral Resources
DOALOS	Division for Ocean Affairs and the Law of the Sea
EC	European Community
ECJ	European Court of Justice
EEZ	exclusive economic zone
EU	European Union
FAO	Food and Agriculture Organization
Fish Stocks Agreement	Agreement for the Implementation of the Provisions of the United Nations Convention on the Law of the Sea of 10 December 1982 relating to the Conservation and Management of Straddling Fish Stocks and Highly Migratory Fish Stocks
Fish Stocks Conference	United Nations Conference on Straddling Fish Stocks and Highly Migratory Fish Stocks
FLR	Federal Law Reports
FSI	flag State implementation
GISIS	Global Integrated Shipping Information System

Guidelines on Deep-Sea Fisheries	International Guidelines for the Management of Deep-Sea Fisheries in the High Seas
HSTF	High Seas Task Force
ICCAT	International Commission for the Conservation of Atlantic Tunas
ICJ	International Court of Justice
ICP	United Nations Informal Consultative Process on Oceans and the Law of the Sea
ICPC	International Cable Protection Committee
ILC	International Law Commission
ILM	International Legal Materials
ILO	International Labour Organisation
ILR	International Law Reports
ILS	International Legal System
IMO	International Maritime Organization
ISA	International Seabed Authority
ITLOS	International Tribunal for the Law of the Sea
ITQs	Individual Transferable Quotas
IUCN	International Union for the Conservation of Nature
IUU fishing	illegal, unreported and unregulated fishing
KB	King's Bench Division (Law Reports, England and Wales)
Kyoto Protocol	Protocol to the Framework Convention on Climate Change
LNTS	League of Nations Treaty Series
London Convention	Convention for the Prevention of Marine Pollution by Dumping of Wastes and Other Matter
London Protocol	Protocol to the Convention on the Prevention of Marine Pollution by Dumping of Wastes and Other Matter
LOS Convention	United Nations Convention on the Law of the Sea
MARPOL	International Convention for the Prevention of Pollution from Ships
MCE	monitoring, control and enforcement
MCS	monitoring, control and surveillance
Moon Treaty	Agreement Governing the Activities of States on the Moon and Other Celestial Bodies
MOU	Memorandum of Understanding
MSC	Maritime Safety Committee
MSP	marine spatial planning
MSR	marine scientific research
NAFO	Northwest Atlantic Fisheries Organization
NEAFC	North-East Atlantic Fisheries Commission
NGO	Non-Governmental Organization
NIEO	New International Economic Order
Nm	nautical mile
NZCA	New Zealand Court of Appeal
NZLR	New Zealand Law Reports

OECD	Organisation for Economic Co-operation and Development
OSPAR Convention	Convention for the Protection of the Marine Environment of the North-East Atlantic
Outer Space Treaty	Treaty on Principles Governing the Activities of States in the Exploration and Use of Outer Space Including the Moon and Other Celestial Bodies
PSC	port State control
QB	Queen's Bench Reports
Registration Convention	United Nations Convention on Conditions for the Registration of Ships
RFMA	regional fisheries management arrangement
RFMO	regional fisheries management organization
RIAA	United Nations Reports of International Arbitral Awards
Rome Conference	International Technical Conference on the Living Resources of the Sea
RSO	regional sea organization
SBSTTA	Subsidiary Body on Scientific, Technical and Technological Advice
SOLAS	International Convention for the Safety of Life at Sea
STCW	International Convention on Standards of Training, Certification and Watchkeeping for Seafarers
TAC	total allowable catch
UKHL	Law Report (UK), House of Lords
UKTS	United Kingdom Treaty Series
UNCED	United Nations Conference on Environment and Development
UNCLOS III	Third United Nations Conference on the Law of the Sea
UNECE	United Nations Economic Commission for Europe
UNGA	United Nations General Assembly
US	United States
UNTS	United Nations Treaty Series
Vienna Convention	Vienna Convention on the Law of Treaties
VMS	vessel monitoring system
WCPFC	Commission for the Conservation and Management of Highly Migratory Fish Stocks in the Western and Central Pacific Ocean

LIST OF ARBITRATIONS, CASES AND JUDGMENTS

Allan Guard v. *Seafood Consortium Ltd and Ors* (United States of America/ United Kingdom) [2001] NZCA 291
Behring Fur Seals Arbitration (1893) RIAA, vol. XXVIII
Case Concerning the Conservation and Sustainable Exploitation of Swordfish Stocks in the South-Eastern Pacific Ocean (Chile v. European Community) (2001) 40 ILM 474
Case Concerning the Territorial Dispute (Libya v. Chad) [1994] ICJ Reports 6
Certain Norwegian Loans case (France v. Norway) [1957] ICJ Reports 9
Commission of the European Communities v. Ireland C-459/03 [2006] ECJ, Official Journal of the European Union 2006/C 165/04
Commission of the European Communities v. United Kingdom Case C-6/04 [2006] ECR [0000]
Cooper v. *AG* [1996] 3 NZLR 480
The Esso Malaysia case [1978] QB 198
Fisheries Jurisdiction case (Spain v. Canada) [1995] ICJ Reports 97
France v. United Kingdom Case 141/78 [1979] ECR 2923
Free Zones case [1932] PCIJ (Ser. A/B) No 4
George Rodney Burt (U.S.) v. Great Britain in F.K. Neilsen *Report on American and British Claims Arbitration under Agreement of August 8, 1910* (GPO, Washington: 1926) 588
Grand Prince case (Belize v. France) case No. 8 [1999] 7 ITLOS 17
Gunn v. AG [1993] NZLR 108
Hoshinmaru case (Japan vs. Russian Federation) case No. 14 [2007] ITLOS
The Iron Rhine Arbitration (Belgium v. the Netherlands) [2005] XXVII Reports of International Arbitral Awards
Islands of Palmas case (Netherlands v. United States) [1928] 2 RIAA 829
Jacobsen v. Norwegian Government [1933] 7 ILR 109
John E. Gowen and Franklin Copeland v. Venezuela [1890] in J.B. Moore *History and Digest of the International Arbitrations to Which the United States has been a Party* (1898) 3354–3359
Jones v. *United* States [1890] 137 US Supreme Court 202
Kuwait Airways Corporation v. *Iraqi Airways Company* [2002] UKHL 19
Land Reclamation by Singapore in and around the Straits of Johor (Malaysia v. Singapore) case No. 12 [2003] ITLOS 10
Legality of the Threat or Use of Nuclear Weapons in Armed Conflict, Advisory Opinion [1996] 1 ICJ Reports 226
Lotus case (France v. Turkey) [1927] PCIJ (Ser. A) No 10
Luthor v. *Sagor* [1921] 3 KB 532
Mabo v. *Queensland (No. 2)* [1992] 175 CLR 1
Milirrpum v. *Nabalco Pty Ltd* [1971] 17 FLR 141
The MOX Plant Case (Ireland v. United Kingdom) (2002) 41 ILM 405
The M/V "SAIGA" (No. 2) case (Saint Vincent and the Grenadines v. Guinea) (1999) 38 ILM 1323

North Sea Continental Shelf cases (Federal Republic of Germany v. Denmark; Federal Republic of Germany v. The Netherlands) [1969] ICJ Reports 3
Norwegian Loans case [1957] ICJ Reports 9
Nottebohm case (Guatemala v. Lichtenstein) [1955] ICJ Reports 4
Ocean Estates Ltd v. Pinder [1969] 2 AC 16
Seawatch International v. *Mossbacher*, 762 F. Supp. 370 (DDC 1991)
Southern Bluefin Tuna (New Zealand v. Japan; Australia v. Japan) (1999) 38 ILM 1624; (2000) 39 ILM 1359
Spain v. United Kingdom Case C-145/04 [2006] ECR I-7917
Te Weehi v. Regional Fisheries Officer [1986] 1 NZLR 680
Tomimaru case (Japan v. Russian Federation) (2007) 46 ILM 1183
Trail Smelter (United States v. Canada) (1941) 3 Reports of International Arbitral Awards 1905, reprinted in (1941) 35 AJIL 684
The Tubantia Hague Court Reports (New York, 1932) 135
Western Sahara case [1975] ICJ Reports 12
Winkworth v. *Christie Manson & Woods* [1980] 1 Ch. 496
The Zollverein Reports of cases decided in the High Court of Admiralty of England, and on appeal to the Privy Council (M.C. Merttins Swabey (ed.)) 96

LIST OF CONVENTIONS, TREATIES AND OTHER INTERNATIONAL INSTRUMENTS

1885 Final Act of the Conference of Berlin, done in Berlin, 26 February 1885, 165 Consolidated Treaty Series 485

1919 Treaty of Peace with Germany, done in Versailles, 28 June 1919, in force 10 January 1920, (1919) 13 AJIL Supplement 151

1920 Treaty concerning the Archipelago of Spitsbergen, done in Paris 9 February 1920, in force 14 August 1925, 2 LNTS 7

1945 Financial Agreement between the Governments of the United States of America and the United Kingdom of Great Britain and Northern Ireland, done in Washington, 6 December 1945, 126 UNTS 13

1959 Antarctic Treaty, done in Washington 1 December 1959, in force in 1961, 402 UNTS 71

1967 The Treaty on Principles Governing the Activities of States in the Exploration and Use of Outer Space Including the Moon and Other Celestial Bodies, done in Washington, 27 January 1967, in force 10 October 1967, 610 UNTS 205

1968 Agreement on the Rescue of Astronauts, the Return of Astronauts and the Return of Objects Launched into Outer Space, done in New York, 22 April 1968, in force 3 December 1968 (1969) 63 AJIL 382

1969 Vienna Convention on the Law of Treaties, done in Vienna, 23 May 1969, in force 27 January 1980, 1155 UNTS 331

1970 Declaration of Principles Governing the Sea Bed and Ocean Floor, and the Subsoil Thereof, beyond the Limits of National Jurisdiction of 17 December 1970 ((1971) 10 ILM 220)

1972 Convention for the Prevention of Marine Pollution by Dumping of Wastes and Other Matter, done in London, 29 December 1972, in force 30 August 1975 (1976) UKTS 43

1973 International Convention for the Prevention of Pollution from Ships, done in London, 2 November 1973, in force 2 October 1983, as amended by the 1978 Protocol, done in London, in force 2 October 1983, 1340 UNTS 61

1974 International Convention for the Safety of Life at Sea, done in London, 1 November 1974, in force 25 May 1980, 1184 UNTS 2

1978 Convention on Future Multilateral Cooperation in the Northwest Atlantic Fisheries, done in Ottowa, 24 October 1978, in force 1 January 1979, 1135 UNTS 369

The International Convention on Standards of Training, Certification and Watchkeeping for Seafarers, done in London, 7 July 1978, in force 28 April 1984, 1361 UNTS 190

1979 Agreement Governing the Activities of States on the Moon and Other Celestial Bodies, done in New York, 18 December 1979, in force 11 July 1984 (1979) 18 ILM 1434

1980 Convention on the Conservation of Antarctic Marine Living Resources, done in Canberra, 20 May 1980, in force 7 April 1982, 1329 UNTS 47

Convention on Future Multilateral Cooperation in the Northeast Atlantic Fisheries, done in London, 18 November 1980, in force 17 March 1982, 1285 UNTS 129

1982 United Nations Convention on the Law of the Sea, done in Montego Bay, 10 December 1982, in force 16 November 1994, 1833 UNTS 396

1986 United Nations Convention on Conditions for the Registration of Ships, done in Geneva, 7 February 1986, not yet into force (1987) 26 ILM 1229

1988 Convention on the Regulation of Antarctic Mineral Resource Activities, Wellington, 2 June 1988, not into force (1988) 27 ILM 868

1991 Protocol on Environmental Protection to the Antarctic Treaty, done in Madrid, 4 October 1991, in force 15 January 1998 (1991) 30 ILM 1455

1992 United Nations Framework Convention on Climate Change, done in New York, 9 May 1992, in force 21 March 1994 (1992) 31 ILM 849

Convention on Biological Diversity, done in Rio de Janeiro, 5 June 1992, in force 29 December 1993 (1992) 31 ILM 818

Convention for the Protection of the Marine Environment of the North-East Atlantic, done in Paris, 22 September 1992, in force 25 March 1998 (1993) 32 ILM 1072 and Annex 5, done in Sintra, 23 September 1998, in force 30 August 2000 (amended and updated text available at ⟨www.ospar.org⟩)

1993 Agreement to Promote Compliance with International Conservation and Management Measures by Fishing Vessels on the High Seas, done in Rome, 24 November 1993, in force 24 April 2003 (1994) 33 ILM 968

1994 Agreement Relating to the Implementation of Part XI of the United Nations Convention on the Law of the Sea of 10 December 1982, done in New York, 28 July 1994, in force 28 July 1996 (1994) 33 ILM 1309

1995 Agreement for the Implementation of the Provisions of the United Nations Convention on the Law of the Sea of 10 December 1982 Relating to the Conservation and Management of Straddling Fish Stocks and Highly Migratory Fish Stocks, done in New York, 4 August 1995, in force 11 December 2001, 2167 UNTS 3

Amendment to the the International Convention on Standards of Training, Certification and Watchkeeping for Seafarers, done in London, 7 July 1995, in force 1 February 1997 (1997) UKTS 61

1996 Protocol to the Convention on the Prevention of Marine Pollution by Dumping of Wastes and Other Matter of 29 December 1972, done in London, 7 November 1996, in force 24 March 2006 (2006) Australian Treaty Series 11

1997 Protocol to the Framework Convention on Climate Change, done in Kyoto, 11 December 1997, in force 16 February 2005, 2303 UNTS 162

1998 UNECE Convention on Access to Information, Public Participation in Decision-making and Access to Justice in Environmental Matters, done in Aarhus, 25 June 1998, in force 30 October 2001, 2161 UNTS 447

2001 Convention on the Protection of the Underwater Cultural Heritage, done in Paris, 2 November 2001, in force 12 January 2009 (2002) 41 ILM 40

International Treaty on Plant Genetic Resources for Food and Agriculture, done in Rome, in force 29 June 2004, ⟨www.fao.org/Legal⟩

2007 International Convention on the Removal of Wrecks, done in Nairobi, 18 May 2007, not yet in force (2007) 46 ILM 694

INTRODUCTION

Erik J. Molenaar and Alex G. Oude Elferink

States and entrepreneurs are becoming increasingly interested in the economic potential of ocean areas beyond the national jurisdiction of coastal States.[1] This concerns both an intensification and spatial extension of existing activities, such as for instance fisheries and the development of new activities such as bioprospecting for genetic resources of the Area.

These developments have led to growing support within the international community to enhance the international legal regime for those areas, among other things to protect and preserve the environment and biodiversity. However, the current debate in international fora indicates that States have widely different interpretations on key aspects of this regime, for instance whether or not bioprospecting for genetic resources of the Area is governed by the principle of the common heritage of mankind.

The purpose of the Fourth J.H.W. Verzijl Memorial Symposium was to contribute to a better understanding of the international law aspects of the ongoing debate on current and future international governance and regulation of areas beyond national jurisdiction (ABNJ). To this end four specific topics were selected, on which papers were presented at four consecutive sessions:

- principles and objectives of the legal regime;
- institutional arrangements for the legal regime;
- entitlements to marine living resources; and
- compliance with international regulations.

In his report, which was presented at the first session of the Symposium, Tullio Treves sheds his light on the substantive dimension of the international legal regime of ABNJ. As a preliminary issue, he explores the reasons why—despite

[1] This concerns the high seas and the Area. Art 1(1)(1) of the United Nations Convention on the Law of the Sea (LOS Convention) provides that the Area "means the seabed and ocean floor and subsoil thereof, beyond the limits of national jurisdiction". Art. 86 of Part VII of the LOS Convention, which is concerned with the high seas, provides that:

> The provisions of this Part apply to all parts of the sea that are not included in the exclusive economic zone, in the territorial sea or in the internal waters of a State, or in the archipelagic waters of an archipelagic State.

Alex G. Oude Elferink and Erik J. Molenaar (eds.), *The International Legal Regime of Areas beyond National Jurisdiction: Current and Future Developments*, pp. 1–3.

broad support for the ecosystem approach—the international community often tends to give priority to addressing issues relating to ABNJ rather than issues relating to areas within national jurisdiction. The main body of his report is devoted to current discussions and models for governance of ABNJ, with two foci: genetic resources of the Area and a general regime for ABNJ—the latter discussion making ample references to the IUCN 'Principles for High Seas Governance' of October 2008. The commentary on Tullio Treves' report by Daniel Owen focuses on two issues in particular, namely on making the 'due regard' concept in international law more precise and on stakeholder participation in decision-making.

Tullio Scovazzi's report to the second session is entitled 'The Seabed beyond the Limits of National Jurisdiction: General and Institutional Aspects'. The principle of the common heritage of mankind plays a pivotal role in his report, both its historical background and current and future relevance, for instance in relation to genetic resources of the Area. His report highlights the controversy surrounding the relevance of the principle in the ongoing debate in the framework of the General Assembly of the United Nations That point is also illustrated by the contribution of the commentator to this session—Nele Matz-Lück—and the title she has chosen for her commentary entitled 'The Concept of the Common Heritage of Mankind: Its Viability as a Management Tool for Deep-Sea Genetic Resources'. In her opinion, the common heritage approach cannot be employed as a legal and institutional model for future instruments on deep-sea genetic resources.

The third and fourth sessions of the Symposium were essentially thematic. Richard Barnes' report for the third session—'Entitlement to Marine Living Resources in Areas Beyond National Jurisdiction' investigates the possibility of regulating marine capture fisheries in ABNJ by means of property rights-based entitlements established within regional fisheries management organizations (RFMOs). In that connection he takes account of experience and practice within several arenas, for instance Antarctica, outer space and the deep seabed. His report concludes with some thoughtful observations on allocations of entitlements under international law. Andrew Serdy's commentary for this session—entitled 'Property Rights in Areas Beyond National Jurisdiction: Not Too Late for a Proper Debate?'—in a sense complements Barnes' report. One of his key concerns is that property rights are in fact already "being unsystematically and fitfully consolidated through the collective hypocrisy of fishing States, who are not being held to account to the generality of States for their past over-exploitation, and with no prospect of compensation for those States affected by the loss of freedom of fishing." This thought illustrates the potential impact of State practice on the principles underpinning the current legal regime of the oceans, in the absence of an accompanying debate on the significance of those principles. It could be argued that this is in a sense a variation of the 'creeping jurisdiction' of coastal States in especially the second half of the 20th century, which also significantly curtailed the scope of application of the regime of the high seas.

The fourth and last session of the Symposium opened with a report by Rosemary Rayfuse entitled 'The Anthropocene, Autopoiesis and the Disingenuousness of the Genuine Link: Addressing Enforcement Gaps in the Legal Regime for Areas Beyond National Jurisdiction'. The inadequacy of the genuine link for dealing with enforcement in ABNJ is among other things discussed in relation to high seas fishing and dumping at sea. Rayfuse concludes with a number of suggestions to address this inadequacy, not only through such mainstream ideas as removing or reducing incentives to engage in undesirable activities but also through progressively developing international law by non-flag State action, possibly culminating in international dispute settlement procedures. Ronán Long's commentary contains valuable insights on the thought-provoking terms 'anthropocene' and 'autopoiesis' and ends with some observations on the role of international dispute settlement, among other things in light of experiences within the European Community.

The debates that ensued on these reports and commentaries were both lively and informative. Louise de La Fayette's interventions during the debates in all sessions were further developed after the Symposium and are incorporated in these proceedings. A welcome first of this Fourth Verzijl Symposium was having a luncheon speech. The written text of that speech by Helmut Tuerk—entitled 'The Contribution of the International Tribunal for the Law of the Sea to International Law'—is also reproduced in the proceedings.

The editors feel these proceedings make a contribution to a better understanding of key international law aspects of the ongoing debate on current and future international governance and regulation of ABNJ. Hopefully also, some of the suggestions identified in these proceedings for addressing gaps and shortcomings in the current regime find their way into the ongoing debate. There can be little doubt that there remains an urgent need for the further elaboration and implementation of the current framework regime for ABNJ to take proper account of the protection and preservation of the marine environment, the conservation of marine biodiversity and the sustainable, fair and equitable use and allocation of their resources.

PART ONE

PRINCIPLES AND OBJECTIVES OF THE LEGAL REGIME GOVERNING AREAS BEYOND NATIONAL JURISDICTION

PRINCIPLES AND OBJECTIVES OF THE LEGAL REGIME GOVERNING AREAS BEYOND NATIONAL JURISDICTION

TULLIO TREVES*

1. *Regime and Machinery*

The idea of 'governance' does not belong to common legal parlance, even though lawyers, under the pressure of political scientists, have started using it. 'Governance' at least as far as the present writer understands it, contains something more than 'government'. It includes the idea of 'good' government, government for the general interest of those governed, on the basis of commonly shared values and with the involvement of stakeholders. Also the idea of 'government' encompassed in that of governance does not coincide with the concept used under that name by lawyers. It has no reference to doctrines such as the separation of powers. It alludes to all forms of regulation and of the enforcement of such regulation in a given area or on a given subject. Sometimes the domestic law concept of 'government' is echoed in the use of the expression 'governance gaps' as against 'regulatory gaps' in opposing the lack of a competent organization to the lack of substantive legal rules in a geographical area or on a given subject. The latter distinction has been proposed recently on subjects concerning the oceans.[1]

Although expressed by other words, this distinction has been present since the beginning of the negotiations leading to the conclusion of the United Nations Convention for the Law of the Sea (LOS Convention).[2] The 1970 Declaration of Principles Governing the Seabed and the Ocean Floor, and the Subsoil thereof, beyond the Limits of National Jurisdiction, a key starting point of that negotiation, as regards the mineral resources of the deep seabed, makes a distinction between a 'regime' and a 'machinery'.[3] It is clear that

* Judge of the International Tribunal for the Law of the Sea; Professor at the University of Milano.

[1] K.M. Gjerde, with the assistance of H. Dotinga, S. Hart, E.J. Molenaar, R. Rayfuse, R. Warner *Regulatory and Governance Gaps in the International Regime for the Conservation and Sustainable Use of Marine Biodiversity in Areas Beyond National Jurisdiction* IUCN Marine Series No. 1 (IUCN, Gland: 2008).

[2] Adopted on 10 December 1982; 1833 UNTS 396.

[3] UN General Assembly resolution 2749 (XXV) of 17 December 1970. Article 9 states in

Alex G. Oude Elferink and Erik J. Molenaar (eds.), *The International Legal Regime of Areas beyond National Jurisdiction: Current and Future Developments*, pp. 7–25.

when current discussions on governance oppose 'regulatory' to 'governance' gaps they allude to the same distinction between a consistent set of rules to pursue certain objectives and the institutional arrangements to ensure its implementation.

It is nevertheless only prudent to underline at the outset that, while the distinction is a convenient analytical tool, in obtaining adequate governance a regime and its machinery are intertwined. Notwithstanding the efforts I will make to keep them separate, some connections will emerge as they are unavoidable.

2. *Why are only Areas Beyond National Jurisdiction Envisaged?*

It is a fact that current discussions envisaging global law of the sea problems, and in particular regulatory and governance gaps, and consequent regime-building possibilities, focus on areas beyond national jurisdiction (ABNJ). To give a few examples, we can recall the discussions concerning marine genetic resources and marine biodiversity, those on deep-sea fishing and most of those concerning illegal, unregulated and unreported (IUU) fishing and the impact of climate change on the seas.

The focus on areas beyond the limits of national jurisdiction is due to the reluctance of States to engage in discussions that might envisage some limits to their jurisdiction as coastal States. Provisions in which activities that may straddle the borderline between areas within and beyond national jurisdiction provide good examples of this. These provisions seem to show that, in adopting them, States, while trying to ensure a proper balance, are more interested in safeguarding the jurisdiction of coastal States than to expand the scope of the regime they establish for ABNJ.

As regards the LOS Convention, in Part XI, concerning the seabed and subsoil beyond national jurisdiction (the Area), we can recall Article 142, entitled "rights and legitimate interests of the coastal States". Paragraphs 1 and 2 of this article envisage the situation of "resource deposits in the Area which lie across limits of national jurisdiction". Activities in the Area concerning them are to be conducted "with due regard to the rights and legitimate interests of any coastal State across whose jurisdiction such deposits lie" (Article 142(1)). Infringements of such rights and interests must be prevented through consultation including prior notification, and, in case activities in the Area result in

---

part: "an international *régime* applying to the area and its resources and including appropriate international *machinery* to give effect to its provisions shall be established by an international treaty of universal character, generally agreed upon" (italics added).

exploitation of resources within national jurisdiction, "the prior consent of the coastal State shall be required" (Article 142(2)). Moreover,

> the regime of the Area does not affect the right of the coastal State to take measures beyond the limits of national jurisdiction to prevent, mitigate or eliminate grave or imminent damage to their coastline or related interests from pollution or threat thereof or from other hazardous occurrences resulting from or caused by any activities in the Area.

The balancing obtained with the 'due regard' concept does not exclude that the final word is given to the coastal State, whose consent is required in paragraph 2, and whose right to intervene in case of pollution caused by maritime casualties is preserved. Thus, this article seems keener to protect the rights and interests of the coastal State than to ensure the application of the Area regime to the adjacent seabed under national jurisdiction. It may be observed that the balance between activities in the Area and the exercise of the freedoms of the high seas is ensured more completely by the requirement of 'due regard' for activities in the Area to be observed in the exercise of the freedoms of the high seas, and especially, by the two symmetrical provisions of Article 147, paragraphs 1 and 3: "Activities in the Area shall be carried out with reasonable regard for other activities in the marine environment"; and: "Other activities in the marine environment shall be carried out with reasonable regard for activities in the Area".

In the time after the adoption of the LOS Convention, States have sometimes envisaged regimes straddling the line between areas within and beyond national jurisdiction. The UN Fish Stocks Agreement,[4] as it deals with stocks that by definition straddle the limit between areas within and beyond national jurisdiction, considers the problem in a number of provisions. The basic idea that has been adopted (Article 3) is that the Agreement applies only to ABNJ with the exception of the general principles set out in Article 5 (that should apply *mutatis mutandis* in areas within national jurisdiction), of the precautionary approach set out in Article 6, which shall apply also within areas under national jurisdiction and of Article 7 on compatibility of conservation and management measures taken within and beyond areas of national jurisdiction. Article 7 on compatibility seems the most advanced attempt in an existing treaty to prevent inconsistencies between the regimes applicable within and beyond the limits of national jurisdiction. Nevertheless, its basic premise is that each of these regimes remains separate. Even the dispute-settlement system set out in the Agreement, which makes the provisions of Part XV of the

[4] Agreement for the Implementation of Provisions of the United Nations Convention on the Law of the Sea of 10 December 1982 Relating to the Conservation and Management of Straddling Fish Stocks and Highly Migratory Fish Stock of 4 August 1995 ((1995) 34 ILM 1547).

LOS Convention applicable to disputes concerning its interpretation and application (Article 30(1)), stops at the limits of the high seas. In fact, Article 32, by making applicable Article 297(3), of the LOS Convention, has the effect of excluding from compulsory adjudication disputes concerning fisheries in exclusive economic zones (EEZs) even when they concern the application and interpretation of the Agreement.[5]

More recently, an FAO Technical Consultation provisionally adopted on 29 August 2008 the International Guidelines for the Management of Deep-sea Fisheries in the High Seas (Guidelines on Deep-Sea Fisheries).[6] While it is far from certain that all the vulnerable marine ecosystems that these guidelines aim to protect from deep-sea fishing lie beyond the limits of national jurisdiction, it was assumed from the beginning that the Guidelines would be applicable only to "fisheries that occur in areas beyond the limits of national jurisdiction" (paragraph 8). The only concession to the relevance for fisheries occurring within national jurisdiction of the principles contained in the Guidelines is in paragraph 10, which states that: "Coastal States may apply these Guidelines within their national jurisdiction, as appropriate".[7] This provision obviously is not much more than a footnote for memory's sake, as States are not bound to apply the Guidelines but can do so with or without it.

Even in the cases of the Fish Stocks Agreement and of the 2008 Guidelines on Deep-Sea Fisheries, in which the ecosystem approach is proclaimed to be applicable, States have preferred to keep separate the regime concerning areas within and beyond the limits of national jurisdiction.

From the observations just made it emerges that the resistance to the adoption of rules encompassing areas within and ABNJ remains strong notwithstanding the fact that widely proclaimed modern approaches originating in international environmental law, such as the ecosystem approach, would militate for such adoption. This is particularly remarkable if one considers that some of these modern principles are set out, albeit in imprecise form, in the LOS Convention in terms that envisage the marine environment in general without distinguishing between areas within and ABNJ. One may recall, in particular, the principle of prior notification (Article 198) and the principle requiring environmental impact assessments (Article 206), as well as, especially, the principle of cooperation (Article 197), that—albeit referring explic-

---

[5] See further T. Treves "The Settlement of Disputes According to the Straddling Stocks Agreement of 1995" in A. Boyle, D. Freestone (eds) *International Law and Sustainable Development* (Oxford University Press, Oxford: 1999) 252–269 at 257–260.

[6] FAO Fisheries and Aquaculture Reports *Report of the Technical Consultation on International Guidelines for the Management of Deep-sea Fisheries in the High Seas* (FAO, Rome: 2008) Appendix F.

[7] *Ibid.*

itly only to the prevention of pollution—has been recognized by the International Tribunal for the Law of the Sea (ITLOS) in its Order in the *Mox Plant* case[8] as "fundamental" under LOS Convention and under general international law. This principle, from which, according to the Tribunal's Order "rights arise",[9] requires recognition that proposals for cooperative endeavours to protect and preserve the marine environment must be taken seriously and never rejected offhand (a consequence strengthened by Article 123(b), as regards enclosed and semi-enclosed seas). It also requires good faith in the pursuance of such endeavours. The indications about the obligation to negotiate given by the International Court of Justice (ICJ) as regards delimitation agreements in the *North Sea Continental Shelf cases* seem relevant also in this context:

> the parties [...] are under the obligation so to conduct themselves that the negotiations are meaningful, which will not be the case when either of them insists upon its own position without contemplating any modification of it.[10]

The principle of cooperation does not *per se* require that regimes straddling the line separating areas within and ABNJ be negotiated and adopted. It merely requires a preference for a collective approach to whatever regime of common interest is discussed or negotiated, including a regime limited to ABNJ. Strengthened cooperation regarding ABNJ may, however, be conducive to results equivalent or similar to those that could be reached by including areas within national jurisdiction in the cooperative approach. The history of international environmental law shows that while approaches and ideas developed in domestic law may influence international agreements, also approaches and ideas developed internationally can influence domestic law. States sometimes recognize that to conform to international regimes within domestic law may be preferable in order to achieve uniformity and establish a level playing field as regards competition.[11]

In light of this, the approach envisaging a regime, or regimes, limited to ABNJ can be seen as flawed in some respects, or at least as not being the theoretically preferable one. One could be less critical of this approach if the existing regimes applying to areas under national jurisdiction were fully satisfactory. It would be imprudent to accept this statement, however.

---

[8] *The MOX Plant Case* (Ireland v. United Kingdom) case No. 10 [2001] ITLOS at 95ff. at para. 82.

[9] *Ibid.*

[10] *North Sea Continental Shelf* cases (Federal Republic of Germany v. Denmark; Federal Republic of Germany v. The Netherlands) [1969] ICJ Reports 3 at para. 85.

[11] See T. Treves "Le role du droit international de l'environnement dans l'élaboration du droit interne de l'environnement: quelques réflexions" M. Prieur and C. Lambrecht (eds) *Les hommes et l'Environnement, Etudes en homage à Alexandre Kiss* (Frison Roche, Paris: 1998) 345–349.

Whatever the assessment to be given on specific instances, it seems safe to say that the different approaches adopted by coastal States entail that the results obtained in the exercise of sovereign rights and jurisdiction in the EEZs and continental shelves are uneven. They could not be otherwise in view of the differences in economic and social development, in domestic government and administrative capability, in the political structure, in the reliance on coastal waters' resources. In some cases the results are by any standards bad or mediocre. Suffice it to say that the fact that the coastal State enjoys exclusive rights over the resources of the EEZs or fishery zones, has not stopped overfishing in many of these zones, bringing enhanced pressure on high seas fisheries. Even in case fisheries in the 200-mile zones are well managed, the lack of uniformity and coordination with high seas fisheries may cause overfishing in less well-managed 200-mile zones and in the high seas.

Why are States insisting to act on the basis of the 'high seas only' approach? The reasons are ideological and historical. State sovereignty is seen as the supreme value: any idea that could question recently obtained and hard-fought extensions of it are considered with suspicion and rejected offhand by a substantial number of States. In the present situation of the world, the vast majority of States does not seem to be ready to consider rules—and, even more so, institution-based management—that could be perceived as taking away parcels of their newly-acquired sovereign rights and jurisdiction over adjacent seas. The very LOS Convention, notwithstanding the many nuances one can find in its provisions, is seen by most States as the consecration of the coastal State approach.[12]

However persuasive the arguments for a different approach, this is a situation of fact at the present time. A growing awareness of the problems of, for instance, the effects of climate change, may bring a change. But it will not come quickly.

For the time being, if one or more regimes are to be developed, it is a political requirement that they will be limited to areas beyond the limits of national jurisdiction.

[12] For other States, however, it is seen as a mechanism to stabilize the maritime claims of States by stopping 'creeping jurisdiction'. I develop the view of the different attitudes of States of the LOS Convention as being either a point of departure for further expansion of coastal States' rights or a point of arrival of the extension of such rights, in T. Treves "Les lectures nationales de la convention de Montego Bay" in *Ministère de la Défense, Colloque "Droits maritimes et défense"* (Ecole militaire, Paris: 1996) 32–42.

3. *Existing Regimes for the Governance of ABNJ*

Before trying to enter into the question of a new regime, or new regimes, for the governance in ABNJ, it must be recalled that two regimes concerning such areas already exist. They are the regime of the Area as defined in Article 1(1) of the LOS Convention and the regime concerning straddling and highly migratory fish stocks set out in the Fish stocks Agreement. Neither of them is a 'self-contained' regime.[13] They build upon the customary and codified rules on the high seas in respect of which they can be seen as *leges speciales*. When rules set out for the regime of the Area do not apply, the general rules on the high seas do; these general rules similarly apply when the rules set out for straddling and highly migratory fish stocks in the Fish Stock Agreement do not apply. The two regimes derogate from the general rules on the high seas in different ways and measure. The regime of the Area denies the idea of freedom, and substitutes it with the concept of the common heritage of mankind; while the Fish Stocks Agreement's regime does not deny the idea of the freedom to fish even though it limits it in order to protect species and the environment as well as biodiversity in general, and to take into account the interests of certain coastal States.

Both regimes concern resources, and, among these, resources intended for human consumption, even though mineral resources of the Area are non-renewable, while fish resources are renewable. Both regimes include a machinery. While the machinery adopted for the Area is a new organization set up for the purposes of the regime, the International Seabed Authority (ISA), the Fish Stocks Agreement utilizes for various purposes of its provisions institutions that already exist or may be established, namely "subregional or regional fisheries management organizations or arrangements" (RFMO/As). The regime and machinery of the Area are centralized, while the Fish Stocks Agreement's regime and machinery are de-centralized.

The provisions of Part XI and of the relevant Annexes III and IV of LOS Convention[14] are very detailed, as are those of the Fish Stocks Agreement. Both are, nonetheless, very narrow as far as their subject matter is concerned. The regime of the Area concerns only the exploration for and the exploitation of resources, and "resources" are narrowly defined as "all solid, liquid or gaseous *mineral* resources *in situ* in the Area at or beneath the seabed, including

---

[13] On the discussions raised by this notion, T. Treves "Fragmentation of International Law: The Judicial Perspective" (2007) 23 *Comunicazioni e Studi* 821–875 at 824–832, 841 and 844–845.

[14] As amended by the Agreement Relating to the Implementation of Part XI of the United Nations Convention on the Law of the Sea of 10 December 1982 of 28 July 1994 ((1994) 33 ILM 1309).

polymetallic nodules" (Article 133, emphasis added). This narrow scope is enhanced by the fact that the regime contained in most provisions of Part XI concerns the exploration and exploitation of polymetallic nodules only. The Fish Stocks Agreement concerns only "straddling" and "highly migratory" fish stocks. Although these stocks are not defined in the Agreement, the definition provided by Article 63 of the LOS Convention for straddling stocks and the list set out in Annex 1 for highly migratory species give some precision to these notions. More precision is added by Article 1(c) of the Agreement that includes in its definition of "fish" molluscs and crustaceans, except when belonging to sedentary species of the continental shelf.

Practice since the entry into force of the LOS Convention and the Fish Stocks Agreement shows that both regimes have a certain degree of flexibility that has permitted them to broaden their scope. The ISA is making progress in expanding the regime of the Area to mineral resources different from polymetallic nodules, in particular polymetallic sulphides and cobalt-rich ferromanganese crusts, and in developing rules, regulations and procedures to ensure the protection of the marine environment in the Area including the prevention of damage to flora and fauna from harmful effects of activities in the Area.[15]

As regards the Fish Stocks Agreement, the 2006 session of its Review Conference encouraged States to consider that the general principles of the Agreement also apply to 'discrete high seas fish stocks', namely stocks that occur only on the high seas and that are often the target of deep-sea fishing.[16] It also stated that RFMO/As with competence to manage straddling fish stocks "have the necessary competence to conserve and manage"[17] discrete high seas fish stocks. These views are also found in recent resolutions of the UN General Assembly. What appears as a mere encouragement to wider application of the Agreement could perhaps be seen as an interpretation agreed by the parties and accepted generally, especially as regards the precautionary and the ecosystem approaches that the Agreement includes in its list of general principles.[18] The Fish Stocks Agreement's Review Conference, which, according to Article 36, was supposed to be held only once, four years after entry into force of the Agreement, has been transformed, through the procedural device of suspending and not closing the 2006 session, into a potentially regular event (the 2006 session is to resume in 2010). The possibility that this conference will achieve a

[15] UN General Assembly resolution A/63/.111 of 5 December 2008, para. 33.

[16] Report of the Review Conference of the UN Fish Stocks Agreement New York 23 to 26 May 2006 (Doc. A/CONF.210/2006.15 of 5 July 2006) 31, para. 2.

[17] *Ibid.*, 33para. 16.

[18] See UN General Assembly resolutions A/60/31 of 29 November 2005, para 12, and, most recently, A/63/112 of 5 December 2008, para 25.

more substantial expansion of the scope of the Fish Stocks Agreement's regime than that achieved in 2006 seems, nevertheless, uncertain. A well-informed observer of the 2006 Review Conference notes that there was little or no support for formally extending the Fish Stocks Agreement to all stocks.[19]

Another aspect that contributes to the flexibility of the two regimes and their capacity to expand is the fact that both are endowed with compulsory mechanisms for the settlement of disputes. Disputes relating to activities in the Area, including contractual and pre-contractual matters, as well as questions of liability relating thereto, can be submitted—as the case may be, by a State party, the Authority or by a contractor or prospective contractor—to the Seabed Disputes Chamber of the ITLOS, whose decision is binding (see the LOS Convention Article 187). Disputes concerning the interpretation and application of the Fish Stocks Agreement may be submitted unilaterally, by a party thereto, to the courts or tribunals competent under Part XV of the LOS Convention, whose judgments are binding. Beyond settling the specific dispute submitted, judgments of international courts or tribunals may seize opportunities for interpretation of the provisions of the LOS Convention and of the Fish Stocks Agreement. In light of the authority of judicial and arbitral bodies, notwithstanding the lack of *stare decisis* in international law, these interpretations may have the effect to enhance the precision of the provisions they refer to or to extend their scope to include activities not encompassed in their literal formulation.

The capacity to expand of the two regimes is not unlimited, however. Judges are not legislators and they can intervene only if a dispute is submitted to them. The amendment mechanisms of the LOS Convention and of the Fish Stocks Agreement are so cumbersome that no serious thought has been given to using them.[20] "Implementing agreements", of which the very Fish Stocks Agreement is the main example, are seen as the most practical way to develop notions insufficiently dealt with in the LOS Convention. These are nonetheless separate agreements, which may attract as parties a group of States smaller or different than that of the parties of the LOS Convention and of other agreements, so involving the risk of a lack of uniformity.

---

[19] E.J. Molenaar "Managing Biodiversity in Areas Beyond National Jurisdiction" (2007) 22 *International Journal of Marine and Coastal Law* 89–124 at 100.

[20] B.H. Oxman "Tools for Change: the Amendment Procedure" in *Proceedings of the Twentieth Anniversary Commemoration of the Opening for Signature of the United Nations Convention on the Law of the Sea, New York, 9 and 10 December 2002* (United Nations, New York: 2003) 195–207; D. Freestone and A.G. Oude Elferink "Flexibility and Innovation in the Law of the Sea: Will the LOS Convention Amendment Procedures Ever be Used?" in A.G. Oude Elferink (ed.) *Stability and Change in the Law of the Sea: the Role of the LOS Convention* (Martinus Nijhoff, Leiden-Boston: 2005)169–221.

4. *Current Discussions and the Models for Governance*

a. *Genetic Resources*

Current discussions relating to governance of ABNJ concern two different, albeit interconnected, subjects. On the one hand, they concern a regime for genetic resources beyond the limits of national jurisdiction and, on the other, the idea of a general regime for ABNJ. The discussions on genetic resources are held within institutional channels, especially the UN General Assembly, including the United Nations Informal Consultative Process on Oceans and the Law of the Sea (ICP) and an ad-hoc Working Group that met in 2006 and 2008 and is scheduled to meet again in 2010[21] and the Convention on Biological Diversity.[22] Discussions on a general regime are the subject of debate in the framework of non-governmental organizations. The latest outcome of these discussion is the resolution on "Principles for High Seas Governance" adopted by the International Union for the Conservation of Nature (IUCN) at its Barcelona Congress in 2008.[23]

As is well known, the main divergence of views in the discussions concerning the regime for genetic resources in ABNJ relate to, on the one side, States holding the opinion that the principle of the common heritage of mankind must be at the centre of such a regime, and, on the other, States holding the view that the principle of the freedom of the high seas should apply.[24] This opposition of views often takes the form of a discussion as to the current status of international law regarding genetic resources in ABNJ. It focuses on

[21] See Res. A/63/111, note 15 at para. 127.

[22] Convention on Biological Diversity of 5 June 1992 ((1992) 31 ILM 818).

[23] IUCN *10 Principles for High Seas Governance* (2008) (available at ⟨http://www.iucn.org/⟩).

[24] A broad literature considers the subject see e.g. T. Scovazzi "Mining, Protection of the Environment, Scientific Research and Bio-prospecting: Some Considerations on the Role of the ISA" in (2004) 19 *International. Journal of Marine & Coastal Law* 383–409; D.K. Leary "Bio-prospecting and the Genetic Resources of Hydrothermal Vents on the High Seas: What is the Existing Legal Position, Where are we Heading and What are our Options?" (2004) 1 *Macquarie Journal of Comparative and Environmental Law* 137–178; D. Tladi "Genetic Resources, Benefit Sharing, and the Law of the Sea: the Need for Clarity" (2007) 13 *Journal of International Maritime Law* 183–193; A.G. Oude Elferink "The Regime of the Area: Delineating the Scope of Application of the Common Heritage Principle and of Freedom of the High Seas" (2007) 22 *International Journal. Marine & Coastal Law* 143–176; E.J. Molenaar "Managing Biodiversity in Areas Beyond National Jurisdiction" in M.H. Nordquist, R. Long, T.H. Heidar, J.N. Moore (eds.) *Law, Science and Ocean Management* (Martinus Nijhoff, Leiden/Boston: 2007) 625–681; M.F. Hayes "Charismatic Microfauna: Marine Genetic Resources and the Law of the Sea" *ibid.* 683–700; F. Millicay "A Legal Regime for the Biodiversity of the Area" *ibid.* 739–850.

whether the regime of the Area encompasses resources other than mineral resources, perhaps on the basis of an analogy with the status of sedentary species on the continental shelf, on whether Article 143 of the LOS Convention concerning marine scientific research in the Area may be invoked to support the idea that prospecting for genetic resources must be conducted "for the benefit of mankind as a whole", on whether the ISA is entitled to play a role, and, more generally, on whether the concept of the common heritage of mankind as formulated in Part XI of the LOS Convention applies to genetic resources.

The very fact that these discussions are held with the evident, although not always clearly stated or acknowledged, view of developing an agreed regime for genetic resources beyond the limits of national jurisdiction, including prospecting and exploitation, causes a measure of confusion between the *de lege lata* and the *de lege ferenda* perspectives. While this is not the case as regards some, but not all, scholarly views, the positions held by States as to the status of international law on the subject have the function to prepare a solid foundation for the positions these States are promoting for the regime to be established. The need to refrain from making concessions too early explains why these positions are often stated in non-nuanced, extreme, terms. This reminds of the discussions of the sixties and seventies (*res communis omnium* or *res nullius*?) about the exploration for and exploitation of polymetallic nodules on the seabed beyond national jurisdiction during the negotiations for the regime of the Area at the UN Seabed Committee and the Third UN Conference on the Law of the Sea.

The peculiarity of the resources under discussion, the difficulty to adopt general assumptions as to whether they belong to the seabed or to the water column, the fact that only samples are needed for subsequent research, and that huge investments are often needed to develop potential applications, make it evident that the regime for the Area set out in the LOS Convention cannot be applied as such to deal with this subject.

Such application would require radical changes in the institutional framework established by Part XI of the LOS Convention. Suffice it to consider that the composition of the Council, a key organ of the ISA, is based on interest groups defined having regard to the polymetallic nodules industry such as, in particular, investors in the industry, consumers of the metals and land-based producers. Such composition would not be appropriate if applied to the management of a regime for genetic resources. The amendments that would be necessary would be tantamount to adopting a new convention. Moreover, certain aspects of the regime of the Area are obsolete. In particular, it ignores the ecosystem approach. Other modern concepts of international environmental law, such as the precautionary approach or the polluter-pays principle, are almost absent from it. The efforts made to include them in regulations of the ISA, although noteworthy, are, nonetheless, limited to the exploration and exploitation of polymetallic nodules.[25]

As a consequence, it seems clear that the aim of the States that refer as a model to Part XI is not necessarily to broaden the powers of the ISA and to apply the regime of the Area to genetic resources. Their objective is to ensure that a new regime to be set up would contain certain general characteristics of that regime, notably its ideological thrust expressed by the notion of the common heritage of mankind. This approach emerges, for instance, in the following excerpt of the summary of their position now under consideration set out in the report of 2007 of the ICP:

> notwithstanding the fact that it was clear under the Convention that marine genetic resources were part of the common heritage of mankind, any future implementing agreement to the Convention should clarify this point.[26]

The opposite position relies on an interpretation of the LOS Convention according to which marine genetic resources, not being mineral resources, do not fall under the regime of the Area, including the principle of the common heritage of mankind. The rules on the freedom of the seas, in particular those on the conservation of the living resources of the high seas set out in Articles 117 and 118 of the LOS Convention should apply, as well as those on the protection of the environment and on scientific research of general applicability or related to the high seas.[27] This would imply basically free access to the genetic resources and the application of rules for the protection of intellectual property to processes and substances developed.

It seems that this position, as the previous one, should be seen as a starting bid in view of a negotiation. The difference is that the States supporting it are not in a hurry to engage in such negotiation. Their concern is that such negotiation might produce an expansion of the common heritage idea (which they consider well constrained within the limits of Part XI as amended in 1994) and bring about obstacles and burdens for private activity by the creation

[25] Regulation 31(2) of the "Regulations on Prospecting and Exploration for Polymetallic Nodules in the Area" adopted in 2000 by the ISA provides for the application by the Authority and the sponsoring States of the 'precautionary approach as reflected in Principle 15 of the Rio Declaration'. The latter is certainly not the most detailed and precise statement of this approach. Sect. 5 of Annex 4 to these Regulations provides in some detail for environmental impact assessments. The regulation and annexes are annexed to the Authority's decision of 13 July 2000 in doc. ISBA/6/A/18 16 *International Organizations and the Law of the Sea, Documentary Yearbook* (2000) 425.

[26] Report of the United Nations Open-ended Consultative Process on Oceans and the Law of the Sea at its eighth meeting, Doc. A/62/169 of 30 July 2007 at para. 72.

[27] *Ibid.*, para. 74.

of new institutions or the expansion of the existing ones with added costs. They do not want to repeat the experience of the setting up of the regime for polymetallic nodules.

The clash between these opposing positions with its ideological connotations does not seem likely to produce a clear victory for either one. Neither side is going to be persuaded by the other. The precedent of the negotiations on Part XI of the LOS Convention and on the Fish Stocks Agreement shows that the road towards agreement on a regime requires going around the ideological questions and adopting practical solutions based on shared values. This seems to be the approach that a number of States—in particular those of the European Community and the Community itself—have in mind. In the 2007 ICP Meeting that approach was presented as requiring "a comprehensive and practical framework for exploring all marine genetic resources in areas beyond national jurisdiction" both for the water column and the deep seabed area. The regulation this group was willing to consider would be "more formal", probably alluding to a binding implementing agreement. The commonly shared concepts proposed to be applied are that an "integrated approach to conservation and sustainable use of marine biodiversity" should be pursued, that the aim should be "to protect and preserve those resources and [...] access and benefit-sharing" and that "the legitimate interests of all States" should be taken into account, while stressing that this would be "without prejudice to the sovereign rights and jurisdiction of coastal States in maritime zones under their jurisdiction".[28] Concepts developed in international environmental law as the "integrated approach" and the purpose to protect and preserve resources are put forward as shared values that should help to produce consensus. In more political terms, a double balancing is alluded to. On the one hand, the balancing between applying the new regime to the water column and to the seabed, thus denying or limiting the ambitions of the ISA, and acceptance of the idea that the new regime would not impinge on areas within national jurisdiction. On the other hand, the balancing is proposed between guaranteeing access and consideration of the interests of all States, and benefit-sharing (the common heritage without mentioning it?). These ideas would be set out in a "formal" instrument, often explained as an implementing agreement to the LOS Convention.

Even taking into account that the ideas set out in this proposal are no more than a point of departure to help the negotiation to abandon the sterile opposition of positions of principle, it would be imprudent to say that there will soon be agreement on a regime for genetic resources in ABNJ and that the

---

[28] *Ibid.*, para. 75.

ingredients of such a regime will correspond to these ideas. It is nonetheless possible to recognize a trend towards adopting a new regime that will correspond to what States will agree to be the solution most appropriate for the specific subject-matter. It seems also possible to surmise that this regime will not be a copy of Part XI or a simple reference to the regime of the high seas. It seems likely that some elements of the Part XI approach and some elements of the general high seas regime and of the regime of the Fish Stocks Agreement will be present. What remains open is the balancing of the various elements, as each side of the negotiation will strive to move such balance in the direction it considers more consonant to its interests. If the precedent of the negotiation of Part XI can teach a lesson, the risk involved is that of going into so much detail that the solution adopted would soon be overcome by changed political and economic circumstances and scientific progress.

b. *General Regime for ABNJ?*

The trends emerging in the discussions on genetic resources seem to indicate that, sooner or later, there will be a third special regime concerning ABNJ in addition to those of Part XI of the LOS Convention and of the Fish Stocks Agreement. We must take this perspective into consideration when examining studies and proposals made in the framework of non-governmental organizations concerning 'governance gaps' in the high seas.

These studies have been engaged into in light of the scientific discoveries about hydrothermal vents, the forms of life that accompany them, and the international attention raised by genetic resources of the high seas. They highlight, however, a number of 'governance gaps' as regards ABNJ apart from matters concerning genetic resources.[29] The interest of these studies and proposals is, on the one hand, linked to the current discussion on a regime for genetic resources. On the other hand, beyond that discussion, and independently of whether one can agree that all the governance gaps mentioned exist and if it is urgent to deal with them, in my view more interestingly, these studies and proposals are useful to highlight the issue whether existing governance gaps, as well as future ones, should continue to be addressed on a case-by-case basis or whether a general framework should

[29] See Gjerde, note 1. See also the Report of the Workshop on High Seas Governance for the 21st Century held in New York on 17–19 October 2007 (available at ⟨www.iucn.org⟩) while the Executive Summary of the Co-Chairs Report is published in D. Freestone, K.M. Gjerde, R. Rayfuse and D. VanderZwaag, "Workshop on High Seas Governance for the 21st Century" (2008) 23 *International Journal of Marine & Coastal Law* 359–363; IUCN Principles, note 23; D. Freestone "Modern Principles of High Seas Governance—The Legal Underpinnings" (2009) 39 (1) *Environmental Policy and Law* 44–49.

be envisaged. Having in mind these studies and proposals, and especially the IUCN 'Principles for High Seas Governance' of October 2008, I submit some reflections of mine, in which, while sharing much of the basic orientation in favour of the protection of the environment and of transparency in the availability of information and decision-making, I assume as a given that there will be a regime for genetic resources (and perhaps other specific regimes) and try to adopt a less idealistic, and I hope, more diplomatically realistic outlook.

In light of the above mentioned assumption that a plurality of regimes is likely for the future, it seems worthwhile to consider how the perceived difficulties and drawbacks of such a development might be overcome. These difficulties and drawbacks consist of the risk of a lack of uniformity and coordination due to the different time of adoption, the possibility of different constituencies, and the different subject-matters. In my view some ideas of a very general character may be proposed. They should be thought of as the contents of a new instrument whose purpose would be to serve as a basic orientation for new regimes and as a 'default' set of concepts for subjects for which no regime has been (or has not yet) been developed. Such an instrument, in my view, should preferably have a 'soft law' character. This would permit its adoption in a relatively short time avoiding the risk of slow processes for entry into force and the situation in which some States would be bound and others would not. A 'declaration of principles' set out in a UN General Assembly resolution could be the appropriate form. It would not lack significant precedents.

The elements that should be set out in the instrument are tentatively mentioned below. While some correspond to broadly held ideas, others are less solid and elaborated. They seem nevertheless worth considering in a discussion.

It should be made clear at the outset that new regimes for ABNJ should be built on the LOS Convention. The basic idea of the freedom of the high seas and of the exclusive responsibility of the flag State should be recognized as the point of departure or as the 'default' rule. Alternative basic approaches such as a further expansion of coastal State jurisdiction to include the whole of the high seas, or, on the opposite side of the spectrum, a centralized system including a powerful machinery with law-making and perhaps enforcement powers would be untenable. The first would subvert the balance of the law of the sea and lead to an exaggerated inequality between States. The second would have the drawbacks already seen in the idea of expanding the existing regime for the Area.

To consider the freedom of the high seas as the starting point does not mean that I disagree with the idea, set out in the IUCN Principles, that:

> the time of treating of the high seas as "open to all without conditions" is over [and that] access to the high seas should be twinned with responsibility and accountability, assured through comprehensive governance that includes effective regulation, monitoring, sanctioning and enforcement.[30]

While perhaps it may be questioned how comprehensive a form of governance acceptable to the international community could be, it seems to me clear that some form of restriction of the freedom of the high seas, based on cooperation and on the acceptance of new obligations by flag States and port States, as well as rights to be exercised collectively by States, perhaps through international organizations, would be the tools to reach the desired results.

In light of the law of the sea rule that the freedoms of the high seas shall be exercised "with due regard" to the interest of other States in exercising such freedoms (Article 87(2) of the LOS Convention), the new instrument should strive to make the "due regard" concept more precise. It should state specific criteria for ensuring coexistence of different activities, and, if necessary, establish priorities, or mechanisms for dealing with conflicts. If a plurality of machineries is to be set up, each regime should make provision for the possibility of efficient contacts and cooperation between them.

The new instrument should assume as a starting point that the resources of the seas are limited and in many cases impoverished and going towards exhaustion and that the capacity of the marine environment to regenerate itself has reached and passed its limit so that any human activity conducted in it may have a negative effect. Consequently, the connection between the protection of the environment and the conservation of biodiversity—as wisely done in the IUCN Principles[31]—should be enhanced. The existing sectoral and regional management approach to fisheries should be submitted to discussion in order to assess gaps and devise mechanisms "to better manage ocean ecosystems and to ensure the conservation and sustainable and equitable use of all high seas resources".[32]

An enhanced status for science seems necessary. This would require the removal of obstacles to marine scientific research activities, and, especially, devising mechanisms for adjusting regimes in light of scientific inputs. Paragraph 4 of the IUCN Principles seems eloquent, as regards the second aspect mentioned:

> Management decisions should be based on the best available science and not on the lobbying of a powerful few. Further scientific research on high seas ecosystems and resources is required to underpin ecologically sustainable use,

---

[30] IUCN Principles, note 23 at para. 1.
[31] *Ibid.*, paras 2 and 3.
[32] *Ibid.*, para. 2.

> to inform the adaptive application of conservation measures and to enhance the development of criteria for monitoring their effectiveness, independent structures should be established so that scientific advice is not diluted for political purposes.

To protect and develop science is not sufficient, however. Information coming from scientists as well as from users should be fully and freely available in order to permit meaningful public participation in decision-making, which should be "transparent, accountable and inclusive" as stressed by the IUCN Principles.[33]

Sustainability should be the key concept permitting to ensure reciprocal "due regard" between rights based on the preservation of the environment and rights relevant specifically for the utilization of marine resources. The idea stressed in the *Iron Rhine* arbitral award that "environmental law and the law on development stand not as alternatives but as mutually reinforcing, integral concepts"[34] should be extended to the relationship between international environmental law and the law of the exploitation of the resources of the seas.

As regards the environmental protection aspects that should be included, the obligations of all States set out in the LOS Convention Articles 192 and 194 to protect and preserve the marine environment and to take measures to prevent, reduce and control pollution, should be enhanced by underlining that non-compliance with these obligations triggers the application of the regime of State responsibility and suggesting that the development of non-compliance mechanisms of the kind now existing for certain multilateral environmental agreements could be useful.

The new instrument should develop seminal ideas to be found, albeit briefly formulated, in recent international judgments and awards. One may recall that the duty of prevention or at least of mitigation of significant harm to the environment, according to the *Iron Rhine* arbitral award, "has now become a principle of general international law";[35] so that, according to the ICJ in its advisory opinion on the *Legality of the Threat or Use of Nuclear Weapons*:

> [t]he existence of the general obligation of States to ensure that activities within their jurisdiction and control respect the environment of other States or of areas beyond national control is now part of the corpus of international law relating to the environment;[36]

---

33 *Ibid.*, para. 9.

34 *The Iron Rhine Arbitration* (Belgium v. the Netherlands) [2005] Reports of International Arbitral Awards vol. XXVII 35, para. 59.

35 *Ibid.*

36 Legality of the Threat or Use of Nuclear Weapons in Armed Conflict, Advisory Opinion [1996] 1 ICJ Reports 226 at 241–242, para. 29.

and that, according to the ITLOS in its *Mox Plant* Order:

> the duty to cooperate is a fundamental principle in the prevention of pollution of the marine environment under part XII of the [LOS] Convention and general international law.[37]

Modern environmental law approaches should be included such as, especially, the ecosystem and precautionary approaches. It may be discussed whether, beyond the statement of the approaches in their simple form of 'principles', it would be preferable to encourage the development, for each regime to be adopted in the future, of ways and means to apply these approaches in the specific field covered. The Fish Stocks Agreement, which specifies in detail how to apply the precautionary approach to the conservation and management of the fish stocks concerned (Article 6, and annex II), may be seen as a precedent. Other modern principles of international environmental law should also be considered, such as the requirement that environmental impact assessments be used whenever necessary.

Notwithstanding the fact that the regimes already existing and under consideration are all focused on resources, it would seem useful that a very general approach to resources be contained in the new instrument. In that approach, in my view, balance must be sought between the ideas of sustainability and of precaution and those of encouraging scientific, technological and industrial investment for the purpose of economic progress and development and for meeting the needs of the poorest components of humankind. This would require encouragement of participation of developing countries and their nationals in the new regimes. Utilization of benefits for purposes of development should be part of the new regimes, even though not necessarily on the basis of the rules set out in the LOS Convention as regards the Area or the outer continental shelf. The idea of reinvestment in development or environmental protection projects could be considered.

Of course, while both requiring the aforementioned very general elements, regimes concerning resources that are extracted for the purpose of their consumption, as mineral resources or fish, are different from regimes concerning resources that are not (or not exclusively or necessarily) consumed or consumed in high quantities, such as genetic resources of the seas.

The remarks made above that some collective rights and obligations have to be developed and that there is a need to take into account the interest of the poorest sections of the international community, raise the question whether the notion of the common heritage of mankind could be a useful

[37] *The MOX Plant Case* (Ireland v. United Kingdom) case No. 10 [2001] ITLOS 95 at 110, para. 82.

means to express the collective rights and need just mentioned. This notion has undoubtedly a powerful ideological appeal and raises a correspondingly strong ideological opposition. Whether it would be useful to repeat it and whether the time has come to give it a more precise definition seems debatable. The danger of the exercise would be to perpetuate the clash between those who see the "common heritage of mankind" as a normative principle from which consequences considered implicit are to be drawn and those who see it as a label to designate a specific set of rules setting out well defined rights and obligations for States.

The role of dispute settlement (a point not addressed in the IUCN Principles) should be indicated as important for clarifying existing rules, for addressing gaps, and especially for reducing tensions and conflicts. Compulsory and binding mechanisms should be preferred as they have a stronger deterrent effect and permit relatively expeditious settlement. States should be encouraged to consider submission of a dispute to judicial or arbitral settlement as a normal event in international relations and not as a hostile act. The mechanism inaugurated by the Fish Stocks Agreement consisting in utilizing the LOS Convention dispute-settlement mechanism also for settling disputes concerning the application and interpretation of other law of the sea instruments[38] should be commended as fostering uniformity.

[38] For a detailed analysis, T. Treves "Dispute-Settlement in the Law of the Sea: Disorder or System?" in M.G. Kohen (ed.) *Promoting Justice, Human Rights and Conflicts Resolution through International Law, Liber Amicorum Lucius Caflisch* (Martinus Nijhoff, Leiden: 2007) 927–949.

PRINCIPLES AND OBJECTIVES OF THE LEGAL REGIME GOVERNING AREAS BEYOND NATIONAL JURISDICTION—COMMENTARY ON TULLIO TREVES

DANIEL OWEN*

Introduction

This short paper is based on the spoken commentary provided by the author at the Fourth J.W.H. Verzijl Memorial Symposium on 21 November 2008, with some subsequent elaboration. Professor Treves' paper proposes "some ideas of a very general character" relevant to the governance of areas beyond national jurisdiction (ABNJ).[1] This commentary focuses on just two matters. The first is one of the ideas raised by Professor Treves, namely that of making the "due regard" concept in international law more precise. The second is the matter of stakeholder participation in decision-making.

The "Due Regard" Concept

In his paper, Professor Treves states that:

> In light of the law of the sea rule that the freedoms of the high seas shall be exercised "with due regard" to the interest of other States in exercising such freedoms (Article 87(2) of the LOS Convention), the new instrument should strive to make the "due regard" concept more precise. It should state specific criteria for ensuring coexistence of different activities, and, if necessary, establish priorities, or mechanisms for dealing with conflicts. If a plurality of machineries is to be set up, each regime should make provision for the possibility of efficient contacts and cooperation between them.[2]

In the Convention on the Law of the Sea (LOS Convention),[3] as indicated by Professor Treves, reference to "due regard" in the context of the exercise of high

* Fenners Chambers, Cambridge, England, UK.

[1] Paper by T. Treves in this volume at 21.

[2] *Ibid.*, 22.

[3] Adopted on 10 December 1982; 1833 UNTS 396.

Alex G. Oude Elferink and Erik J. Molenaar (eds.), *The International Legal Regime of Areas beyond National Jurisdiction: Current and Future Developments*, pp. 27–37.

seas freedoms can be found in Article 87(2). In the specific context of "activities in the Area", as defined in Article 1 of the LOS Convention, Article 147 provides that "[a]ctivities in the Area shall be carried out with *reasonable regard* for other activities in the marine environment" and, reciprocally, "[o]ther activities in the marine environment shall be conducted with *reasonable regard* for activities in the Area".[4] It is not clear what, if anything, accounts for or flows from the difference in terminology in Article 87 ("due regard") and Article 147 ("reasonable regard").

Professor Treves, in the extract from his paper provided above, considers that any new instrument, in seeking to make the "due regard" concept more precise, "should state *specific criteria for ensuring coexistence* of different activities, and, if necessary, *establish priorities, or mechanisms for dealing with conflicts*".[5] In addition, the various regimes involved "should make provision for the possibility of *efficient contacts and cooperation* between them".[6] These specific points, and particularly the first, bring to mind the concept of marine spatial planning (MSP).

MSP is a tool that is increasingly being adopted and developed by coastal States to deal with growing competition for the use of ocean space.[7] Marine internal waters, territorial seas, continental shelves and exclusive economic zones (EEZs) are becoming more and more crowded with human activities. Some of these activities are actually or potentially incompatible with each other (for example activities that each require unimpeded access to the seabed of a given area). MSP involves the making of strategic decisions about the use of marine space, whether in relation to the surface, water column, seabed or subsoil. Whilst the desire may be to make the best overall use of such space, perhaps with a view to achieving sustainable development, there will be instances where difficult choices have to be made about which of two or more incompatible activities (including nature conservation) should take priority in a particular area.

Under the LOS Convention, many of the activities in a coastal State's waters are, in broad terms, under the exclusive competence of that State. Examples include fisheries (subject to duties of cooperation in respect of certain stocks and species), extraction of non-living resources (such as aggregates or oil and

---

[4] LOS Convention, Article 147(1) and (3) (emphasis added).

[5] Paper by T. Treves in this volume at 22 (emphasis added).

[6] *Ibid.*, 22 (emphasis added).

[7] For more background on marine spatial planning in the European Community context, see Communication from the Commission *Roadmap for Maritime Spatial Planning: Achieving Common Principles in the EU* COM(2008) 791; MRAG *et al. Legal Aspects of Maritime Spatial Planning* (October 2008) final report to DG Mare.

gas) and renewable energy generation. The coastal State is in principle able to exercise MSP unilaterally in respect of such activities, subject to any additional obligations it may have (such as, in the case of coastal Member States of the European Community (EC), under the EC's common fisheries policy). For some other activities, the ability of a coastal State to exercise MSP is more curtailed by the LOS Convention. The principal example in that regard is navigation, since foreign-flagged ships enjoy the right of innocent passage in the territorial sea and the freedom of navigation in the EEZ.

Of course, MSP need not be confined to coastal State waters. In principle, it may also be applied to ABNJ—whether at the level of an ocean basin or at a smaller scale such as a regional sea or a particular feature within a regional sea. However, in ABNJ there are, in contrast to coastal State waters, no activities over which a single coastal State has exclusive control. The result is that, in practice, MSP in ABNJ is far more difficult to achieve from a competence point of view. The onus needs to be placed on relevant international organizations, and potentially on individual operators or flag States, to cooperate to achieve MSP, including by taking difficult decisions about which activities should take priority over others. MSP in ABNJ is one means by which practical application could be given to Professor Treves' points, mentioned above, about identifying "specific criteria for ensuring coexistence of different activities" and establishing "priorities, or mechanisms for dealing with conflicts".[8]

Relevant international organizations include, *inter alia*, those responsible for control of exploration and exploitation of mineral resources in the Area (the International Seabed Authority (ISA)), fishing (regional fisheries management organizations (RFMOs)), shipping (the International Maritime Organization) and whaling (the International Whaling Commission). Regional seas organizations (RSOs), where these encompass ABNJ, are also potentially very relevant, not just in terms of the fields in respect of which they have competence but also potentially as brokers for coordination. For some activities there are no international organizations with a management role, except to the extent that RSOs may have a mandate. Examples include marine bioprospecting, submarine cable laying and, to a large degree, marine scientific research. For the latter activities, individual flag States as well as the relevant operators themselves in principle have an important role to play. In some cases, such as with straddling resources, it may be necessary to involve adjacent coastal States.

[8] Paper by T. Treves in this volume at 22.

Given the existence of various sectoral international organizations with the mandate to manage activities in ABNJ, the question is how MSP may be achieved in practice in such areas. One possibility could be the establishment of a mechanism for the relevant organizations to consult with each other in respect of any particular area and make strategic decisions between themselves, based on a common understanding of principles as well as common processes, about the use of the relevant marine space. If activity X under the competence of organization A is not compatible with activity Y under the competence of organization B, for any given area, some rules, or at least guidance, may be necessary to assist decision-making between the organizations in question.

An example of potentially incompatible activities can be provided by reference to seamounts. Seamounts are an important location for some commercially important fish stocks. They also support habitats that may be sensitive to the use of certain fishing gears. Cobalt-rich ferromanganese crusts may also occur on seamounts.[9] Thus it is conceivable that a particular seamount may be of interest for the purpose of commercial fishing, seabed mining and nature conservation; yet these may all be incompatible with each other. Potentially, a difficult decision will need to be made as to which takes priority. Such a decision could potentially involve the relevant RFMO, the ISA and the relevant RSO. In principle, such a decision could be made on a case-by-case basis in the absence of any MSP or, alternatively, it could be facilitated by prior adoption of a system of MSP between the organizations in question.

An example of a step towards coordination between international organizations is provided by the memorandum of understanding (MOU) between the North-East Atlantic Fisheries Commission (NEAFC, an RFMO) and the OSPAR Commission (an RSO), which has been applicable since September 2008.[10] The underlying justification for the MOU is the recognition that "NEAFC and the OSPAR Commission have *complementary competences and responsibilities* for fisheries management and environmental protection, respectively, within the North-East Atlantic including in areas beyond national jurisdiction ...".[11] The MOU commits the NEAFC and the OSPAR Commission to, *inter alia*:

---

[9] See further the ISA's brochure entitled *Cobalt-Rich Crusts* (available at ⟨www.isa.org.jm⟩).

[10] OSPAR Agreement 2008–4 (available at ⟨www.ospar.org⟩).

[11] *Ibid.*, 2 (emphasis added). See further, in particular, 1992 Convention for the Protection of the Marine Environment of the North-East Atlantic (32 ILM 1072), Annex V, Article 4(1) (available at ⟨www.ospar.org⟩).

> *discuss jointly* their respective concerns over the management of human activities that impact on the marine environment and the living marine resources in the North-East Atlantic including in areas beyond national jurisdiction and *possible actions and measures* to address them;[12]

The MOU contains an express reference to MSP, in that the two organizations "will cooperate regarding marine spatial planning and area management".[13] There is no elaboration on how cooperation on MSP will be achieved. However, a general provision states that:

> Cooperation on specific issues within the scope of this [MOU] may, if necessary, be specified in further detail through the development of separate sub-agreements between NEAFC and the OSPAR Commission.[14]

The author is not aware of any such sub-agreements, whether on MSP or other subjects covered by the MOU, in existence at the time of writing.

It remains to be seen how effective the MOU between the NEAFC and the OSPAR Commission will be in practice. However, good practice under this MOU may stimulate further MOUs in other parts of the world's oceans. In the case of the example above featuring an RFMO, an RSO and the ISA, one possibility is that a trilateral MOU, or three separate bilateral MOUs, could be adopted between the three organizations. In this respect, the latest annual report of the Secretary-General of the ISA states that the OSPAR Heads of Delegation, in November 2008, *inter alia*:

> welcomed a suggestion to develop a memorandum of understanding between the OSPAR Commission and the [ISA] in order to ensure appropriate coordination of measures between the two organizations.[15]

However, it is to be emphasized that the adoption of a cooperative framework is just one step, whereas adoption of a meaningful system of MSP between organizations may be a far greater challenge.[16]

---

[12] MOU, para. 1(b) (emphasis added).

[13] *Ibid.*, para. 1(d).

[14] *Ibid.*, para. 3.

[15] *Report of the Secretary-General of the International Seabed Authority under Article 166, paragraph 4, of the United Nations Convention on the Law of the Sea* (23 March 2009) ISBA/15/A/2 para. 21 (and see also paras 19–21 generally and para. 105).

[16] On MSP in areas beyond national jurisdiction, see further, e.g., J. Ardron, K. Gjerde, S. Pullen and V. Tilot "Marine Spatial Planning in the High Seas" (2008) 32 *Marine Policy* 832–839.

Stakeholder Participation in Decision-Making

In his paper, Professor Treves refers to the International Union for Conservation of Nature (IUCN) "Principles for High Seas Governance".[17] Principle 6 of the IUCN Principles states, *inter alia*, that:

> there is an urgent need to ensure greater transparency and increased participation by stakeholders in managing high seas resources. [...] it is critical that decision-making processes are conducted in a manner that is transparent and accountable *to minimise the likelihood of disputes and to promote international cooperation*. Regional and global organizations need to promote the meaningful participation of all interested stakeholders *in decision making*, provide observers access to all meetings and documents and receive advice from all interested observers.[18]

Broadly speaking, the stakeholders in ABNJ comprise States; international organizations; industry, comprising various sectors; environmental non-governmental organizations and other civil society groups; and the marine scientific research community. When considering States as stakeholders, it is important not to overlook those States that may have a presence or role in the region or issue in question (e.g. as flag States of fishing vessels) but which are not parties to the relevant treaty or members of the relevant international organization.

The forums at which stakeholders have a role are not necessarily limited to meetings of relevant international organizations. There may be other relevant intergovernmental forums, including, *inter alia*, meetings to negotiate new treaties or other agreements, the meetings of the States Parties to the LOS Convention, the Review Conference on the Fish Stocks Agreement and the United Nations Open-ended Informal Consultative Process on Oceans and the Law of the Sea. In addition, various informal international conferences on the governance of ABNJ, such as those convened primarily at the initiative of a particular State or environmental non-governmental organization, potentially provide an opportunity for all stakeholders to have a say on the matters under discussion.

For any given sea area or economic activity, it may be quite hard to identify *all* the relevant stakeholders, particularly those from economic sectors and the marine scientific research community. For example, regarding submarine cable laying, there is a body called the International Cable Protection Committee (ICPC). As at 18 April 2009, the ICPC had 94 members.[19] Full Membership is available to "Telecommunications and Power Transmission Submarine

---

[17] IUCN *10 Principles for High Seas Governance* (2008) (available at ⟨http://www.iucn.org/⟩).
[18] Emphasis added.
[19] Member List of the ICPC (available at ⟨www.iscpc.org⟩ (20 April 2009)).

Cable Owners and Maintenance Authorities", and Provisional Membership is available to "applicants who are planning the installation of new submarine cable systems but have not yet obtained a Cable Landing License".[20] In general, membership is available to "governmental administrations or commercial companies owning or operating submarine cables".[21]

The ICPC's "vision statement" refers to its desire "[t]o be *the premier* international Submarine Cable Owners' Association providing leadership and guidance on issues related to submarine cable planning, installation, operation, maintenance, protection and retirement".[22] A page of the ICPC's website, entitled "Cable Database",[23] notes that the information in the database "may not include cables which are owned/operated by *non* ICPC members".[24] Overall, the implication is that some international submarine cable owners or operators may fall outside the ICPC's membership.

Therefore, while contacting the ICPC would presumably be a sensible action for any international organization wishing to establish contact with the submarine cable laying sector,[25] it does not follow that all relevant stakeholders in this sector would necessarily be identified by this action. It would presumably be necessary for the international organization concerned to ascertain what proportion of relevant international submarine cable owners and maintenance authorities is *not* covered by the ICPC's membership, and hence how much further the international organization should go in its search to identify *all* relevant stakeholders in the sector. This example is provided merely to illustrate the general point made above that identifying all the relevant stakeholders in a given sector may not necessarily be straightforward.

Treaties focusing on stakeholder participation are relatively rare. To the author's knowledge, the principal treaty in this respect is the 1998 United Nations Economic Commission for Europe (UNECE) Convention on Access to Information, Public Participation in Decision-making and Access to Justice in Environmental Matters (Aarhus Convention).[26] At the time of writing, this treaty had 42 parties (all in Europe and central Asia). It has three pillars, as indicated by its title, including one on public participation in decision-making. The latter comprises Articles 6, 7 and 8 of the treaty.

---

[20] ⟨www.iscpc.org⟩ (20 April 2009).

[21] *Ibid.*

[22] *Ibid.* (emphasis added).

[23] *Ibid.* The page states: "This page was last updated on 10 October 2007."

[24] Emphasis added.

[25] See, for example, *Report of the Secretary-General of the International Seabed Authority under Article 166, paragraph 4, of the United Nations Convention on the Law of the Sea* (23 March 2009) ISBA/15/A/2, para. 22.

[26] Adopted on 25 June 1998; 2161 UNTS 447.

Article 6 relates to "specific activities", comprising those activities listed in Annex I to the treaty as well as any other activities that the party considers "may have a significant effect on the environment". It requires parties to inform the public concerned "early in an environmental decision-making procedure, and in an adequate, timely and effective manner" about the public participation procedure that will apply. It requires parties to, *inter alia*, provide for "early public participation, when all options are open and effective public participation can take place"; allow sufficient time for the public "to prepare and participate effectively"; and provide for access to certain information about the proposed activity and for submission of comments. In the decision, "due account" must be taken "of the outcome of the public participation" and reasons for the decision must be provided.

Article 7 relates to plans, programmes and policies. Regarding plans and programmes relating to the environment, the public that may participate is to be "identified by the relevant public authority", taking into account the objectives of the treaty. The requirements for public participation are less specific than those set out in Article 6. Some, but not all, of the principles from Article 6 are to be applied, including providing for early participation when options are still open; allowing sufficient time for the public to prepare and participate effectively; and taking due account of the outcome of the public participation. These principles are to be part of "a transparent and fair framework" for public participation. Regarding policies relating to the environment, a much more qualified and less specific duty applies.

Article 8 relates to preparation by "public authorities" of "executive regulations and other generally applicable legally binding rules that may have a significant effect on the environment". The treaty's definition of the term "public authority" excludes "bodies or institutions acting in a judicial *or legislative* capacity".[27] In contrast to Articles 6 and 7, most of the language of Article 8 is exhortatory rather than mandatory. In summary, draft rules should be published; time-frames allowing effective participation should be fixed; the public should be given an opportunity to comment; and the result of public participation is to be taken into account, but only "as far as possible".

One of the general provisions of the Aarhus Convention, Article 3(7), states that:

> Each Party shall promote the application of the principles of this Convention in international environmental decision-making processes and within the framework of international organizations in matters relating to the environment.

---

[27] Aarhus Convention, Article 2(2) (emphasis added).

Thus the treaty imposes on its parties a duty to promote its principles on, *inter alia*, public participation in decision-making within international organizations in matters relating to the environment. In 2005, the parties to the Aarhus Convention adopted the so-called Almaty Guidelines,[28] which provide guidance on the implementation of Article 3(7) including in relation to public participation.[29] As a basic proposition, the Almaty Guidelines state that "[e]fforts should be made to *proactively* seek the participation of relevant actors, in a transparent, consultative manner, appropriate to the nature of the forum"[30] and that:

> Participation of the public concerned in the meetings of international forums, including their subsidiary bodies and other groups established by the forums to contribute to the decision-making, in matters relating to the environment should be allowed at all relevant stages of the decision-making process, unless there is a reasonable basis to exclude such participation according to transparent and clearly stated standards that are made available, if possible, in advance.[31]

The Almaty Guidelines introduce the possibility of a test of standing for stakeholders "if this is necessary and unavoidable for practical reasons". Principles are suggested for applying such a test.[32] The Guidelines suggest possible forms of participation at meetings in international forums, including, *inter alia*, observer status, "advisory committees open to relevant stakeholders" and "forums and dialogues open to members of the public".[33] They state that, without prejudice to "the ability of international forums to prioritize their business and apply their rules of procedures", participation of the public concerned at meetings of such forums should include "the entitlement" to: (a) "have access to all documents relevant to the decision-making process produced for the meetings", (b) "circulate written statements" and (c) "speak at meetings".[34] Some of the principles from Article 6 of the Aarhus Convention (see above) are in effect repeated in the Almaty Guidelines, albeit with some supplementary suggestions.[35]

---

[28] Second Meeting of the Parties *Promoting the Application of the Principles of the Aarhus Convention in International Forums* (May 2005) Decision II/4. See also Third Meeting of the Parties *Promoting the Application of the Principles of the Convention in International Forums* (June 2008) Decision III/4.

[29] Regarding the implementation of Article 3(7) and the Almaty Guidelines, see ⟨www.unece.org/env/pp/ppif.htm⟩ (20 April 2009).

[30] Almaty Guidelines, para. 28 (emphasis added).

[31] *Ibid.*, para. 29.

[32] *Ibid.*, para. 31.

[33] *Ibid.*, para. 33.

[34] *Ibid.*, para. 34.

[35] *Ibid.*, paras 32 and 35–37.

Meaningful involvement of relevant stakeholders in decision-making is potentially time-consuming and expensive. However, the potential benefits of serious investment in stakeholder participation may include enhanced implementation and minimization of the likelihood of disputes. Many international organizations with a role in management of ABNJ allow stakeholders, both State and non-State, from outside their membership to be observers at their meetings. The participation rights that flow from observer status vary from one international organization to another. If the task is, say, to ensure compliance with management rules for a marine protected area or to minimize negative interactions between two economic activities, targeted and innovative forms of stakeholder participation may be required.

An example of an international organization with a marine management role that has started to tackle the matter of stakeholder participation in a specific way is the OSPAR Commission, in relation to its marine protected areas program. In 2008, the OSPAR Commission's Biodiversity Committee agreed to adopt, on a trial basis, "Guidance for good practice for communicating with stakeholders on the establishment & management of marine protected areas".[36] The guidance document states that its "final goal" is "to work towards a solid and secure stakeholder involvement process, based on the experience already available and the incorporation of professional approaches to communication tools".[37] The document does not have a specific section on ABNJ, but is instead of general application to the maritime area covered by the OSPAR Commission.

Conclusion

This short paper has addressed the related themes of MSP and stakeholder participation in ABNJ. On stakeholder participation, it has sought to explain that this is a relevant process for such areas, for example to help ensure compliance with management rules for marine protected areas or to minimize negative interactions between economic activities. However, it is a difficult process to define and not much attention has been paid to it in treaty law to date. An exception is the Aarhus Convention, which requires that treaty's principles to be promoted within international organizations in matters relating to the environment. The Almaty Guidelines seek to implement this requirement. In terms of practice by international organizations with a marine management role, the

[36] OSPAR, Agreement 2008–2 (available at ⟨www.ospar.org⟩). Regarding the document's adoption, see *ibid.*, para. 4.

[37] *Ibid.*, para. 6.

OSPAR Commission's guidance for good practice regarding communication with stakeholders in connection with marine protected areas represents a start in the involvement stakeholders in a specific initiative in, *inter alia*, ABNJ.

Regarding MSP, the paper has sought to show that this tool need not be confined to zones under the sovereignty or jurisdiction of coastal States. However, its use in ABNJ will require a variety of international organizations and potentially individual operators and flag States too, as well as adjacent coastal States in some cases, to work together. The beginnings of cooperation between relevant entities, with a view to developing MSP in ABNJ, can already be seen in the North-East Atlantic. These developments may be regarded as a prelude to rendering more precise the "due regard" concept in international law. However, the more difficult work to "state specific criteria for ensuring coexistence of different activities, and, if necessary, establish priorities, or mechanisms for dealing with conflicts", as called for by Professor Treves in his paper,[38] is still to come.

[38] Paper by T. Treves in this volume at 22.

PRINCIPLES AND OBJECTIVES OF THE LEGAL REGIME GOVERNING AREAS BEYOND NATIONAL JURISDICTION—COMMENTARY ON TULLIO TREVES

Louise A. de La Fayette*

I agree with Judge Treves that the distinction between beyond and within national jurisdiction is artificial and contrary to the ecosystem approach. Unfortunately, some states insist upon having absolute sovereign rights over the living resources within their exclusive economic zones (EEZs) and will not accept the obligation of compatibility between measures taken in the EEZ and on the high seas. They regard the requirement of compatibility as against their interest and a violation of their sovereign rights, not understanding that compatibility is a mutual obligation and may require either compromise on both sides or even that the rights of the coastal State take precedence in light of article 116 of the United Nations Convention on the Law of the Sea (LOS Convention).[1] This mistrust of the compatibility requirement as formulated in Article 7 of the Fish Stocks Agreement[2] is one of the reasons why some States, especially those in Latin America, refuse to become parties to the Agreement.[3] Unless they can be persuaded that they have misread the provision, for the time being at least, the unnatural dividing line across ocean ecosystems will remain.

I also agree that the mandate of the International Seabed Authority (ISA) cannot and should not be expanded to include *all* activities beyond national jurisdiction. However, as I have argued in a recent article, one could consider expanding the mandate of the ISA to cover only the conservation of biodiversity and bioprospecting in the Area.[4] The ISA already has a mandate to

* Visiting Professor, Maritime Institute, University of Greenwich, London.

[1] Adopted on 10 December 1982; 1833 UNTS 396.

[2] Agreement for the Implementation of the Provisions of the United Nations Convention on the Law of the Sea of 10 December 1982 Relating to the Conservation and Management of Straddling Fish Stocks and Highly Migratory Fish Stocks of 4 August 1995 ((1995) 34 ILM 1542).

[3] See, for example, D. Diz Pinto *et al.* "Summary of the Eighth Round of Informal Consultations of States Parties to the United Nations Fish Stocks Agreement (ICSP-8): 16 to 19 March 2009" (2009) 7 *Earth Negotiations Bulletin of the International Institute for Sustainable Development* No. 64 (available at ⟨www.iisd.ca⟩). The official report is in document ICSP8/UNFSA/REP/INF.6, available at www.un.org/Depts/los.

[4] L. de La Fayette "A New Regime for the Conservation and Sustainable Use of Marine Biodiversity and Genetic Resources beyond the Limits of National Jurisdiction", 24 (2009) *International Journal of Marine and Coastal Law* pp. 221–280.

Alex G. Oude Elferink and Erik J. Molenaar (eds.), *The International Legal Regime of Areas beyond National Jurisdiction: Current and Future Developments*, pp. 39–40.

protect the marine environment and fauna and flora from seabed mining and has already sponsored scientific research and workshops on marine biodiversity in the Area. Therefore, the ISA has a partial mandate and the background information necessary to protect seabed biodiversity from all activities, albeit in cooperation with other relevant organisations. Furthermore, the ISA already has an extensive mandate concerning marine scientific research (MSR). Since bioprospecting is closely linked to MSR, it would be logical and reasonable to entrust the ISA with the regulation of bioprospecting, especially as the organisms that interest bioprospectors are co-located and often inextricably attached to mineral resources.

Judge Treves considers that the various activities in areas beyond national jurisdiction could not realistically be brought together and regulated by one all-encompassing international organisation, a World Oceans Organisation or Authority. Although such a consolidation of authority might be desirable to ensure an integrated, ecosystem approach to ocean management, it would probably be politically impossible. The existing sectoral institutions could not be expected to abolish themselves. Furthermore, they have developed a certain degree of specialised expertise which should be preserved.

However, an implementing agreement to the LOS Convention could be elaborated setting out the relevant principles, including those in Part XII of the LOS Convention, as well as the ecosystem approach and the precautionary approach, which were articulated subsequently at the United Nations Conference on Environment and Development (UNCED). This new agreement could establish a process under the UN General Assembly for discussion of the issues, for coordinating the sectoral regimes, and for evaluating their effectiveness. The current Ad Hoc Open-ended Informal Working Group to study issues relating to the conservation and sustainable use of marine biological diversity beyond areas of national jurisdiction could be developed to serve as such a process. The Fish Stocks Agreement with its yearly meetings of States parties and its Review Conference could serve to a certain extent as a model.

As Judge Treves so usefully suggests, a UN Declaration of Principles in a General Assembly resolution could serve as the basis for such an agreement, just as declarations of principles set the scene for the negotiation of the LOS Convention and the Outer Space Treaty.[5] Such declarations are carefully negotiated and have a great deal of influence and effectiveness in determining the actions of states and organisations.

---

[5] General Assembly resolution 1962 (XVIII) of 13 December 1963: Declaration of Legal Principles Governing the Activities of States in the Exploration and Use of Outer Space; General Assembly resolution 2749 (XXV) of 17 December 1970: Declaration of Principles Governing the Sea-Bed and the Ocean Floor.

PART TWO

INSTITUTIONAL ARRANGEMENTS FOR THE LEGAL REGIME GOVERNING AREAS BEYOND NATIONAL JURISDICTION

THE SEABED BEYOND THE LIMITS OF NATIONAL JURISDICTION: GENERAL AND INSTITUTIONAL ASPECTS

Tullio Scovazzi*

The Concept of Common Heritage of Mankind

The main innovation of the United Nations Convention on the Law of the Sea (LOS Convention),[1] with respect to the previous law of the sea regime, is the concept of the common heritage of mankind. While other important innovations included in the LOS Convention, such as the exclusive economic zone (EEZ), may be considered to be the result of a foreseeable evolution in the international law of the sea, the concept of common heritage of mankind has a revolutionary character. It presupposes a third kind of regime which is completely different from both the traditional concepts of sovereignty, which applies in the territorial sea, and of freedom, which applies on the high seas.

The idea of the common heritage of mankind was launched in a memorable speech made at the United Nations General Assembly on 1 November 1967 by the representative of Malta, Mr. Arvid Pardo.[2] The practical opportunity for proposing a new regime was given by the technological developments which were expected to lead in a relatively short time to the commercial exploitation of polymetallic nodules lying on the surface of the deep seabed and containing various minerals of appreciable economic value, such as manganese, nickel, cobalt and copper.

* Professor at the University of Milano-Bicocca, Milan, Italy.

[1] Adopted on 10 December 1982; 1833 UNTS 396.

[2] The only precedent is a proposal made in 1927 by the Argentine jurist José León Suárez. He was entrusted by the League of Nations Experts Committee for the Progressive Codification of International Law with the drafting of a report on the international rules relating to the exploitation of marine living resources. Mr. Suárez proposed that the living resources of the sea, and whales in particular, should be considered a heritage of mankind:

> Les richesses de la mer, en particulier les richesses immenses de la région antarctique, constituent un patrimoine de l'humanité, et notre Commission, constituée par la Société des Nations, est tout indiquée pour proposer au Gouvernement un moyen d'action avant qu'il ne soit trop tard (Société des Nations *Comité d'Experts pour la Codification Progressive du Droit International, Rapport au Conseil de la Société des Nations* (Genève: 1927) 123).

Alex G. Oude Elferink and Erik J. Molenaar (eds.), *The International Legal Regime of Areas beyond National Jurisdiction: Current and Future Developments*, pp. 43–60.

The application of the scheme of sovereignty was likely to lead to a series of competitive extensions of the limits of national jurisdiction on the seabed. The application of the scheme of freedom was likely to lead to a rush towards the exploitation of economically and strategically valuable minerals falling under the regime of freedom of the high seas ("first-come-first-served" rule). According to Mr. Pardo's speech, the consequences of both possible scenarios would have been equally undesirable. They would have encompassed political tension, economic injustice and risks of pollution. In a few words, "the strong would get stronger, the rich richer".[3]

The basic elements of the regime of common heritage of mankind, applying to the seabed beyond the limits of national jurisdiction, are the prohibition of national appropriation, the destination of the Area[4] for peaceful purposes, the use of the Area and its resources for the benefit of mankind as a whole with particular consideration for the interests and needs of developing countries, and the establishment of an international organization entitled to act on behalf of mankind in the exercise of rights over the resources.[5]

---

[3] As was observed by Ambassador Pardo:

> The known resources of the seabed and of the ocean floor are far greater than the resources known to exist on dry land. The seabed and ocean floor are also of vital and increasing strategic importance. Present and clearly foreseeable technology also permits their effective exploration for military or economic purposes. Some countries may therefore be tempted to use their technical competence to achieve near-unbreakable world dominance through predominant control over the seabed and the ocean floor. This, even more than the search for wealth, will impel countries with the requisite technical competence competitively to extend their jurisdiction over selected areas of the ocean floor. The process has already started and will lead to a competitive scramble for sovereign rights over the land underlying the world's seas and oceans, surpassing in magnitude and in its implications last century's colonial scramble for territory in Asia and Africa. The consequences will be very grave: at the very least a dramatic escalation of the arms race and sharply increasing world tensions, also caused by the intolerable injustice that would reserve the plurality of the world's resources for the exclusive benefit of less than a handful of nations. The strong would get stronger, the rich richer, and among the rich themselves there would arise an increasing and insuperable differentiation between two or three and the remainder. Between the very few dominant powers, suspicions and tensions would reach unprecedented levels. Traditional activities on the high seas would be curtailed and, at the same time, the world would face the growing danger of permanent damage to the marine environment through radioactive and other pollution: this is a virtually inevitable consequence of the present situation (A. Pardo *The Common Heritage—Selected Papers on Oceans and World Order* (International Ocean Institute, Valletta: 1975) 31).

[4] Article 1 of the LOS Convention provides that 'Area' means "the sea-bed and ocean floor and subsoil thereof, beyond the limits of national jurisdiction".

[5] The word 'heritage' itself, which renders the idea of the sound management of a resource to be transmitted to the heritors, was preferred to the word 'property', as the latter could have recalled the *jus utendi et abutendi* (right to use and misuse) that private Roman law gave to the owner (E. Mann Borgese "Introduction" in Pardo, note 3).

The institutional aspect is one of the main components of the concept of common heritage of mankind and cannot be separated from the others.

The Common Heritage of Mankind in the LOS Convention

All the basic elements mentioned above can be found in Part XI of the LOS Convention ("The Area"). The Area and its resources are the common heritage of mankind (Article 136). No State can claim or exercise sovereignty over any part of the Area, nor can any State or natural or juridical person appropriate any part thereof (Article 137(1)). The Area is open to use exclusively for peaceful purposes (Article 141). All rights over the resources of the Area are vested in mankind as a whole, on whose behalf the International Sea-Bed Authority (ISA)—the international organization created by the LOS Convention (Article 137(2))—is entitled to act. Activities in the Area[6] are carried out for the benefit of mankind as a whole, irrespective of the geographical location of States, whether coastal or land-locked, and taking into particular consideration the interests and needs of developing States (Article 140(1)). The ISA provides for the equitable sharing of financial and other economic benefits derived from activities in the Area through an appropriate mechanism (Article 140(2)).

However, the concrete incorporation of the idea of common heritage of mankind into the LOS Convention does not fully reflect all the aspects included in the original proposal made by Malta. Under the Maltese draft,[7] all the natural resources, whether living or non-living, existing beyond the 200-mile limit were to be managed by international institutions, to ensure the equitable sharing by all States of the benefits derived from the development of these resources and taking into particular consideration the interests and needs of poor countries. Moreover, within the 200-mile limit, the coastal State was bound to make contributions to the international community in exchange for the financial benefits derived from the extension of its rights to the resources contained therein.

The above mentioned aspects of the Maltese proposal were not retained in the LOS Convention regime for the Area. The resources to which the principle of common heritage applies are limited to the mineral resources. The

---

[6] Article 1((1)(3)) of the LOS Convention provides that activities in the Area "means all activities of exploration for, and exploitation of, the resources of the Area". For the purposes of Part XI resources "means all solid, liquid or gaseous mineral resources *in situ* in the Area at or beneath the seabed, including polymetallic nodules" (LOS Convention, Article 133).

[7] Text in Pardo, note 3 at 381.

contributions that the coastal State is called to make through the ISA are related to the exploitation of the non-living resources of the continental shelf beyond (and not within) the 200-mile limit (Article 82).

Yet the differences between the proposal by the promoting State and the regime resulting in the LOS Convention do not detract from the importance of the ideal embodied in the concept of common heritage of mankind. For the first time in the historical development of international law of the sea a regime based on the management of resources by an international organization was included in a treaty of codification. The common heritage of mankind is a third conceptual option (*tertium genus*) which applies to a particular kind of resources located in a specific marine space. It does not eliminate the traditional notions of freedom or sovereignty for the remaining resources and the remaining marine spaces. But it provides for a different and much more equitable approach.

The Common Heritage of Mankind in the Amended Text of the LOS Convention

The text of the LOS Convention was not adopted by consensus. It was submitted to a vote after all efforts to reach consensus had been exhausted. It received 130 votes in favor, 4 against and 17 abstentions. Many developed States were among those which cast a negative vote or abstained. The main criticisms were addressed at the regime of the Area. According to many industrialized States, the LOS Convention regime would have discouraged mining activities by individual States and private enterprise, would have unduly favored a monopoly of activities by the ISA, would have burdened the contractors with excessive financial and other obligations relating also to the field of transfer of technology and would have disregarded the interests of industrialized countries in the decision-making procedures of the Council, the executive organ of the ISA.

In 1994 it was clear that the LOS Convention was expected to formally enter into force without the participation of many developed countries, that is, without the participation of the limited number of States having the command of the technological and financial capability required to engage in deep seabed mining activities. To avoid the substantial failure of a regime based on the principle of common heritage of mankind, the United Nations promoted a new negotiation on Part XI of the LOS Convention. It resulted in the 1994 Agreement,[8] which was annexed to Resolution 48/263, adopted by the General

[8] Agreement Relating to the Implementation of Part XI of the United Nations Convention on the Law of the Sea of 10 December 1982 of 28 July 1994 ((1994) 33 ILM 1309).

Assembly on 17 August 1994. Resolution 48/263, while reaffirming that the Area and its resources are the common heritage of mankind, recognizes that "political and economic changes, including in particular a growing reliance on market principles, have necessitated the re-evaluation of some aspects of the regime for the Area and its resources".

The provisions of the 1994 Agreement and those of Part XI of the LOS Convention "shall be interpreted and applied together as a single instrument".[9] However, in the event of any inconsistency between the 1994 Agreement and Part XI, the provisions of the former shall prevail. In fact, the label of 'implementing agreement' is a fig leaf that covers the evident reality that in 1994 the LOS Convention was amended and several aspects of the original concept of common heritage of mankind were substantively changed.[10]

For instance, the obligation of States Parties to finance the deep seabed mining operations of the Enterprise, the organ of the ISA which is to carry out mining activities in the Area directly, is abrogated and the independent activities by the Enterprise are delayed until it is able to conduct mining operations through joint-ventures. A contractor which has contributed a particular area to the ISA as a reserved area has the right of first refusal to enter into a joint-venture arrangement with the Enterprise for exploration and exploitation of that area. If the Enterprise does not submit an application for a plan of work for activities with respect to a reserved area within 15 years, the contractor which contributed the area is entitled to apply for a plan of work for that area, provided that it offers in good faith to include the Enterprise as a joint-venture partner. The Enterprise and developing States wishing to obtain technology for deep seabed mining shall seek to obtain it on fair and reasonable commercial terms and conditions on the open market or through joint-venture arrangements. The decision-making procedure by the Council is modified by the introduction of the rule that, if all efforts to reach consensus have been exhausted, decisions on questions of substance are taken by a two-thirds majority, provided that such decisions are not opposed by a majority in any one

---

9 1994 Agreement, Article 2.

10 As has been observed:

> The 1994 Implementation Agreement is a curious creature. The 1982 LOSC does not permit reservations (Articles 309, 310) and the procedures for its amendment are both protracted and open only to State parties (Articles 311–317). Neither route was suitable for modifications of the Convention sought by the industrialised States that remained outside the Convention. Instead, the 1994 Implementation Agreement was made, its title disingenuously implying that it was concerned to put into effect the 1982 provisions rather than to change them. In fact, it stipulates that several provisions of Part XI of the LOSC 'shall not apply' and modifies the effect of others" (R.R. Churchill and A.V. Lowe *The Law of the Sea*, 3rd ed. (Manchester University Press, Manchester: 1999) 20).

of the Council's chambers. This means that any of the five chambers of States established under Part XI of the LOS Convention (for example, the chamber composed of four of the major consumer or importer States) can veto the taking of decisions by the Council.

Following the adoption of the 1994 Agreement, the LOS Convention has achieved an almost universal participation.[11] However, the exception remains the United States, the main industrialized country and the main potential investor in the field of deep seabed mining, which is not yet a party to the LOS Convention.

While adapted (or, under a less optimistic perspective, diluted) in the 1994 text of the LOS Convention, the principle of common heritage of mankind still applies. It remains a major source of inspiration for a codification treaty designed to:

> contribute to the realization of a just and equitable international economic order which takes into account the interests and needs of mankind as a whole and, in particular the special interests and needs of developing countries, whether coastal or land-locked.[12]

The Uncertain Prospects for Commercial Mining in the Deep Seabed

Since several years, the ISA has been working on the subject of exploration of the different mineral resources of the Area. On 13 July 2000 the ISA Assembly approved the Regulations on Prospecting and Exploration for Polymetallic Nodules in the Area (the so-called mining code).[13] This has enabled the ISA to sign, between 2001 and 2005, contracts for exploration with eight investors.

Mining activities for resources different from polymetallic nodules have also been envisaged. The ISA Council is presently reviewing a second "mining code", the "Regulations on Prospecting and Exploration for Polymetallic Sulphides in the Area", and work is going on for another similar instrument relating to cobalt-rich ferromanganese crusts. Unlike polymetallic nodules which

---

[11] However, the original text of the LOS Convention is still in force today in the relationships between twenty-four States which have became parties to the LOS Convention prior to the adoption of the 1994 Agreement and have not yet completed the procedural steps to became parties to the 1994 Agreement.

[12] LOS Convention, preamble.

[13] Polymetallic nodules have been defined as:

> lumps of metallic ore, between golf ball and soccer ball in size, scattered loosely in expansive fields on abyssal plains. Their quantity in a given area can be assessed simply by photographing the ocean bottom. They can be scooped up by mechanical harvesters with little physical damage to the seabed (ISBA, *Press Release* SB/9/1 (23 July 2003) 2).

cover extensive areas of the deep seabed, sulphides[14] and crusts[15] are found in localized deposits. Concentrations of methane hydrates[16] are also found in the Area and their exploration and exploitation may also require further regulation by the ISA in the future.

A number of factors have inhibited progress towards commercial exploitation of polymetallic nodule deposits. These factors include the hostile environment in which exploration and mining will take place both as regards the open-ocean surface environment and the great depths at which polymetallic nodule deposits occur, the high costs involved in research and development of mining technology and the fact that, under current economic conditions, deep seabed mining remains uncompetitive compared to land-based mining.

Recently, the ISA Secretary-General remarked in his report that the present eight contractors for exploration for polymetallic nodules in the Area have so far limited their exploration activities to the analysis of existing information and the opportunistic collection of environmental baselines data through scientific research cruises. There are no proposals to carry out research on matters related to future commercial exploitation of the resources, such as the physical problems of recovering nodules from the seabed and transferring them to transport ships:

> Although this situation may be considered reasonable, given the technological and economic conditions relating to seabed mining that prevailed until recently, it must also be recalled that the resources of the deep seabed are the common heritage of mankind and that the fundamental objective of the regime established by the Convention and the Agreement is to encourage the development of those resources for the benefit of mankind as a whole. This is why

[14] Hydrothermal polymetallic massive sulphides:

> occur typically in chimney-like structures, called smokers, surrounding undersea hot-spring vents. Their minerals come mainly from magma, the mass of molten rock deep beneath the earth's crust, where it breaches the ocean bottom in volcanic regions along the margins of ocean basins. Individual deposits are small and scattered. Mining would require the destruction of the smokers, with potentially catastrophic consequences for the exotic animal communities that live in the superheated, oxygen-deprived water and cannot exist in a normal environment dependent on sunlight (*ibid.*).

[15] Cobalt-rich ferromanganese crusts:

> derived like the nodules from metals precipitated out of seawater, are fused to the seabed in layers up to tens of centimetres thick, often buried beneath other seabed deposits. They are found on the flanks and ridges of globe-encircling, mid-ocean mountain range. Assessment of their occurrence and metal content and their eventual exploitation will require digging or drilling the ores out of a solid rock bed (*ibid*).

[16] Concentrations of methane hydrates are ice-like materials that occur in abundance in marine sediments and store immense quantities of methane.

> the Agreement provides for a time-limit of 15 years, during which time contractors have exclusive rights to explore the areas allocated to them. The expectation is that, after 15 years, in the absence of special circumstances, contractors will either move to the exploitation phase or surrender the areas allocated to them. The current leisurely pace of activities, however, would suggest that the contractors will basically continue to sit on the sites and seek multiple extensions of their contract if they are to retain the allocated areas. Prolonged blocking of access to the resources is neither an efficient nor an equitable way of administering the resources, which belong to mankind as a whole.[17]

Yet the concept of common heritage of mankind, which is a third and more equitable scheme different from both the schemes of freedom or sovereignty, has actually been put in place under an international regime and an international organization has been established to manage marine economic resources falling under this regime. But what seems now to be missing is the possibility to reach the resources to which the regime was intended to apply!

The Prospects of the Exploitation of Genetic Resources in the Deep Seabed

While the prospects for commercial mining in the deep seabed are uncertain, the exploitation of commercially valuable genetic resources is becoming another activity taking place on the deep seabed. The deep seabed is not a desert, despite extreme conditions of cold, complete darkness and high pressure. It is the habitat of diverse forms of life associated with typical features, such as hydrothermal vents, cold water seeps, seamounts or deep water coral reefs. It supports biological communities that present unique genetic characteristics. For instance, some animal communities live in the complete absence of sunlight where warm water springs from tectonically active areas (so called hydrothermal vents).[18] Several species of microorganisms, fish, crustaceans, polychaetes, echinoderms, coelenterates and mollusks have been found in hydrothermal vent areas. Many of them were new to science. These communities, which do not depend on plant photosynthesis for their survival, rely on specially adapted micro-organisms able to synthesize organic compounds

---

[17] Report of the Secretary-General of the International Seabed Authority under Article 166, Paragraph 4, of the United Nations Convention on the Law of the Sea Doc. ISBA/14/A/2 of 14 April 2008, para. 59.

[18] Hydrothermal vents may be found both in the Area and on the seabed falling within the limits of national jurisdiction under the definition of continental shelf given by Article 76 LOS Convention.

from the hydrothermal fluid of the vents (chemosynthesis).[19] The ability of some deep seabed organisms to survive extreme temperatures (thermophiles and hyperthermophiles) and other extreme conditions (extremophiles) makes their genes of great interest to science and industry.

But what is the present international regime of bioprospecting and exploitation of the genetic resources of the Area, also considering that neither the LOS Convention nor the 1992 Convention on Biological Diversity (CBD)[20] provide any specific legal framework for this activity?[21] The factual implications of the question are pointed out in a document issued in 2005 by the Subsidiary Body on Scientific, Technical and Technological Advice (SBSTTA) established under the CBD.[22]

Only few States and private entities have access to the financial means and sophisticated technologies needed to reach the deep seabed:

> Reaching deep seabed extreme environments and maintaining alive the sampled organisms, as well as culturing them, requires sophisticated and expensive technologies. [...] Typically, the technology associated with research on deep seabed genetic resources involves: oceanographic vessels equipped with sonar technology, manned or unmanned submersible vehicles; *in situ* sampling tools; technology related to culture methods; molecular biology technology and techniques; and technology associated with the different steps of the commercialization process of derivates of deep seabed genetic resources. With the exception of basic

[19] The discovery of hydrothermal vent ecosystems has given rise to a new theory as to how life originated on earth. It could have originated and evolved in association with hydrothermal vents in the primeval ocean during the early Archaean period (about 4,000 million years ago).

[20] Convention on Biological Diversity of 5 June 1992 ((1992) 31 ILM 818).

[21] On this question see L. Glowka "The Deepest of Ironies: Genetic Resources, Marine Scientific Research, and the Area" (1996) *Ocean Yearbook* 154–178; T. Scovazzi "Mining, Protection of the Environment, Scientific Research and Bioprospecting: Some Considerations on the Role of the International Sea-Bed Authority" (2004) *International Journal of Marine and Coastal Law* 383–409; S. Arico and C. Salpin *Bioprospecting of Genetic Resources in the Deep Seabed: Scientific, Legal and Policy Aspects* (United Nations Institute of Advanced Studies, Yokohama: 2005); F. Armas Pfirter "The Management of Seabed Living Resources in 'the Area' under UNCLOS" (2006) 11 *Revista Electrónica de Estudios Internacionales*; D.K. Leary *International Law and Genetic Resources of the Deep Sea* (Martinus Nijhoff, Leiden: 2006); E.J. Molenaar "Managing Biodiversity in Areas beyond National Jurisdiction" (2007) 22 *International Journal of Marine and Coastal Law* 89–124; A.G. Oude Elferink "The Regime of the Area: Delineating the Scope of Application of the Common Heritage Principle and Freedom of the High Seas" (2007) 22 *International Journal of Marine and Coastal Law*, 2007 143–176. See also the report of the international seminar *Towards a New Governance of High Seas Biodiversity*, sponsored by IDDRI (Institut du Développement Durable et des Relations Internationales), held in Monaco on 20–21 March 2008.

[22] *Status and Trends of, and Threats to, Deep Seabed Genetic Resources beyond National Jurisdiction, and Identification of Technical Options for their Conservation and Sustainable Use* Doc. UNEP/CBD/SBSTTA/11/11 of 22 July 2005.

> molecular biology techniques, most of the technology necessary for accessing the deep seabed and studying and isolating its organisms is owned by research institutions, both public and private. To date, only very few countries have access to these technologies.[23]

The prospects for commercial application of bioprospecting activities seem promising:

> Deep seabed resources hold enormous potential for many types of commercial applications, including in the health sector, for industrial processes or bioremediation. A brief search of Patent Office Databases revealed that compounds from deep seabed organisms have been used as basis for potent cancer fighting drugs, commercial skin protection products providing higher resistance to ultraviolet and heat exposure, and for preventing skin inflammation, detoxification agents for snake venom, anti-viral compounds, anti-allergy agents and anti-coagulant agents, as well as industrial applications for reducing viscosity.[24]

Prospects for profits seem promising as well:

> The commercial importance of marine genetic resources is demonstrated by the fact that all major pharmaceutical firms have marine biology departments. The high cost of marine scientific research, and the slim odds of success (only one to two percent of pre-clinical candidates become commercially produced) is offset by the potential profits. Estimates put worldwide sales of all marine biotechnology-related products at US $ 100 billion for the year 2000.[25]

An important element to take into consideration in assessing the legal aspects of deep seabed bioprospecting and exploitation of genetic resources is that the patent legislation of several States does not compel the applicant to disclose the origin of the genetic materials used:

> Assessing the types and levels of current uses of genetic resources from the deep seabed proves relatively difficult for several reasons. First, patents do not necessarily provide detailed information about practical applications, though they do indicate potential uses. Moreover, information regarding the origin of the samples used is not always included in patent descriptions.[26]

---

[23] *Ibid.*, paras 12 and 13. "A limited number of institutions worldwide own or operate vehicles that are able to reach areas deeper than 1,000 meters below the oceans' surface, and can therefore be actively involved in deep seabed research" (*ibid.*, para. 16).

[24] *Ibid.*, para. 21.

[25] *Ibid.*, para. 22.

[26] *Ibid.*

The Present Discussion on the Regime for Genetic Resources in the Deep Seabed

In February 2006 the subject of the international regime for the genetic resources in the deep seabed was discussed within the Ad Hoc Open-ended Informal Working Group to study issues relating to the conservation and sustainable use of marine biological diversity beyond areas of national jurisdiction,[27] established by United Nations General Assembly Resolution 60/30 of 29 November 2005. Opposite views were put forward by the States concerned.

Some States took the position that the LOS Convention principle of common heritage of mankind and the mandate of the ISA should be extended to cover also bioprospecting:

> Several delegations reiterated their understanding that the marine genetic resources beyond areas of national jurisdiction constituted the common heritage of mankind and recalled article 140 of the Convention, which provides that the activities in the Area shall be carried out for the benefit of mankind and that particular consideration should be given to the interest and needs of developing States, including the need for these resources to be used for the benefit of present generations and to be preserved for future generations. [...] A number of delegations mentioned that the International Seabed Authority constituted an existing mechanism in this area and that consideration should accordingly be given to the possibility of broadening its mandate.[28]

Other States relied on the LOS Convention principle of freedom of the high seas, which would imply a right of freedom of access to, and unrestricted exploitation of, deep seabed genetic resources:

> Other delegations reiterated that any measures that may be taken in relation to genetic resources in areas beyond national jurisdiction must be consistent with international law, including freedom of navigation. In their view, these resources were covered by the regime of the high seas, which provided the legal framework for all activities relating to them, in particular marine scientific research. These delegations did not agree that there was a need for a new regime to address the exploitation of marine genetic resources in areas beyond national jurisdiction or to expand the mandate of the International Seabed Authority.[29]

In the summary of trends prepared after the 2006 meeting, the co-chairpersons of the Working Group took the view that:

---

[27] Hereinafter, Working Group.

[28] *Report of the Ad Hoc Open-ended Working Group to Study Issues Relating to their Conservation and Sustainable Use of Marine Biological Diversity beyond Areas of National Jurisdiction* Doc. A/61/65 of 20 March 2006, para. 71.

[29] *Ibid.*, para. 72.

> further discussion on the legal status of marine biological diversity, including genetic resources beyond national jurisdiction, is needed in order to clarify how such resources may have to be regulated, whether existing tools and arrangements are sufficient or whether new tools are required for their conservation and sustainable use, including consideration of access and benefit sharing.[30]

The Working Group held a second meeting from 28 April to 2 May 2008.[31] The general understanding on the importance of marine genetic resources was repeated:

> Delegations agreed that marine genetic resources provided important ecosystems goods and services to humankind. Therefore, ensuring the conservation and sustainable use of marine biodiversity beyond areas of national jurisdiction was essential.[32]

As regards the legal aspects of the question, the starting point was the following:

> The United Nations Convention on the Law of the Sea was recognized as the legal framework for all activities in the oceans and seas, including in respect of genetic resources beyond areas of national jurisdiction.[33]

However, while moving from the same starting point, the States participating to the 2008 meeting of the Working Group reached two very opposite conclusions as regards the regime to be applied to marine genetic resources, repeating the difference of views which had already taken place in 2006:

> In that regard, divergent views were expressed on the relevant legal regime on marine genetic resources beyond areas of national jurisdiction, in particular whether those marine genetic resources were part of the common heritage of mankind and therefore fell under the regime of the Area, or were part of the regime for the high seas.[34]

An attempt was made by a number of delegations to get out of the deadlock of a theoretical battle on what the LOS Convention might have to say as regards marine genetic resources. The States belonging to the European Union proposed to concentrate the discussion on practical measures and to address

---

[30] *Ibid.*, para. 12 of Annex I.

[31] The United Nations Open-Ended Informal Consultative Process on Oceans and the Law of the Sea also addressed the subject of marine genetic resources at its 2007 meeting. However, the meeting was unable to reach overall agreement on the elements to be suggested to the UN General Assembly as regards the legal regime of such resources. See the co-chairpersons' possible elements to be suggested in the annex to UN Doc. A/62/169 of 30 July 2007.

[32] *Joint statement of the Co-Chairpersons of the Working Group* Doc. A/63/79 of 16 May 2008, para. 32.

[33] *Ibid.*, para. 36.

[34] *Ibid.*

the crucial question of benefit sharing, taking into consideration, as a possible reference, the International Treaty on Plant Genetic Resources for Food and Agriculture, concluded in 2001 under the auspices of the Food and Agriculture Organization (FAO). This treaty includes a mechanism on benefit sharing. It could be studied as a possible model to provide, *mutatis mutandis*, solutions in discussing the question of benefit sharing in the field of marine genetic resources:

> some delegations proposed focusing on practical measures to enhance the conservation and sustainable use of marine genetic resources. It was proposed that such practical measures could address, among others, options for benefit-sharing. In that regard, several delegations expressed interest in considering a proposal to use the multilateral system developed under the International Treaty on Plant Genetic Resources for Food and Agriculture as a possible reference point for the discussions.[35]

This approach is reflected in the concluding remarks presented by the Co-Chairpersons of the Working Group, who believe that there is a need for further consideration on, *inter alia*:

> (e) Practical measures to address the conservation and sustainable use of marine genetic resources in areas beyond national jurisdiction, without prejudice to ongoing discussions on the relevant legal regime on marine genetic resources beyond areas of national jurisdiction.[36]

Some Legal Elaboration on the Ongoing Discussion

The present discussion on the international regime of bioprospecting for deep seabed genetic resources leaves a sentiment of dissatisfaction. Why do two groups of States, moving from the same starting point, namely that the LOS Convention is the legal framework for all activities taking place in the sea, reach two completely opposite conclusions as regards the matter in question? Who is wrong? A possible (and also intellectually attractive) answer to the question is that there is something wrong in the very starting point. Such a view needs some elaboration.

The LOS Convention is a great achievement in the field of codification of international law. It has been rightly qualified as a "Constitution for Oceans", "a monumental achievement in the international community", "the first comprehensive treaty dealing with practically every aspect of the uses and resources of the seas and the oceans", an instrument which "has successfully accommodated

[35] *Ibid.*, para. 38.
[36] *Ibid.*, para. 54.

the competing interests of all nations".[37] This may explain why it is repeatedly stated by States and in United Nations General Assembly Resolutions that the LOS Convention "sets out the legal framework within which all activities in the oceans and seas must be carried out".[38]

But this statement is only partially true. In fact, the LOS Convention, as any legal text, is linked to the period when it was negotiated and adopted (1973–1982). Being itself a product of time, the LOS Convention cannot stop the passing of time. While it provides a solid basis, it would be illusory to think that the LOS Convention is the end of legal regulation. Yet international law of the sea is subject to a process of natural evolution and progressive development which is linked to State practice and presents several aspects. Due to limits of space, it is not possible to elaborate here on the instances where changes with respect to the original LOS Convention regime have been integrated into the LOS Convention itself (evolution by integration), where different interpretations of the relevant LOS Convention provisions are in principle admissible and State practice may be important in making one interpretation prevail (evolution by interpretation), where the relevant legal regime is to be inferred only from State practice, for the reason that the LOS Convention does not provide any clearly defined regime (evolution in another context) or where, due to the fact that the LOS Convention regime is clearly unsatisfactory, a new instrument of universal scope has been drafted to avoid the risk of undesirable consequences (evolution by further codification).[39]

Interestingly enough, the main point that needs to be stressed here goes close to a banality: the LOS Convention cannot produce miracles. In particular, it cannot regulate activities that its drafters cannot be supposed to have regulated for the simple reason that the activities themselves were not foreseeable in the period when the treaty was being negotiated. It may thus be asked how much of the subject matter of genetic resources of the Area can reasonably be understood as falling under the LOS Convention regime. Four considerations seem important in this regard.

First, the LOS Convention does not provide any specific regime for the exploitation of marine genetic resources of the Area. At the time when the LOS Convention was being drafted, very little was known about the genetic qualities of deep seabed organisms. For evident chronological reasons, the

---

[37] See T. Koh "A Constitution for the Oceans" *The Law of the Sea—Official Text of the United Nations Convention on the Law of the Sea with Annexes and Index* (United Nations, New York: 1983) xxiii.

[38] See Resolution 62/215 on "Oceans and the Law of the Sea" of 22 December 2007.

[39] For more elaboration see T. Scovazzi "The Evolution of International Law of the Sea: New Issues, New Challenges" *Hague Academy of International Law*, 286 *Recueil des cours* (2001) 39–52.

potential economic value of the units of heredity of this kind of organisms was not considered by the LOS Convention negotiators. When dealing with the resources of the Area, they had only mineral resources in mind. In fact, the resources of the Area are limited in the LOS Convention to "all solid, liquid or gaseous mineral resources *in-situ* in the Area at or beneath the sea-bed, including polymetallic nodules" (Article 133(a)). The term "activities" in the Area is narrowly defined in the LOS Convention as "all activities of exploration for, and exploitation of the resources of the Area" (Article 1(1)).

Second, despite the narrow definitions of resources and activities, not all of the LOS Convention should be left aside when envisaging a future regime for marine genetic resources of the Area. The scope of the regime of the Area is already broader than it may be believed to be at first sight. Under the LOS Convention, the legal condition of the Area has an influence also on the regulation of matters and activities that, although different from minerals and mining activities, are located in that space. Besides the main field of competence, the regime of the Area already encompasses matters which are more or less directly related to mining activities, such as marine scientific research,[40] the preservation of the marine environment[41] and the protection of underwater cultural heritage.[42]

While a specific regime for the exploitation of genetic resources is lacking, the aim of sharing the benefit among all States, which was the main aspect of the seminal proposal made by Arvid Pardo, can still be seen as the paramount objective embodied in the LOS Convention for everything that takes place in the Area. Also in the field of genetic resources, the application of the principle of freedom of the sea (that is the 'first-come-first-served' rule) leads to inequitable and hardly acceptable consequences.[43] New cooperative schemes have to be envisaged at the international level, based on the objective of the benefit of all States. This is also in full conformity with the principle of fair and equitable sharing of the benefits arising out of the utilization of genetic resources set forth by Article 1 of the CBD.

Third, the activity of bioprospecting, that is the search for commercially valuable genetic resources of the deep seabed, could already be considered as falling under the LOS Convention regime of marine scientific research. The LOS Convention does not provide any definition of "marine scientific research". Article 246, which applies to the EEZ and the continental shelf, makes a distinction between two kinds of marine scientific research projects,

---

40 Article 143. See also *infra*.
41 See LOS Convention, Article 145.
42 See *ibid.*, Article 149.
43 "The strong would get stronger, the rich richer" (see note 3).

namely those carried out "to increase scientific knowledge of the marine environment for the benefit of all mankind" (para. 3) and those "of direct significance for the exploration and exploitation of natural resources, whether living or non-living" (para. 5(a)).

This distinction supports the conclusion that, under the LOS Convention regime, research activities directly related to the purpose of commercial exploitation of resources, such as bioprospecting, fall under the general label of "marine scientific research".[44] Also bioprospecting is consequently covered by Article 143 of the LOS Convention, which applies only to the Area and sets forth the principle that "marine scientific research in the Area shall be carried out exclusively for peaceful purposes and for the benefit of the mankind as a whole".[45] This provision refers to any kind of marine scientific research and is not limited to research on mineral resources. Under Article 143(2), the ISA, besides carrying out marine scientific research concerning the Area and its resources, shall promote and encourage the conduct of research and co-ordinate and disseminate the results and analysis when available.[46] Article 143(3), grants to the States the right to carry out scientific research in the Area, but binds them to co-operate with other States and the ISA in various fields, including dissemination of results. Also this provision refers to any kind of marine scientific research in the Area.

Yet the reading of Article 143 in combination with Article 246 contradicts the unwarranted assumption that there is an absolute freedom to carry out bioprospecting in the Area. States which are already active in bioprospecting in the Area should be required to explain how they activities contribute to the benefit of mankind as a whole.[47]

[44] Yet there is an inextricable factual link between marine scientific research (either pure or applied) and bioprospecting. A research endeavor organized with the intent to increase human knowledge may well result in the discovery of commercially valuable information on genetic resources.

[45] Article 241 of the LOS Convention is also relevant in a discussion on the legal condition of the genetic resources of the deep seabed. It provides that "Marine scientific research activities shall not constitute the legal basis for any claim to any part of the marine environment or its resources".

[46] The provision deals with the carrying out of "marine scientific research concerning the Area and its resources" and, given the narrow definition of "resources" (Article 133), could be interpreted as limited to mineral resources. But the provision can also be read as relating to research concerning either the Area in general or its specific mineral resources.

[47] "The principle of common heritage in its substantive aspect is, like any norm of international law, capable of being applied in a decentralised manner by states. Even in the absence of *ad hoc* institutions every state is under an obligation to respect and fulfil the principle of the common heritage by ensuring that subjects within its jurisdiction do not act contrary to its

Fourth, as regards the institutional aspects of the issue, the mandate of ISA deserves close scrutiny, especially if it is to be understood not only as an entity involved in marine mining activities in competition with others, but as the international organization which bears the main responsibility to realize a just and equitable economic order of the oceans and seas.[48] Nothing prevents States from expanding the mining focus of the ISA and granting to it some broader management competences within the Area. All the stakeholders should play a role in the endeavor of drafting a future regime on the exploitation of genetic resources of the Area, together with the ISA, which is already entitled to exercise a range of preferential or cooperative responsibilities in the field of marine scientific research and protection of the environment in the deep seabed. This does not mean that the ISA should become the overarching regulatory body in the field of the exploitation of genetic resources of the Area.[49] Nor does this mean that the rights acquired by public and private entities which have made consistent investments and developed a sophisticated technological capacity in the field of bioprospecting shall be ignored. It simply means that the ISA, the principles that it represents, as well as its already existing competences and cooperative role, need to be taken into consideration when the States decide to fill the legal gap of the regime of deep seabed genetic resources.

Prospects for a future discussion of the questions related to the Area in a broader context that would involve several fora and institutions have emerged during the 2008 meeting of the Working Group:

> Several delegations expressed support for the continuation of discussions on marine genetic resources beyond areas of national jurisdiction under the authority of the General Assembly and within the framework of the United Nations Convention on the Law of the Sea. Reference was also made to the need to take

---

object and purpose. This would be the case if a state authorised or negligently failed to prevent biotechnological activities in common spaces that had the effect of causing severe and irreversible damage to the unique biodiversity of that space. Similarly, a state would fail the common heritage if it authorised exclusive appropriation of genetic resources without requiring equitable sharing of pertinent scientific knowledge and without ensuring that a fair portion of economic benefits accruing from their exploitation be devoted to the conservation and sustainable development of such common resources" (F. Francioni "Genetic Resources, Biotechnology and Human Rights: The International Legal Framework" in F. Francioni (ed.) *Biotechnologies and International Human Rights* (Oxford: 2007) 14).

[48] As stated in the 2008 report of the ISA Secretary-General, Mr. Nandan, "the Authority represents a unique experiment in international relations. It is the only international body with the responsibility of administering a global commons for the benefit of mankind" (Doc. ISBAISA/14/A/2 of 14 April 2008, para. 102).

[49] See also the part of the Joint statement of the Co-Chairpersons of the Working Group reproduced in the text at note 50 below.

into account the work under other relevant forums, such as the Convention on Biological Diversity, FAO, the World Intellectual Property Organization and the World Trade Organization.[50] The Working Group is expected to meet again in 2010.

[50] *Joint Statement of the Co-Chairpersons of the Working Group* note 32, para. 39.

THE CONCEPT OF THE COMMON HERITAGE OF MANKIND: ITS VIABILITY AS A MANAGEMENT TOOL FOR DEEP-SEA GENETIC RESOURCES

Nele Matz-Lück*

1. *Genetic Resources and the Common Heritage Approach*

Many living organisms in the deep sea possess unique genetic dispositions due to their adaptation to a particularly hostile environment in darkness, cold and high pressure.[1] Such resources are often labeled 'genetic resources' to distinguish them *inter alia* from other marine living resources which are exploited for consumption. Strictly speaking the term 'genetic resources' refers not to the living organism as such but only to genetic material, i.e. to "any material of plant, animal, microbial or other origin containing functional units of heredity".[2] Hence, when it comes to genetic resources the focus of human activity is not the living organism hosting the genetic material but the material itself. The collection of samples of living organisms with potentially useful genetic material is usually sufficient for further research and cannot be compared to the harvesting of living organisms for consumption. This distinction is relevant for a regime on the management of genetic resources and standards for their protection from adverse human influences.

The actual or potential value of genetic resources requires research activities, e.g. the taking of samples of organisms in the deep sea, which are extremely costly, while the value of marine genetic resources for the development of technologies and pharmaceuticals is difficult to assess. Although some believe in the development of e.g. anti-cancer drugs from marine organisms, it cannot be excluded that a legal regime for marine genetic resources in areas outside national jurisdiction will share the fate of the one for mineral resources of the Area.

---

* Senior Research Fellow, Max-Planck-Institute for Comparative Public Law and International Law, Heidelberg, Germany.

[1] On characteristics of the environment see L. Glowka "The Deepest of Ironies: Genetic Resources, Marine Scientific Research and the International Deep Sea-bed Area" (1996) 12 *Ocean Yearbook* 154–178, 156.

[2] This is the definition of 'genetic material' given by Article 2 of the Convention on Biological Diversity (CBD) of 5 June 1992 ((1992) 31 ILM 818 et seq.).

Alex G. Oude Elferink and Erik J. Molenaar (eds.), *The International Legal Regime of Areas beyond National Jurisdiction: Current and Future Developments*, pp. 61–75.

Genetic resources located in the water column of the sea outside areas of national jurisdiction or on the seabed beyond the continental shelves of coastal States[3] are not addressed specifically by any relevant international agreement. While the Convention on the Law of the Sea (LOS Convention)[4] deals specifically with mineral resources of the Area and establishes an institutional regime based upon the concept of the common heritage of mankind for them, genetic resources are not mentioned. Although the concept itself is still subject to misunderstandings and divergences in interpretation, the LOS Convention seems clear that the concept of the common heritage of mankind only applies to the mineral resources located at, on or under the deep seabed.[5] Article 136 LOS Convention states that "[t]he Area and its resources are the common heritage of mankind". However, Article 133(a) LOS Convention defines the notion of "resources" in Part XI as "all solid, liquid or gaseous mineral resources". This limitation has also consequences for a potential institutional set-up for the management of genetic resources of the deep sea as it is relevant for the competences of the International Seabed Authority (ISA) and its structural design.

Neither is the Convention on Biological Diversity (CBD)[6] directly applicable to the resources of the water column of the high seas or the deep seabed.[7] Due to the reliance upon resources under national jurisdiction, the CBD does not mention the common heritage approach. The formulation of the conservation of biological diversity as a "common concern" in the preamble was chosen deliberately to avoid any implications of a general regime of shared resources.[8] The access and benefit-sharing regime envisaged by the Convention relies upon specific bilateral agreements and is subject to further elaborations to overcome difficulties[9] and inequalities in North-South relations.[10] By its very

---

[3] On the determination whether features with communities of living organisms are located in the Area or in the waters superjacent to the Area see A.G. Oude Elferink "The Regime of the Area: Delineating the Scope of Application of the Common Heritage Principle and Freedom of the High Seas" (2007) 22 *International Journal of Marine and Coastal Law* 143–176 at 148 et seq.

[4] Adopted on 10 December 1982; 1833 UNTS 296.

[5] A.G. Oude Elferink, note 3 at 174 comes to a different conclusion and affirms that living resources of the Area are included in the common heritage approach.

[6] See note 2.

[7] Beyond the limits of national jurisdiction the Convention only applies to processes and activities under the control of States regardless where their effects occur (Article 4 lit. b) CBD).

[8] Likewise the International Treaty on Plant Genetic Resources of 3 November 2001 (available at ⟨www.planttreaty.org⟩) only mentions the "common concern" and not the concept of a common heritage of mankind.

[9] On the discussion see M. Dross and F. Wolff "Do We Need a New Access and Benefit sharing Instrument?" (2004) 15 *Yearbook of International Environmental Law* 95–118.

[10] On unfair patterns of exchange between the North and the South see I. Mgbeoji "Beyond Rhetoric: State Sovereignty, Common Concern, and the Inapplicability of the Common Heritage Concept to Plant Genetic Resources" (2003) 16 *Leiden Journal of International Law*, 821–837 at 822 et seq.

nature a bilateral scheme is not applicable to resources in areas outside national jurisdiction. An effective multilateral access and benefit-sharing regime could only be established if powers to manage genetic resources are transferred to an international institution by (universal) agreement.

Since the living resources on, or close to, the deep seabed are not covered by the concept of the common heritage of mankind, there is no obligation to share benefits resulting from research or applications and technologies that were derived from marine genetic resources located in the deep sea.[11] It is subject to discussion whether the lack of specific regulation on marine genetic resources in the high seas and on the ocean floor is a gap that should be filled or whether the rules on marine scientific research and the protection of the marine environment including its living resources under the LOS Convention are sufficient.[12]

The notion of a gap implies an existing system of regulation and governance which strives for comprehensiveness but suffers from certain deficiencies. The LOS Convention as the 'constitution of the oceans' comprehensively regulates an extensive quantity of legal matters concerning the seas within and outside areas of national jurisdiction. Even if issues are not subject to detailed substantive regulations the LOS Convention addresses them by providing for the legal framework for further governance. Like all treaties it is a product of the time in which it was negotiated. Certain issues such as the protection and exploitation of genetic resources, the implications of climate change or the relationship to human rights law were unknown or not considered relevant at that time. From our perspective today such shortcomings may be considered 'gaps' in an otherwise all-encompassing agreement. Likewise, the perspective of adequate protection of all components of biological diversity regardless of their location reveals shortcomings in international law that may be labeled 'gaps'. It is not the intention of the author, however, to allege that all issues lacking specific legal regulation are 'gaps' and should be filled by international agreement. Recognized deficiencies in regulatory regimes can be overcome in different ways, e.g. by the dynamic interpretation of existing rules, by implementation agreements or by a new treaty which is not formally linked to existing

---

[11] D. König "Genetic Resources of the Deep Sea—How Can They Be Preserved?" in D. König, P.T. Stoll, V. Röben and N. Matz-Lück (eds) *International Law Today: New Challenges and the Need for Reform?* (Springer, Berlin: 2008), 141–163 at 149 with further references.

[12] While many voices call for international action to fill the alleged gap, see König note 11 at 141 et seq.; R. Wolfrum and N. Matz "The Interplay of the United Nations Convention on the Law of the Sea and the Convention on Biological Diversity" (2000) *Max-Planck Yearbook of United Nations Law* 445–480 others emphasize the existing rules codified in the LOS Convention, see A. Proelss "Marine Genetic Resources under UNCLOS and the CBD" (2009) 51 *German Yearbook of International Law* 417–446.

ones. The institutional dimension becomes particularly relevant if a new agreement is envisaged which focuses upon the management of the exploitation of/bioprospecting for genetic resources e.g. by licenses for access and/or a procedure for the sharing of benefits.

2. *A New Instrument?*

Although activities such as mining, oil and gas exploration and exploitation or deep-sea fisheries pose severer threats to the preservation of marine biological diversity than marine scientific research and bioprospecting, the latter shall not be underestimated. The taking of samples of living organisms with unique genetic dispositions is unlikely to deplete the resources as a result of overexploitation and may not be compared to fisheries.[13] However, research activities can have adverse effects on the vulnerable environment of the deep sea and an increase in research activities may lead to the destruction of specific habitats.[14] Research on genetic resources is not specifically addressed by international regulation. Consequently, the specific problems that may result from research activities concerning genetic resources of the deep sea are not subject to control or, potentially, restrictions. Article 240 LOS Convention refers only in a general manner to consistency with the Convention's regulations for the protection and preservation of the environment.

Those voices who perceive the current regulation—or rather the lack thereof—as a potential threat to genetic resources and as unfair with a view to States that are incapable of engaging in such research and the subsequent development of technologies usually call for a new instrument on genetic resources of the deep sea which provides for a benefit-sharing mechanism. Although it generally seems a promising approach to conclude new instruments specifically designed to solve contemporary problems in international relations, the proliferation of treaties and other binding or non-binding regulations on different levels bears its own difficulties.[15] Those who favor a new instrument or the extension of the regime for mineral resources to genetic resources often

---

[13] Wolfrum and Matz note 12 at 456. This is also brought forward as a reason why the rules on living resources, which are clearly designed for fisheries, are inadequate to preserve and manage genetic resources.

[14] See examples at König, note 11 at 147 et seq.

[15] Overlapping or colliding regulations derived from international treaties have lately been discussed as part of a 'fragmentation' of public international law, see e.g. Report of the Study Group of the ILC on *Fragmentation of International Law: Difficulties Arising from the Diversification and Expansion of International Law*, Finalized by M. Koskenniemi, UN Doc. A/CN.4/L.682 of 13 April 2006; see also R. Wolfrum and N. Matz *Conflicts in International Environmental Law* (Springer, Berlin: 2003).

seem to take for granted that a comprehensive approach should be based upon the common heritage concept. However, it must be questioned whether the concept of the common heritage of mankind as it is framed today is a feasible basis for a management regime.

3. *Content and Value of the Concept of the Common Heritage of Mankind*

The establishment of an instrument on genetic resources of the deep sea which is based upon the concept of the common heritage of mankind would certainly be a radical difference to exclusive sovereignty on the one hand and complete freedom on the other. In between these extremes the law of the sea also knows a *sui generis* system of specific sovereign rights without the establishment of full sovereignty e.g. for the Exclusive Economic Zone (EEZ) and also for the deep seabed. The allocation of exclusive rights to exploit mineral resources of the deep seabed, even if benefits have to be shared with the international community, would not be in conformity with the freedom of the high seas and exemplify the *sui generis* status of the deep seabed.[16] Whether it is a viable approach to establish an operational regime for genetic resources which relies upon the concept of the common heritage of mankind depends upon the content of and consequences from such an approach and the institutional design for managing resources accordingly.

A regime for the management and use of resources based upon the common heritage of mankind relies upon considerations of solidarity between all participating States and particularly with regard to the weaker members.[17] So far the concept of designating resources as the common heritage of mankind is more an underlying philosophy but does not give indications concerning the formal or substantive contents of a legal regime in a general sense.[18] Despite the lack of a general legal content, in regard to the Area one might consider a positive integrative effect due to designating all mankind as participants in the use of mineral resources of the deep seabed.[19]

---

[16] R. Wolfrum "Hohe See und Tiefseeboden" in Wolfgang Graf Vitzthum (ed.) *Handbuch des Seerechts* (C.H. Beck, München: 2006) 287–345 at 336.

[17] *Ibid.*, 338 et seq.

[18] On the legal content with examples from the governance of other resources outside national jurisdiction see E. Guntrip "The Common Heritage of Mankind: An Adequate Regime for Managing the Deep Seabed?" (2003) 4 *Melbourne Journal of International Law* 376–405.

[19] On integration of States into an organized system by the concept of mankind see R.J. Dupuy "The Area as the Common Heritage of Mankind" in R.J. Dupuy and D. Vignes (eds) *A Handbook on the New Law of the Sea* (Martinus Nijhoff Publishers, Dordrecht: 1991) 579 at 582.

Despite the inclusion of the idea of a common heritage in different agreements on areas outside national jurisdiction such as celestial bodies and, to some extent, Antarctica[20] one might question whether it is a legal principle.[21] The common heritage of mankind has been labeled a principle, concept, notion, doctrine, regime, ideal, theory, right, or legal term of art.[22] This demonstrates scholarly uncertainty as to the legal content and status. Although the inclusion in the LOS Convention is indeed revolutionary for exchanging the freedom of the high seas with a management regime, the latter has not yet become fully operational. The common heritage approach as incorporated in the law of the sea is the result of compromise and different interpretations and has no generally accepted and reliable legal content that could serve as a model. The elements commonly referred to in the realm of the management of mineral resources of the deep seabed are the abstention from sovereignty claims, the use for peaceful purposes, the use of the resources for the benefit of mankind as a whole and with particular consideration of the interests of developing countries, i.e. by a sharing of benefits, and the management by an international organization.[23]

It is a matter of methodology whether the common heritage concept is a legal principle from which one can deduct the necessary legal consequences or whether it is an idea that is reflected in different treaty provisions. Certainly, one could establish a new instrument, incorporate rules on access, monitoring and the sharing of benefit which are managed by an international institution and sell this result as an expression and new example of the common heritage approach. To take the common heritage approach as the outset, however, does not give the necessary guidance on the details unless one would rely exclusively upon the legal rules for the Area. Yet, this seems uncertain ground due to the lack of practice concerning the operation of the exploitation of mineral resources of the deep seabed by the ISA. Without defined legal content, a deductive method for drafting a new instrument seems impossible.

The wish to improve the protection of genetic resources from the adverse effects of human activities alone cannot be decisive for the establishment of a regime that relies upon the concept of the common heritage of mankind. The

---

[20] See also Guntrip, note 18 at 394 et seq.

[21] R. Wolfrum "The Principle of the Common Heritage of Mankind" (1983) 43 *Heidelberg Journal of International Law* 312–337 uses both the terms "principle" and "concept".

[22] J. Frakes "The Common Heritage of Mankind Principle and the Deep Seabed, Outer Space, and Antarctica: Will Developed and Developing Nations Reach a Compromise?" (2003) 21 *Wisconsin International Law Journal* 409–434 at 410 in footnote 4.

[23] On these elements and the implications of the term 'heritage' instead of 'property' see T. Scovazzi "Mining, Protection of the Environment, Scientific Research and Bioprospecting: Some Considerations on the Role of the International Sea-Bed Authority" (2004) 19 *International Journal of Marine and Coastal Law* 383–409 at 385.

current regime may not be sufficient to protect genetic resources but, from the perspective of better conservation, the relevant rules must not necessarily be based upon benefit-sharing or a substantive management scheme. To achieve better protection, already a modification of the current regime by rules on notification of research activities, i.e. who is doing research where, and a sharing of data without the need to establish a fully-fledged management authority may improve the situation. Likewise restrictions on all or certain research activities aiming at higher protection standards would not require a system based upon a common heritage approach. Restricting marine scientific research for areas outside national jurisdiction in order to protect genetic resources from the adverse effects of research would require a substantive modification of the current rules under the LOS Convention. The establishment of such restrictions, particularly, if only certain activities are to be regulated, and the management of research activities might also benefit from some institutional structure, e.g. to control compliance. This, however, could be considered independently from a regime based upon the common heritage of mankind. For the latter the set-up of an international organization seems indispensible, if the characteristics as established for mineral resources of the Area are taken as the basis.

4. *The Institutional Dimension*

Cooperation between States is the essential element to effectively address marine issues. While the LOS Convention requires each Member State to abide by its rules and regulations the drafters were very conscious of the fact that the marine environment does not mind the somewhat artificial borders and different sea-zones established by States. The water itself and marine species travel regionally and even globally, as does pollution. Human activities e.g. the overexploitation of edible fish species, by-catch, pollution, installations or other alterations of the marine environment have significant effects on marine ecosystems and in many cases also affect other States and their potential use of the sea. Many objectives of the LOS Convention can only be promoted or achieved, if States cooperate.

If cooperation involves more than two States and if the issues are complex, it may be particularly effective when it is institutionalized and, hence, formalized. The establishment of permanent institutions has the benefit of being able to provide for formal structures for meetings, the exchange of information, decision-making, compliance and expertise. Forms of institutionalized cooperation can be manifold and include *inter alia* international agreements with permanent organs, joint authorities and international organizations in a legal sense, i.e. subjects of international law with a legal personality that is independent from the Member States. What form is suitable to meet the needs of the cooperating States to a large extent depends upon the issue which they wish to address. The regular exchange of scientific data, for example, may only require a secretariat that administers an internet platform, while the continuous management of a resource with scientific experts, substantive decision-making and compliance control may require a permanent institution with different organs and, potentially, independent legal personality.

Likewise the question whether institutions shall be set up on a regional or global level generally depends upon the issue in question and upon political realities. Some issues have a clear subregional or regional dimension, e.g. the conservation and sustainable use a transboundary coral reef. Others, like the resources of the deep seabed, are of a global nature. Smaller regional institutions benefit from the lower number of actors, which may allow easier and faster decision-making, while global institutions may strive for wide acceptance of uniform standards.

In addition to direct cooperation between States the LOS Convention strongly encourages the establishment of international organizations and the cooperation with existing ones to implement its objectives. In the relevant articles the LOS Convention mainly refers to cooperation through "competent international organizations". Article 212(2) LOS Convention offers the alternative option of a diplomatic conference for the elaboration of rules and standards on pollution from or through the atmosphere. The level of cooperation, subregional, regional or global, depends upon the issue. In some provisions, e.g. Article 212(2) LOS Convention any reference to the level of the international organization is missing, while others e.g. Article 197 seem to give preference to the global level and allow for regional cooperation "as appropriate", and yet others mention subregional, regional and global organizations (Article 119 (2) UNCLOS).

Cooperation seems particularly relevant to the issues of marine living resources and environmental protection of the seas. For fisheries and the relevant sustainable use of living resources the LOS Convention calls for cooperation either directly or through international organizations.[24] As far as the dissemination of scientific information, statistics and other data on living resources of the high seas is concerned Article 119(2) LOS Convention calls for an exchange through "competent international organizations, whether subregional, regional or global". Likewise Article 244 LOS Convention obliges States and competent international organizations to cooperate to make avail-

[24] See e.g. Article 63(2) and Article 64(1).

able knowledge resulting from research and to transfer knowledge especially to developing States. Article 197 LOS Convention emphasizes the necessary co-operation for the protection and preservation of the marine environment. The provision mentions both the global and, where appropriate, the regional level for the formulation and elaboration of international rules, standards and recommended practice.

The specific institutional dimension results from the linkage to the common heritage elements established for mineral resources of the Area, i.e. management and benefit-sharing between all States of the international community, rather than the need to agree upon specific rules for the conservation and exploitation of genetic resources. International standards for the protection of genetic resources from harmful human activities could either be adopted under Article 197 LOS Convention or outside the convention if specific obligations are carried out in a manner consistent with it (Article 237 LOS Convention). In principle, these general provisions of the LOS Convention could hence serve as a basis for standards on genetic resources. States are generally free to agree upon further regulations *inter se* if they do not derogate from provisions which are essential for the effective execution of the Convention (Article 311(3) LOS Convention). Hence, States could even restrict research activities between them if this would serve the protection of genetic resources and transfer the relevant competences to an international organization. However, this would not have any effects on non-members to this new instrument and organization.

Notification of research activities and a sharing of data, for example, could be established by a clearing-house mechanism that could operate with a minimum of an institutional structure. The general provision on the sharing of knowledge resulting from marine scientific research, Article 244 LOS Convention, is silent on the form and level of cooperation. It mentions both States and international organizations that shall make available information either individually or jointly through appropriate channels. As mentioned above already the establishment of specific restrictions to free marine scientific research on the high seas and on genetic resources on or near the sea-bed would benefit from an institutional background. A proper management scheme, however, would require a well-funded and staffed institution with different organs. The sharing between all States, like the regime for the management of mineral resources on the deep seabed, needs a procedure on access with a licensing scheme, the dissemination of results and monitoring of further economic development and utilization, if such benefits are made part of the benefit-sharing regime.

If the concept of the common heritage of mankind is taken as the basis for benefit-sharing amongst all States the competent institution must operate on the global level. For mineral resources Article 140 LOS Convention mentions benefits for "mankind as a whole, irrespective of the geographical location of States, whether coastal or land-locked". The safeguarding of these interests necessarily requires that the institution is also open for participation of all States. While, as mentioned above, regional organizations seem particularly viable tools to address issues concerning certain groups of States because a smaller number of actors may result in more effective decision-making, genetic resources on the deep seabed have to be perceived a global issue.

Any institution which bases its rules and regulations upon the common heritage of mankind will have to ask itself, whether the decision-making process meets democratic and participatory needs. Management in the name of the common heritage of mankind implies integration that has to be reflected by the relevant structures and processes of the institution.[25] The ISA tries to take account of the interests of different groups by *inter alia* involving in the Council certain quora of States Parties which are commodity consumers, which have the largest investments in conducting activities in the Area, which are net exporters of those minerals to be extracted from the deep seabed and developing countries with special interests (Article 161(1) LOS Convention).

While the sharing of benefits may be easy if minerals are extracted and sold on the world-market, for a regime on genetic resources it will be essential to define what is meant by this notion. A sharing of benefits could range from developing countries' participation in research activities, the sharing of information[26] on research and a transfer of technologies to process the relevant data to the sharing of economic benefits resulting from the application of technologies developed from marine genetic resources. The LOS Convention generally encourages marine scientific research and obliges States to share information on the results (Article 244 LOS Convention). This also applies to marine scientific research conducted in the Area. Article 143 LOS Convention is silent on the issue of research, i.e. whether marine scientific research in the Area is understood to be research on mineral resources or on all issues of interest, e.g. geological, biological etc. The only explicit "restriction" given by Article 143 LOS Convention refers to the peaceful purposes of research.[27]

---

[25] Dupuy, see note 19 at 582.

[26] The issue of an exchange of information raises the question of intellectual property rights. Despite it being a broad framework it is questionable whether this should be regulated under the roof of the LOS Convention. However, due regard must be paid to existing international regulations on intellectual property.

[27] The other general principles for the conduct of marine scientific research (LOS Convention, Article 240) are also applicable by reference to Part XIII under Article 143(1) of the LOS Convention.

The provision on cooperation in research activities in Article 143(3) LOS Convention already incorporate the idea of participation of developing countries, capacity building and effective dissemination of data and analysis. However, such provisions cannot be qualified as benefit-sharing in the sense of sharing the economic benefits. The LOS Convention does not distinguish between fundamental research and applied research for activities in areas outside national jurisdiction. For marine scientific research on the continental shelf and the EEZ of States the situation differs. In this context coastal States may withhold consent *inter alia* if research is of direct significance for the exploitation of resources (Article 246(5)(a)). Hence, the LOS Convention generally acknowledges specific interests in applied research but does not provide for a specific regime for the Area or the high seas. All States have the right to conduct scientific research in the Area and the water column in areas beyond the EEZ of coastal States (Articles 256 and 257 LOS Convention) regardless of whether their activities qualify as fundamental or applied research.[28] Consequently benefits from applied research such as later technologies developed from bioprospecting are not addressed by the Convention.

As far as the creation of a new organization which could be responsible for controlling research and manage a sharing of benefits is concerned it shall also be noted that States have become particularly reluctant to transfer powers and financial resources to a growing number of international organizations or institutions necessary to operate modern treaty regimes. From this perspective it seems beneficial to make use of the already existing ISA to manage genetic resources of the Area. Although the institution is primarily responsible for the management of mineral resources, its mandate already includes issues like the coordination of marine scientific research in the Area and the protection of the marine environment. This makes the competences of the ISA already broader than commonly believed.[29] Due to the restriction to mining activities, however, the ISA has currently no mandate to restrict or regulate marine scientific research on genetic resources of the Area.[30]

If the ISA should be employed as an international organization responsible for the management and protection of genetic resources the restriction of its mandate to mining activities must be abolished. As mining activities may destruct ecosystems of living organisms with particular genetic material the integrated management of mining and genetic resources seems beneficial.[31] Otherwise a new global organization responsible for the coordination and

[28] See also König, note 11 at 151.

[29] Scovazzi, note 23 at 391.

[30] König, note 11 at 152.

[31] *Ibid.*, 160.

restriction of research on deep sea genetic resources, their management and the sharing of potential benefits derived from such resources would have to closely cooperate with the ISA in order to prevent contradictions and to coordinate activities. This, however, would initiate another potentially lengthy process: the drafting of a memorandum of understanding or a joint working plan between the institutions, implementation of the standards and procedures and, if necessary revision. Cooperation between institutions is an issue that is very important in the light of the growing number of institutions (governmental and non-governmental). However, from the perspective of effectiveness and coherence it seems more viable to expand the mandate of existing institutions than to create more and more specialized ones with partially overlapping competences. In practice, the expansion of the mandate of the ISA seems as unlikely as the creation of a new instrument and institution based upon the common heritage approach and incorporating a benefit-sharing scheme due to the diverse political interests of States.

Despite the arguments in favor of extending the mandate of the ISA to also deal with genetic resources, it must be noted that not only the mandate but the whole impetus of the organization must be changed. As mining may threaten habitats of organisms valuable for their genetic characteristics the focus of the ISA must change towards specific environmental protection of relevant ecosystems. General environmental protection is already one of the tasks of the ISA but the facilitation of the exploration and exploitation of mineral resources is clearly the centre of activities. A balancing between interests in deep seabed mining and the management of genetic resources must be agreed on the normative level in order for the ISA to effectively manage both issues. Furthermore, the current institutional design which allows for participation of different groups with particular interests in deep-sea mineral resources may be the main argument against the expansion of the ISA's mandate[32] as it will be difficult to alter the compromise reached for such resources in the light of a second focus on genetic resources. Hence, not only the mandate and the standards but also the structure and decision-making procedures would have to be adapted to accommodate the new management tasks.

As it seems difficult to distinguish between genetic resources of the seabed and of the surrounding water column, institutional competences may even be designed to encompass all marine genetic resources in areas outside national jurisdiction. No matter how far-reaching the management capacity will be, it seems that the change in competences can only be based upon a new instrument. If a new institution is established or if the authority of the ISA is modified

[32] *Ibid.*

to include the management of genetic resources, decision-making procedures and, particularly, participation of different stakeholders and the weighing of votes must be expected to be prominent features. Even if no new institutions are set up, the mandate of the existing ones must be altered considerably to take account of standards for the regulation of genetic resources and potential restrictions on marine scientific research.

5. *Future Prospects*

The idea of the common heritage of mankind implies equitable solutions for resources in areas outside national jurisdiction. The sharing of benefits may be desirable but the reasoning is political rather than legal. If, for political considerations, we believe genetic resources in areas outside national jurisdiction should be used for the benefit of mankind, we must define this benefit, establish a procedure and management criteria and create and fund the relevant institutions. The current legal regime, however, does not give indications why genetic resources of the deep seabed or the high seas should be managed according to principles derived from the concept of the common heritage of mankind. From a legal perspective it is very difficult to give reasons for a distinction between mineral, genetic, living or any other resources in such areas. The common heritage approach to mineral resources of the Area as it was originally envisaged must be regarded as the result of ideas concerning the New International Economic Order and the specific situation of developing countries as exporters of minerals extracted from land. For genetic resources of the high seas and the seabed the situation is different.

The significant disparities in financial and technical capacity between the North and the South call for capacity-building and the transfer of financial resources and technologies.[33] However, it cannot fully explain why genetic resources in areas outside national jurisdiction should be shared, if this included the sharing of benefits derived from the development of pharmaceuticals or other applications. The underlying fact that a technically advanced status of developed countries allows for different activities is to some degree also true for high seas fisheries. Modern fishing fleets on the high seas are

---

[33] Although the right to development is still an issue under debate as far as the recognition as part of customary international law and the relevant consequences are concerned, there is political consensus on substantive assistance. The objective of the designation of 0.7% of the relevant GNP for development assistance, however, is still not met by the great majority of industrialized States. In addition to these general commitments, many modern international agreements contain further provisions on transfers of technologies and other resources, e.g. CBD, Article 16.

more commonly operated by companies from technically advanced countries while developing States rely upon traditional coastal fisheries. However, so far a benefit-sharing or management scheme to overcome disparities in capabilities has not been envisaged for high seas fisheries. Environmental principles like common but differentiated responsibilities are not applicable in this context.

The lack of benefit sharing for high-sea fisheries may not explain why there is no such scheme for genetic resources of the Area but it serves an example for a lack of will of States to provide for equality of result when it comes to the sharing of resources to which access is, in principle, free. Equal opportunity for access to areas and resources outside national jurisdiction can be based upon a general notion of equality of States. Whether substantive equality as to the gains from such opportunities is aimed for to compensate developing States for their lack of capacity is mainly a political question. With the exception of mineral resources of the Area attempts to provide for preferential treatment of developing countries have not gone as far as to establish a full benefit-sharing regime.

Certainly, the exploration of genetic resources and later technologies bear particularly potential and point to the continuous misbalance between industrialized and developing countries but it is questionable whether their location outside national jurisdiction can be decisive to manage them under a benefit-sharing regime. It would be different if all genetic resources regardless of jurisdictional questions would be perceived as the common heritage. To avoid such arguments, however, States are very cautious to emphasize sovereignty over their natural resources and only declare them a "common concern" of humankind.[34]

The developing countries feared implications for their sovereignty over their biological resources and insisted upon a "common concern" instead of the "common heritage" in the realm of the CBD. The common heritage concept for genetic resources outside national jurisdiction seems likely to be opposed from those industrialized States capable of engaging in research and bioprospecting in these areas, if this included a sharing of all benefits derived from applications. When balancing the different interests and considering equity one shall not forget that, if the common heritage approach is taken seriously, all States should participate not only in sharing the benefits but also in the immense costs. Despite all rightful claims to a transfer of technologies and capacity-building by developing countries, the technical and financial capacity of developed States cannot lead to the conclusion that they should bear the costs alone but share the benefits if applications are developed. A

[34] On sovereignty over natural resources and the common heritage approach as mutually exclusive concepts see Mgbeoji, note 10 at 836 et seq.

complete lack of benefit-sharing and lack of reference to the common heritage of mankind, however, is likely to fail due to resistance of the developing world. Hence, it seems that the main difficulty lies in defining benefit-sharing in the context of marine genetic resources in areas outside national jurisdiction.

The current 'solution' to such a dilemma is undesirable from the perspective of better protection of genetic resources: the *status quo* under the LOS Convention. With a view to the necessary regulations—which should be developed by either modification of the existing law of the sea or by a new agreement—it seems that from a legal perspective the common heritage approach serves as a metaphor and may have turned into a myth[35] but is an exception to the general situations of either sovereignty and unrestricted sovereign rights over resources or freedom of use by all States and cannot be employed as a legal and institutional model for future instruments.

[35] M.C.W. Pinto "'Common Heritage of Mankind': From Metaphor to Myth, and the Consequences of Constructive Ambiguity" in J. Makarczyk (ed) *Theory of International Law at the Threshold of the 21st Century* (Kluwer, The Hague: 1999) 249–268.

INSTITUTIONAL ARRANGEMENTS FOR THE LEGAL REGIME GOVERNING AREAS BEYOND NATIONAL JURISDICTION—COMMENTARY ON TULLIO SCOVAZZI

Louise A. de La Fayette*

As usual, I agree with my good friend Professor Scovazzi on almost everything. He provides an excellent summary of the discussions at the United Nations Marine Biodiversity Working Group on the regime for genetic resources beyond national jurisdiction.[1]

Professor Scovazzi refers to the decision to include only mineral resources in Part XI of the LOS Convention[2] and to the differences in the final text from Ambassador Pardo's original idea of including living resources in the regime of the Area. While it is true that only mineral resources were included, it is at least possible, if not probable, that if delegates had known about the economic potential of genetic resources on the seabed at the time that the LOS Convention was being negotiated, they would have included them in the regime of Part XI.

The fact that they did not do so in the 1970s does not prevent us now from creating a new regime based upon the principles in the LOS Convention. Here I disagree with Professor Scovazzi. He underestimates the dynamism of the LOS Convention. He considers only *partially true* the statement that the LOS Convention "sets out the legal framework within which all activities in the oceans and seas must be carried out". He says that the law of the sea is subject to a process of natural evolution and progressive development. True, but this evolution and development is called for in the LOS Convention itself. It does not take place entirely outside the the LOS Convention regime.

* Visiting Professor, Maritime Institute, University of Greenwich, London.

[1] See: 'Report of the Ad Hoc Open-ended Informal Working Group to study issues relating to the conservation and sustainable use of marine biological diversity beyond areas of national jurisdiction' (2006) UN Doc. A/61/65; Letter from the Co-chairpersons of the Ad Hoc Open-ended Informal Working Group to study issues relating to the conservation and sustainable use of marine biological diversity beyond areas of national jurisdiction addressed to the President of the General Assembly (15 May 2008) UN Doc. A/63/79 (both available at ⟨www.un.org/depts/los⟩). When I was at the UN, I worked for several years on marine biodiversity and genetic resources, supervising and contributing to the UN reports on the issue. I attended both meetings of the Working Group, first as a member of the secretariat and second, as the representative of the Advisory Committee on Protection of the Sea.

[2] Adopted on 10 December 1982; 1833 UNTS 396.

Alex G. Oude Elferink and Erik J. Molenaar (eds.), *The International Legal Regime of Areas beyond National Jurisdiction: Current and Future Developments*, pp. 77–79.

Throughout the Convention text, many provisions call for elaboration in separate agreements. This is the case with respect to navigation, fisheries, and especially the protection of the environment addressed in Part XII, which requires States to adopt agreements addressing various sources of marine degradation and to keep them up to date. Furthermore, agreements on new issues are authorised in Article 237, provided that they adhere to the general principles in the LOS Convention. These general principles can be applied to a broad range of new issues as they arise, including marine biodiversity and genetic resources. Article 311 also foresees the possibility of new agreements, while preserving the basic principle of the common heritage of mankind.

Any State that claims the LOS Convention is the end of legal regulation is misreading the text or not reading it at all, for the LOS Convention was designed to evolve in accordance with changing circumstances. This includes those States which insist that genetic resources fall within the regime of freedom of the high seas. They are misreading the Convention in several respects. The freedom of the high seas means that all States may engage in activities on the high seas. It does not mean that such activities are unregulated and that States and individuals may do as they please. All traditional activities are regulated and any new activities should be regulated as well, in order to preserve the rights and interests of all States.

In any event, Professor Scovazzi's analysis in the rest of his paper shows that the LOS Convention is indeed applicable to new issues. However, it is applicable precisely at the level of general principles. Because it was negotiated in the 1970s the LOS Convention does not deal adequately, or in some cases not at all, with issues that were then of little interest and have subsequently assumed importance, and with some principles and concepts that did not exist at the time, such as the precautionary principle and the ecosystem approach. Yet, a basis for all issues arising after the LOS Convention is present in the Convention if one does not read it too literally, if one takes a 'dynamic' approach to interpretation, and above all, if one bears in mind the objectives of the LOS Convention declared in the preamble and reiterated throughout the Convention.

Referring to genetic resources, in his first conclusion, Professor Scovazzi points out that the LOS Convention cannot provide any specific regime for the exploitation of the genetic resources of the Area. This is true: genetic resources are not mentioned in the text of the LOS Convention and there is no applicable regime. Part XI only applies to minerals. Yet, bearing in mind the objectives of the Convention as a whole, the purpose of the 'common heritage of mankind' principle, the fact that the Area itself is the common heritage of mankind, the nature of genetic resources, and the fact that only wealthy, advanced countries have the resources to exploit them, the analogy with mineral resources is clear, and it also seems clear that genetic resources should be considered as the common heritage of mankind. Because of this analogy with mineral resources the Convention itself requires this conclusion. Therefore, States are authorised to negotiate a regime for the conservation and sustainable use of marine genetic resources based upon the objectives and the general principles of the Convention. Professor Scovazzi says that the Convention cannot work miracles; however, States can, if they read the Convention creatively and apply its principles and objectives to new situations and activities.

Indeed, in his second concluding point, Professor Scovazzi recognises that not all of the Convention should be set aside. He points out that the regime of the Area encompasses other matters besides mining, including marine scientific research (MSR), the preservation of the environment and the protection of underwater cultural heritage. He recognises that the aim of activities benefiting all States is the paramount objective in the the LOS Convention. This is true, and this objective should guide the development of a regime for marine genetic resources.

His third point is that the activity of bioprospecting could be considered as falling under the regime for MSR. I agree and believe that this could be the key to the elaboration of the 'sustainable use' part of a regime for marine genetic resources, for the regime for MSR requires benefits to be provided to all mankind, and cooperation and assistance to be provided to developing countries. All the provisions for MSR could be applied to genetic resources, including the requirement for protection of the environment.

The fourth point, about the institutional aspects of a future regime, refers to the need to bear in mind the mandate and responsibilities of the International Seabed Authority (ISA). I agree with him on that point as well.

Finally, Professor Scovazzi mentions what he considers to be difficulties posed by the provisions of the LOS Convention in Article 303 relating to underwater cultural heritage. I think he has been listening too long to those who impose their own restrictive interpretations on the Convention. One should be bolder and more confident, and bear in mind the objectives and principles of the Convention. In my view, the preservation of the law of salvage in Article 303 is not a bar to the protection of underwater cultural heritage, because it is clear that the law of salvage has nothing to do with archaeology or with underwater cultural heritage. Salvage law applies to recent casualties, while the law relating to underwater cultural heritage applies to historic material of archaeological and cultural value. Article 303 merely preserves the difference.

To conclude, I entirely agree with Professor Scovazzi's substantive views on marine genetic resources and underwater cultural heritage, but I do not believe that the LOS Convention is an obstacle to achieving the goals that we share.

PART THREE

ENTITLEMENTS TO MARINE LIVING RESOURCES

ENTITLEMENT TO MARINE LIVING RESOURCES IN AREAS BEYOND NATIONAL JURISDICTION[1]

Richard Barnes*

1. *Introduction*

Entitlement to living resources involves three particular questions: Entitlement to what?; who determines entitlement?; and what process is used to determine entitlement? This paper is concerned with the latter issue and, in particular, the role that property has to play in determining entitlements to natural resources. The focus of this paper is essentially upon the marine living resources of the high seas and the marine genetic resources of the deep seabed, although it is important to note that the issues at stake would apply in principle to other areas such as Antarctica or outer space.[2] The question of who determines entitlement is a little more complicated, and requires, initially, a slight clarification. The label 'areas beyond national jurisdiction' (ABNJ) is perhaps misleading, for it is always, at least theoretically speaking, possible to regulate activities according to the nationality principle, whereby the acts of legal persons or things, such as ships, are governed by the law of the State of which they are nationals. However, as I will discuss in more detail below, resource regulation is more effective and commercially viable when exclusive access and use rights are established. These are not readily supported through the exercise of mere personal jurisdiction. So, for present purposes, what we are really speaking about is areas beyond exclusive spatial jurisdiction. This observation is important because it brings into focus the point that the question of who determines entitlement is, at least initially, fundamentally a question of international law. This means that the answer to the second question raised above is that States determine entitlement, at least initially. The more controversial issue is which States? All States, through the generation of rules of general international law, or groups of States, through regional mechanisms?

[1] I would like to thank the participants at the Verzijl Symposium, and, in particular, Erik Molenaar and Alex Oude Elferink for their comments on the original paper. Of course, the current text remains my own responsibility.

* Senior Lecturer, University of Hull.

[2] See sections 4.2 and 4.3 below.

Alex G. Oude Elferink and Erik J. Molenaar (eds.), *The International Legal Regime of Areas beyond National Jurisdiction: Current and Future Developments*, pp. 83–141.

Finally, there is the question of how entitlements are allocated. This is by far the most difficult issue, and one that is bound up with the question of who determines entitlement. In the law of the sea, the traditional approach to matters of allocation has been to extend jurisdiction or sovereign rights to coastal States who then decide more specific allocations of resources to individuals under domestic law. The continental shelf and excusive economic zone (EEZ) are cases in point. This may suggest a rather simple approach to the question of entitlement, through the continued extension of exclusive (spatial) coastal State jurisdiction. However, further creeping jurisdiction of States seems to be an unlikely prospect, destroying as it would the carefully negotiating settlement found in the United Nations Convention on the Law of the Sea (LOS Convention).[3] As such it may be more useful to consider how international law addresses questions of entitlement, other than through the allocation of competence to States.[4]

In the remainder of this section and section 2, I explore in more detail the nature of marine living resources, showing why they tend to be regulated in a particular way. This is done through the lens of property rights, which are increasingly prevalent as a means of regulating marine resources within domestic legal systems. I then introduce the possibility of regulating activities in ABNJ through the introduction of property rights-based entitlements, and consider if such an approach could be utilized through a regional fisheries management organization (RFMO). Of course, any solution is not quite as simple as privatizing the oceans. Certain qualities of the resource and regulatory structures may limit the scope for the use of property rights. Moreover, property rights must accord with certain fundamental values of the community within which they arise. Whilst such values may include 'preference maximizing' or maximizing economic returns, they may also include guaranteeing certain basic needs, promoting liberty and ensuring good order. In ABNJ, where regulation primarily takes place through international law, it is the values of the international community that become immediately relevant to questions of form and entitlement to rights-based holdings. In sections 3 and 4 I explore how property rights-based holdings may operate on the high seas and in other ABNJ. In section 4, I also explore some of the procedures and values that have shaped the crucial question of entitlement. This reveals how property rights-based entitlements are contingent upon some institutional framework that is capable of delimiting and regulating the enti-

[3] Adopted on 10 December 1982; 1833 UNTS 296.

[4] Of course, it should be recalled that international law may still have a role to play in determining entitlements, by placing limits on how States may exercise their sovereign rights. See for example Articles 61–62 of the LOS Convention.

tlements. In section 5, I explore the critical role of treaties and objective regimes in providing such institutional support, and indicate some of the difficulties in establishing adequate institutional support for rights-based entitlements.

Despite many legal and political obstacles to the use of property rights-based entitlement, there remains considerable interest in exploring their potential to improve upon current regulatory approaches. However, as I indicate in the final section, care needs to be taken to ensure that rights-based regimes are sensitive to ecosystem and biodiversity considerations, and inclusive of distributional values inherent in international law. This is particularly crucial in the absence of strong institutional machinery capable of protecting such community-type interests, and, in turn, risks the prioritization of narrowly drawn interests in the purely commercial exploitation of resources.

1.1. *A Role for Property Rights?*

Resources located firmly within the exclusive spatial jurisdiction (e.g. EEZ) of a single State are subject to domestic law. In most cases this involves the institution of property. Indeed, much of the world's exploited resources are subject to some form of ownership, be it private, State or common ownership. Marine living resources have until recently remained beyond the scope of ordinary property rules, although as I indicate below this is no longer the case. Entitlements to living resources can assume quite varied and complex forms in practice, including limited access rights, regulatory entitlements, usufructs and forms of holding where the incidents of control are split between different agents, as in the case of trusts. In each case, it is important to note that the form of holding and any legal rights or duties attaching thereto are ultimately the product of the particular values of the community within which the resource is located; hence the preference for forms of communitarian holding in socialist States and private ownership in capitalist societies.

If entitlements are determined according to the values of the community within which they are located, then how are entitlements to resources in ABNJ to be determined? At this point I want to emphasize that the political, social and economic values (priorities) of the international community may differ from the values that are pursued in domestic legal communities. This occurs because the international community has a different constituent basis and organizational structure from domestic legal orders. As a result, international law may produce different forms and allocations of natural resources than those that occur under domestic law. This much appears to account for the strong redistributionary agenda pursued by States under the new international economic order (NIEO), which influenced the formulation of

Part XI of the LOS Convention and the Agreement Relating to the Implementation of Part XI of the LOS Convention (1994 Agreement).[5]

Whilst we cannot presume that property in general, and private property in particular, constitute the favored *modus operandi* of all States, or something that is encouraged by international law, we can witness an increasing interest in its use, and of market-based forms of regulation, to tackle important environmental issues.[6] Consonant with the preference for market-based regulatory systems, property rights-based fisheries management systems have come to prominence in Australia, Canada, Iceland, New Zealand, Norway and the United States.[7] There is also some interest in furthering rights-based fisheries through RFMOs.[8]

If forms of exclusive, proprietary control of resources are desirable, and the exclusive spatial jurisdiction of coastal States is not to be extended so as to facilitate this, then the question is whether or not property rights-based entitlements may arise under international law. Before considering this, it is necessary to consider the common pool nature of fisheries, how this contributes to over-exploitation of natural resources, and why property rights provide an attractive regulatory solution to the current crises in the world's commercial fisheries.[9]

1.2. *Common Pool Natural Resources*

The world's oceans and their resources are common pool natural resources. This means that it is difficult or costly to exclude individuals from the resource, and that the benefits consumed by one person are subtracted from the benefits available to others.[10] This says nothing about the actual legal status of a

[5] Agreement Relating to the Implementation of Part XI of the United Nations Convention on the Law of the Sea of 10 December 1982 ((1994) 33 ILM 1309).

[6] See e.g. Agenda 21 (1992) UN Doc. A/CONF/151/4/ section 30.9. More generally, see A. Gillespie *International Environmental Law, Policy and Ethics* (Oxford University Press, Oxford: 1997) 28–61.

[7] Chile, Morocco, Namibia, the Netherlands, Nicaragua and South Africa have introduced weaker forms of individual transferable quota (ITQ) systems. See C. Stewart *Legislating for Property Rights in Fisheries* (FAO, Rome: 2004). See A. Hatcher *et al.* "Future Options for UK Fish Quota Management" (2002) *CEMARE Rep. No. 58* at 18–23 and 34–38. An important review of practice is to be found R. Shotton (ed.) *Use of Property Rights in Fisheries Management* (FAO, Rome: 2000).

[8] T. Aqorau "Moving Towards a Rights-Based Fisheries Management Regime for the Tuna Fisheries in the Western and Central Pacific Ocean" (2007) 22 (1) *International Journal of Marine and Coastal Law* 125–142.

[9] See further R. Barnes *Property Rights and Natural Resources* (Hart, Oxford: 2009).

[10] E. Ostrom, R. Gardner and J. Walker *Rules, Games and Common-Pool Resources* (University of Michigan Press, Ann Arbor: 1994) 6.

resource, which may be subject to private, public and common ownership, or even non-ownership. However, experience shows that access to such resources remains open due to the cost and difficulty of excluding users from it. There is widespread recognition of the adverse consequences of open access for the sustainability and effective exploitation of marine living resources. This is most frequently illustrated by reference to Hardin's seminal paper on the tragedy of the commons.[11]

The common pool qualities of marine resources were appreciated at an early stage in the development of the legal regime for ocean spaces. Indeed, as Grotius observed, because the oceans could be neither bounded nor exhausted by use, they were common property in perpetuity, whether viewed from the point of navigation or fisheries.[12] This provided the basis for his doctrine of *mare liberum*, which has since shaped the legal regime for the high seas. Whilst there may be good reason to support certain aspects of the freedom of the high seas, this has since become problematic in that alternative regulatory approaches to high seas resources will inevitably represent a degree of incursion into this long established legal principle. The law has ossified a regime that contributes to both over-exploitation and inefficient use of natural resources.

1.3. *Uneconomic and Unsustainable Exploitation of Resources*

Not only can the common pool nature of a resource, when combined with open access, result in resource degradation, it can also incentivize uneconomic activities, such as fishing. Firstly, open access leads to the dissipation of economic rent. Economic rent is the "surplus income derivable from certain scarcities of goods in the area, where the price of the good deviates from the exact cost of bringing them to the market".[13] If no-one can stop people from capturing the benefits of a resource, for example by fishing, this causes an unproductive race to capture as much fish as possible.[14] Eventually, a point will be reached when resource exploitation is saturated and no rent is gained.[15] For example,

---

[11] G. Hardin "Tragedy of the Commons" (1968) 162 *Science* 1243–1248.

[12] H. Grotius *Mare Liberum* (1608) trans. R.V.D. Magoffin (Oxford University Press, Oxford: 1916) 30.

[13] J. Christman *The Myth of Property* (Oxford University Press, New York: 1994) 20.

[14] Again the effectiveness of access limitation is crucial. On the high seas, States may limit access by vessels flying their flag, but this may simply prejudice their own nationals vis-à-vis other States' nationals in the absence of universal agreement to restrict access and so be politically unacceptable. Moreover, such limits may be circumvented by flagging out. The position is different in coastal waters, where the coastal State in principle can limit access and thereby take fisheries out of the commons.

[15] See H.S. Gordon "The Economic Theory of a Common Property Resource: The Fishery" (1954) 62 *Journal of Political Economy* 124–142.

it may be better to permit only 20 fishermen to harvest a species, and generate an optimum rent of $ 20,000, rather than have 100 fishermen produce a rent of $ 20. The surplus 80 fishermen might be engaged in productive fishing activity and harvesting more fish than the smaller group. However, the extra effort expended by each additional fisherman produces a diminishing marginal return. Arguably, they could be better deployed in other more economically productive activities. As Hannesson indicates, whilst there may be no wider social purpose to be served by allowing this rent to accrue to individuals, it is in societies' interests to maximize the return from the resources at its disposal.[16]

Secondly, when open-access regimes are combined with regulatory controls intended to ensure sustainable fishing, they tend to exacerbate unproductive fishing effort. The most common forms of regulatory control in commercial fisheries are input controls.[17] These include gear restrictions, closed seasons and vessel size restrictions.[18] Such measures seek to limit the number of people fishing or control the efficiency of fishing effort, rather than directly control how much fish are taken from the oceans.[19] They are usually simple to design and easy to implement, hence their popularity.[20] However, they only have limited success in controlling fishing effort because fishermen react by channeling their fishing effort into areas that are not subject to restriction.[21] For example, the use of limited fishing seasons often leads to 'fishing derbies', where fishermen use bigger and more powerful vessels to catch as much as possible in the shorter fishing season. Under conditions of scarcity and in the absence of capital and labor controls, fishermen intensify their fishing effort in order to obtain a larger share of the catch, with the result that more capital (vessels and equipment) and effort are expended than is necessary to catch the same amount of fish. This results in low productivity. Input controls can be combined to prevent this type of response, but this may lead

---

[16] R. Hannesson *The Privatization of the Oceans* (MIT Press, Cambridge, Mass: 2004) 51. Of course, what counts as optimum utilisation is to be determined by the State, and this may include other social objectives such as maintaining high levels of employment or participation in primary industries.

[17] See generally, OECD *Towards Sustainable Fisheries: Economic Aspects of the Management of Living Marine Resources* (OECD, Paris: 1997).

[18] See National Research Council *Sharing the Fish. Towards a National Policy on Individual Fishing Quotas* (National Academy Press, Washington: 1999) 115.

[19] They are termed input controls as they effectively increase the cost to the fisherman of participating in the fishery. D. Wesney "Applied Fisheries Management Plans: Individual Transferable Quotas and Input Control" in P. Neher *et al.* (eds) *Right Based Fishing* (Kluwer, Dordrecht: 1988) 153 at 163.

[20] See generally, M.P. Sissenwine and J.E. Kirkley "Fishery Management Techniques: Practical Aspects and Limitations" (1982) 6 (1) *Marine Policy* 43–57.

[21] L.G. Anderson *The Economics of Fisheries Management* (John Hopkins University Press, Baltimore: 1977) 204.

to complex and cumbersome regulatory structures, which are difficult and expensive to enforce.[22] Such management systems have also been criticized for requiring too much government intervention, which in turn increases the costs of fishing and generates hostility and possibly non-compliance in fishing communities.[23] Furthermore, high transaction and enforcement costs will be incurred if the participants in the resource regime try to devise rules to reduce the detrimental effects of overuse.[24] Crucially, input controls do not offer fishermen any incentive to decrease their share of the catch, and it is generally agreed that these measures have contributed much to collapses of fish stocks.[25]

Not only is fishing uneconomic in these circumstances, but fishing may be pushed beyond sustainable levels. As noted above, in an open access regime, no fisherman has an incentive to restrict his or her catch because if he does so then other fishermen will take what is left. Fishermen will be attracted to enter the fishery as long as the potential revenue from fishing exceeds the costs of fishing. Of course, each additional vessel in the fishery will reduce the size of the stock and reduce the potential return from the fishery. This means that entry into the fishery will continue until equilibrium is reached when marginal revenues cease. It may be that this equilibrium point is reached at or below the maximum sustainable yield, in which case fishing would be sustainable. However, there is evidence to suggest that natural factors may prevent a sustainable equilibrium from being reached. For example in the 1960s, North-East Atlantic and North Sea herring stocks collapsed due to overfishing.[26] The crisis appears to have resulted from the fact that herring stocks naturally aggregate. Despite a serious decline in stock numbers, herring still gathered in large shoals. This meant that the catch per boat was unaffected and fishing remained profitable beyond the point at which the stock could sustain large catches. The stock collapsed and only a total ban allowed stocks to recover. Unsustainable fishing will result in cases where the equilibrium stock level lies beyond the sustainable stock yield.

---

[22] B. Muse and K. Schelle *Individual Fishermen's Quotas: A Preliminary Review of Some Recent Programs* (CFEC, Alaska: 1989). *Cf.* Sissenwine and Kirkley, note 20.

[23] Wesney, note 19 at 164.

[24] H. Demetz "Toward a Theory of Property Rights" (1967) 57 (2) *American Economic Review* 347–359.

[25] F.T. Christy "The Death Rattle of Open Access and the Advent of Property Rights Regimes in Fisheries" (1996) 11 *Marine Resource Economics* 287–304; P.H. Pearse "From Open Access to Private Property: Recent Innovations in Fishing Rights as Instruments of Fisheries Policy" (1992) 23 *Ocean Development and International Law* 71–83.

[26] Hannesson, note 16 at 47.

1.4. *Regulatory Failings*

Although the common pool nature of resources lends itself to over-exploitation, it is really the absence of effective alternatives to open access that result in the over-exploitation of fisheries. Initially, this was the product of ignorance. As noted above, the freedom of the high seas was predicated upon some misconceptions about the nature of the seas and their resources, which served to impede alternative regulatory solutions. However, by the twentieth century, the causes and impacts of over-fishing were well-understood. One of the assumptions underpinning the extension of exclusive coastal State authority over the EEZ was the realization that this was a pre-requisite for conservation measures aimed at limiting access to and preventing over-exploitation of fish stocks.[27] Indeed, economists such as Christy, who advocated the use of private property rights-based regimes, provided intellectual support for the EEZ enclosure movement.[28] Thus, States, as 'owners' of the resource, could limit access to fisheries thereby preventing the tragedy of the commons. Many States were quick to use this power of 'ownership' to exclude foreign fishermen from their coastal waters. Unfortunately, all that resulted was an expansion of domestic fishing effort to fill the vacuum left by foreign fishermen and the relocation of distant-water fishing effort onto the high seas. The tragedy of the commons was perpetuated by domestic fishermen in the EEZ, and intensified on the high seas by foreign fishing fleets dislocated from traditional fishing grounds.[29]

A considerable body of literature, primarily in the fields of economics and political science, is devoted to exposition and advocacy of the potential benefits of property rights-based fisheries management.[30] Studies by economists show how the introduction of private property rights remedies the above inefficiencies and vest the rights holder with an interest in the maintenance of the resource.[31] Private property rights-based mechanisms, such as individual

---

[27] D. Christie "The Conservation and Management of Stocks Located Solely Within the Exclusive Economic Zone" in E. Hey (ed.) *Developments in International Fisheries Law* (Kluwer Law, The Hague: 1999) 395 at 396.

[28] F.T. Christy, Jr. "Fisheries Goals and the Rights of Property" (1969) 2 *Transactions of the American Fisheries Society* 369–378.

[29] G. Pontecorvo "The Enclosure of the Marine Commons: Adjustment and Redistribution in World Fisheries" (1988) 12 *Marine Policy* 361–372.

[30] For a review of the emergence of economics as a key factor in fisheries management systems see S. Cunningham "The Increasing Importance of Economics in Fisheries Regulation" (1983) 34 *Journal of Agricultural Economics* 69–78.

[31] A.A. Alchian "Some Economics of Property Rights" (1961) *Rand Paper No 2316*. See also Demetz, note 24. More particular to fisheries was the influential works of Gordon, note 15 and A.D. Scott "The Fishery: The Objectives of Sole Ownership" (1955) 63 *Journal of Political Economy* 116–124.

transferable quotas (ITQs), grant exclusive capture rights to individual fishermen or fishing interests, such as companies or trusts.[32] By limiting the number of such grants to fishermen, entry to a fishery is limited, thereby tackling the problem at the heart of the tragedy of the commons. When entry to a fishery is limited, and individual quotas are set in advance, fishermen are no longer required to engage in destructive and inefficient competition to catch as many fish as possible. Furthermore, as it is in their interest to maximize the value of the catch taken and reduce the costs of taking it, exclusive rights result in rent maximization. In theory, individual quotas also vest fishermen with an interest in the health of a stock and encourage more selective fishing practices.[33] Simply put, the better the condition of the stock, the more valuable the individual quota holder's stake in the resource. It is also claimed that because each fishermen has an interest in the capital, i.e. the fish stock, then this will encourage greater self-policing of the fishery, because illegal, unreported and unregulated (IUU) fishing is directly reducing the value of each 'owner's' interest. However, this appears to be more complicated, and contingent upon variables such as individual conscience, culture, size and location of a fishery and the effectiveness of monitoring and enforcement mechanisms.[34]

There is evidence that property rights-based instruments have been successful in protecting fish stocks and making fishing effort more efficient.[35] For example, it is generally agreed that the long-running ITQ program in New Zealand has resulted in increased profitability, improved product quality and reduced fishing effort.[36] The quota system in Canadian sable fish and halibut fisheries has also led to increased profitability.[37] Secondly, there are suggestions that such instruments result in better resource conservation. For example,

---

[32] Strictly speaking the proprietary interest is in the quota, rather than the fish stock *per se*. However, as property rights cannot readily be established in pre-capture fisheries, quotas operate as a surrogate right in *ferae naturae*.

[33] A. Hatcher *et al.*, note 7 at 62.

[34] P. Copes "A Critical Review of Individual Quotas as a Device in Fisheries Management" (1986) 62 *Land Economics* 278–291.

[35] See E. Brubaker *Making the Oceans Safe for Fish: How Property Rights Can Reverse the Destruction of the Atlantic Fisheries* (1995); Christie, note 25; R.Q. Grafton *et al.* "Private property rights and crises in world fisheries: Turning the tide?" (1996) 14 *Contemporary Economic Policy* 90.

[36] See C.M. Dewees, "Assessment of the implementation of individual transferable quotas in New Zealand's inshore fishery" (1989) 9 *North American Journal of Fisheries Management* 131; Pearse, note 25; R. Connor "Trends in Fishing Capacity and Aggregation of Fishing Rights in New Zealand Under Individual Transferable Quota" in Shotton, note 7, vol. 2 at 267; J.H. Annala "New Zealand's ITQ System: Have the First Eight Years Been a Success or a Failure?" (1996) 6 *Reviews in Fish Biology and Fisheries* 43–62; C.J. Batstone and B.M.H. Sharp "New Zealand's quota management system: The first ten years" (1999) 23 *Marine Policy* 177–190.

[37] R.W. Crowley and H. Palsson "Rights based fisheries management in Canada" (1992) 7 *Marine Resource Economics* 1–21.

there is evidence that fisheries utilizing rights-based systems have increased the biomass of some fish stocks.[38] However, this is not a universal benefit in all rights-based fisheries, and it has been suggested that rights-based measures may lead to excess effort being relocated into non-quota fisheries, resulting in their depletion.[39] Despite some disagreement about the precise benefits and consequences of property rights-based fisheries, economists have been strong advocates of private property systems.[40]

1.5. *Property Rights: The Right Solution?*

Economic theory shows how efficiency and conservation gains are contingent on fishermen having an exclusive, permanent and secure interest in the stock.[41] Indeed, the stronger the exclusivity, the more secure the title, the greater the extent of transferability and the longer the duration of the holding, then the more valuable the right and the greater the interest in its preservation. However, not all commentators agree that property rights-based instruments are a good thing. Firstly, there is evidence that property rights-based measures have not prevented destructive fishing practices, such as high-grading, discards, or by-catches.[42] Quotas tend to encourage high-grading in order to maximize the individual return from the fishery, as the costs of this (harmful fishing practice that may damage the sustainability of a stock) are dissipated across all quota holders for a given stock.[43]

Secondly, rights-based mechanisms are objected to because they put an end to a valuable common or public right of access to a resource.[44] Litigation concerning reduction in fishing entitlements,[45] and the exclusion of part-

[38] Hatcher, note 7 at 62.

[39] *Ibid.*

[40] See generally, F.T. Christy and A. Scott *The Common Wealth in Ocean Fisheries* (John Hopkins Press, Baltimore: 1965); Neher *et al.* (eds) note 19; P.H. Pearse "Fishing rights, regulations and revenues" (1981) 15 *Marine Policy* 135–146; R. Arnason "Ocean fisheries management: recent developments" (1993) 17 *Marine Policy* 334–339; B.L. Crowley (ed.) *Taking Ownership. Property Rights and Fishery Management on the Atlantic Coast* (AIMS, Halifax: 1996); Grafton *et al.*, note 35; Hannesson, note 16.

[41] A.D. Scott "Conceptual Origins of Rights Based Fishing" in Neher *et al.* (eds), note 19 at 47–48.

[42] See Hatcher, note 7 supra, at 32.

[43] R. Arnason "On Catch Discarding in Fisheries" (1994) 9 *Marine Resource Economics* 189–207; Annala, note 36 at 54; H.H. Gissurarson, *Overfishing: The Icelandic Solution* (IEA, London: 2000) 56.

[44] For allocation disputes in Iceland see Gissurarson, note 43 at 26. In New Zealand, Maori groups challenged the Fisheries Act establishing right-based fisheries in *Te Weehi v. Regional Fisheries Officer* [1986] 1 NZLR 680.

[45] See, for example, *Cooper v. AG* [1996] 3 NZLR 480; *Allan Guard v. Seafood Consortium Ltd and Ors* [2001] NZCA 291 paras 16–20.

time[46] and recreational fishing interests has been a feature of the post-privatization fishery.[47] These criticisms may be mitigated by ensuring that historic users retain comparable entitlements to access post-privatization fisheries. Indeed, initial quota allocations in domestic rights-based fisheries are usually made on the basis of historic fishing patterns. However, allocations on this basis have been criticized for granting windfall gains to those most responsible for over-fishing.[48] Moreover, this approach does not generally address the concerns of more diffuse interests affected by the reduction of a general freedom to fish. Notably, no State has raised a levy on initial allocations, and few have sought to subsequently extract some of the rent from a fishery, through fees or taxes, in order to compensate for the loss of a public right to fish. Principally, this was done to secure the political support of the key participants in the fishery for the new management system. Subsequently, most States seem content to recover the costs of managing the fisheries, rather than actively redistributing the wealth generated by the resource regime. This suggests a pragmatic rather than principled approach to resource management, and one that might be seen to be strongly at odds with international requirements to ensure equitable use of resources or, in the case of the Area, benefit sharing.[49] Arguably, a similarly pragmatic approach underpins the use of a 'real interest' test to determine access to fisheries regulated under a RFMO, where emphasis is on historic participation in a fishery. This suggests that States are prepared to sacrifice public rights or freedoms to fish if this results in improved fisheries management.

Thirdly, the creation of strong private property rights-based holdings may make it more difficult for governments to regulate fisheries. Quota holders are often highly resistant to regulatory changes that reduce the commercial value of their quotas, for example by general reductions in the total allowable catch (TAC) set by the State. In the short term, holders of quotas have an interest in maintaining higher catch levels. This arises when there is either ignorance of the adverse effects of overfishing on the stock in which they have an interest, or when the 'costs' of overfishing are deliberately postponed to a future, indeterminate date. This is exacerbated by the fact that conservation measures may be taken on the basis of the best, but still incomplete scientific advice, or even a precautionary basis. A short-term interest in maintaining high TACs can be critical to measures taken to reduce quotas for the long-term sustainability of a fishery. In practice, there is scope for considerable pressure

---

[46] *Gunn v. AG* [1993] NZLR 108. See also, Hatcher, note 7 supra, at 94.

[47] R.E. Kearney "Fisheries Property Rights and Recreational/Commercial Conflict: The Implications of Policy Development in Australia and New Zealand" (2001) 25 *Marine Policy* 49–59.

[48] See the points raised in *Seawatch International* v. *Mossbacher*, 762 F. Supp. 370 (DDC 1991) at 375–381.

[49] See subsection 4.4 infra.

to be placed on regulators to maintain high catch levels to mollify commercial fishing interests, who as quota holders are the most important stakeholders in the fishery.

Finally, there is a more general problem that results from the privatization of only one component of the marine environment. Privatized fisheries have a determinable economic value, as represented by the market value of a fishing quota. Other uses of the marine environment do not possess this value. Although efforts are underway to try and provide a better understanding of the value of social and ecological goods, this endeavor is far from complete.[50] This means that any cost-benefit analysis about how to manage activities may be flawed or skewed in favor of those things that can be analyzed in terms of economic value.

The jury is still out on the success of property rights-based instruments, especially given their relatively short history and evolving nature. In any event, it is not the purpose of this paper to fully evaluate what are purely economic arguments. Rather, assuming that they do provide positive results, then what role does law play in delineating such rights and ensuring that non-economic interests are protected.

2. *Property Rights*

Economists view property rights in terms of exclusivity, duration, security and transferability.[51] Exclusivity refers to the holder's freedom to enjoy their property free of interference, either from other persons, or the State. Exclusivity may operate in respect of the typical incidents of ownership, such as possession, use and management. Duration corresponds to the incident of term, and is important because a right with little or no duration will have little economic value. Duration also enables the rights holders to receive any returns for investing in the property in later years. Security relates to the extent to which the right can and will be protected from interference and the extent to which exclusive-use rights will be guaranteed. Transferability relates to the right of the holder to alienate his property through sale or similar mechanism. In short, the greater the extent of these qualities that are held by the property holders, the more valuable their right. This tends to support strong forms of private property, free of State interference. This in turn may result in conflicts between rights holders and State machinery that enforces environmental standards or ensures

---

[50] R.K. Turner *et al.* "Valuing Nature: Lessons Learned and Future Directions" (2003) 46 *Ecological Economics* 493–510.

[51] A. Scott "Introducing Property in Fisheries Management" in Shotton, note 7 vol. 1.

certain welfare needs are met. The tension between such interests is evident in ITQ systems. Whilst certain use rights are in the hands of the fishermen, general management responsibilities remain in the hands of the State. These are powers that quota holders are keen to secure.

In law, property rights concern the legal relationship between people in respect of things.[52] A property right entitles one party, the right holder, to make a claim on an act or forbearance of another party, the right-regarder, in respect of a thing. This right has the force of law behind it, meaning that failure of the duty bearer to comply with the right will justify the use of coercive measures to ensure compliance or compensation in lieu of performance. It also means that law can be used to ensure the holder exercises the right in accordance with any restrictions imposed upon it. Property involves a complex range of rights and responsibilities, including the right to possess, the right to use, the right to manage, the right to the income of a thing, the right to the capital of a thing, the right to security, the rights or incidents of transmissibility and absence of term, the duty to prevent harm, liability to execution, and the incident of residuarity.[53] Not all forms of property locate these incidents in the hands of a single person, nor do all persons possess the same quality of incidents. Property is a social institution, a means to certain ends, and so the quality of a holding is determined according to how a particular society deems it necessary to allocate competence, and power, in respect of things.

Recent scholarship has distilled property down to the idea of excludability: the rights holder's authority to exclude other persons from the *res*.[54] This is not exclusion *per se*, because it might not be exercised, and it is not exclusiveness because other persons can have interests in the *res*; rather it is excludability in the sense that it is the owner's legal right to decide whether or not to exclude others from his or her property. Understood thus, property rights only exist when certain conditions are met: a thing must be capable of being subject to excludability, there must be a legal system that can support excludability, and the legal rights must be capable of being enforced in practice.[55]

---

[52] B.A. Ackerman *Private property and the constitution* (Yale University Press, New Haven: 1977) 26.

[53] See A.M. Honoré "Ownership" in A.G. Guest (ed.) *Oxford Essays in Jurisprudence* (Oxford University Press, London: 1961) 107. These incidents are self-explanatory with the exception of residuarity, which entails that other incidents of ownership revert to the legal owner upon the expiry of the term of the grant or in the event of a breach of the condition of the grant.

[54] See J. Waldron *The Right to Private Property* (Clarendon Press, Oxford: 1990) 89 ff.; J. Penner *The Idea of Property in Law* (Clarendon Press, Oxford: 1997) chapter 4; L. Underkuffler, *The Idea of Property: Its Meaning and Power* (Oxford University Press, Oxford: 2003); Christman, note 13.

[55] Here we may observe a distinction between *de jure* and *de facto* rights. Although a person may have a legal right of property, unless that right can be articulated and enforced in practice,

Gray defines property by its physical, legal and moral excludability.[56] Physical excludability exists only when it is reasonably practicable to exclude others from the benefits of a thing in its existing form.[57] This is illustrated by Grotius' assertion that because the oceans could be neither bounded nor exhausted by use, they were not susceptible to national appropriation.[58] Until the advent of legal excludability through the law of maritime delimitation, most of the world's seas and oceans remained beyond the scope of exclusive coastal State jurisdiction. Marine fisheries are a fungible and unascertained good. Property rights in specific fish in their natural state cannot be allocated because they simply cannot be identified. In most States it remains the case that property rights in fish only arise upon their capture. Of course, the advent of sophisticated fishing quotas has challenged this position through the grant of exclusive harvest rights to predetermined quantities of fish. Although this does not constitute *de jure* ownership of fish in their natural state, it amounts to a *de facto* allocation of the resource among the quota holders.[59]

When exclusive rights are established, care must be taken to ensure that non-exclusive interests are protected. Although fish may be owned, or exclusive capture-rights granted, certain non-exclusive interests inhere in all fisheries, or are necessary to sustain them. Thus the water column provides a habitat and food supply for the captured fish. This is generally not subject to exclusive ownership-type claims under domestic law. In economic terms this produces a negative externality because some of the production costs of a fishery (i.e. animal feed) are not born by the quota holder. The existence of such externalities is important to fisheries regulation, because a failure to properly take

---

it tends to be rendered an empty vessel. This is particularly important in the context of marine living resources, where exclusive rights are undermined by the absence of effective means of protection, for example through the occurrence of IUU fishing activities. Property requires both *de jure* and *de facto* elements to be present.

[56] K. Gray "Property in Thin Air" (1991) 50 *Cambridge Law Journal* 252–307 at 269.

[57] The qualifier of form is an important one. For example, wild animals are not physically excludable unless they are somehow reduced into captivity. This reduction to captivity may be regarded as a change in the form of the resource. Hence the qualitative difference between a quota right to capture wild fish and ownership of the caught fish.

[58] Grotius, note 12.

[59] It is notable that the phrase 'fishing opportunity' is commonly used to describe 'participatory rights' in fisheries regulated under RFMOs. This reaffirms the idea that actual fish are not being allocated, merely permission to fish. See R. Rayfuse "Regional Allocation Issues or Zen and the Art of Pie Cutting" (2007) *University of New South Wales Faculty of Law Research Paper Series*, 10 section 2.2 In practice most entitlements resemble access rights and therefore possess weak proprietary attributes. However, this does not preclude the future use of property rights-based measures, although ultimately this will be contingent on how the principle of the freedom to fish on the high seas is constrained. Ultimately, the determinative issue here, as in EEZ fisheries, is the quality of the entitlement held by the fisherman rather than the nomenclature.

them into account may result in destructive fishing practices, such as bottom trawling. A quota holder may have little regard for components of the marine environment that are not his or her property. The costs of his or her trawling in terms of reef destruction are externalized to the 'unowned' marine environment. Here regulatory constraints will be necessary to ensure that externalities are properly controlled, thus undercutting some of regulatory benefits of using rights-based instruments.

Legal excludability can be used as a proxy for physical excludability. In large part it is contingent upon recognition of the legitimacy of the rule of exclusion, and upon the law possessing effective legal means for ensuring exclusivity and sanctioning breaches of the rule. This is fundamental to maritime zones such as the EEZ. Brilmayer and Klein point out that as occupation or possession of water is not practicable, States must base their authority on something else: reciprocal legal recognition.[60] Crucially, reciprocal legal recognition is only likely to succeed if the regime is perceived to have been established in accordance with rules and procedures that are fair.[61] This shows a strong link between legal excludability and moral excludability. In every society there are powerful and compelling reasons why natural resources are subject to particular forms of holding, or are excluded from property regimes altogether. This is particularly the case for essential natural resources.[62] For example, undesirable or intolerable consequences, such as food shortages, might follow if one person, or a group of persons, would be permitted to control access to those resources. Through legal institutions such as the legislature and courts, society engages in a process of converting moral limits to property into legal norms in order to ensure that property remains consistent with highly regarded human values and needs.

Before considering these values, it is important to note that property rights or legal excludability can only be serviced through a legal system. In legal terms, ownership denotes a relationship between persons in respect of things. More specifically, a property right consists of a complex of rights and privileges all of which must be *in rem*, i.e. good against the entire world, and not merely against specific persons.[63] Crucially, the effectiveness of any proprietary

---

[60] L. Brilmayer and N. Klein "Land and Sea: Two Sovereignty Regimes in Search of a Common Denominator" (2001) 33 *New York University Journal of International Law and Politics* 703–768 at 736.

[61] See section 6 infra.

[62] Gray, note 56 at 280.

[63] It is sometimes contended that a right *in rem* is a conglomeration of separate rights *in personam*, since every right will be exercised against persons. However, the essence of the right *in rem* is that it is effective against an open or unspecified class of persons, whereas the right *in personam* is only available against a specific person or persons.

right depends upon a title or source from which it is derived. As Fitzgerald notes, "title is the *de facto* antecedent of which the right is the *de jure* consequence."[64] In domestic legal orders property rights are effective because the State acts as the guarantor of title. Clearly, such title is good only in so far as the State is a recognized authority for the territory in which the property is located and has sufficient authority to guarantee that title. Under international law this authority is rooted in the notion of sovereignty, and, more particularly, territorial sovereignty.[65] The importance of exclusive authority in a geographically circumscribed area or territory needs to be stressed. Territorial sovereignty is a basic building block of the international legal order, allowing for a clear and secure delimitation of legal competence between formally equal sovereign agencies. It provides a basic framework for the regulation of things. When a *res* moves from one State to another, property rights, that is to say the rights between persons in respects of things, are not extinguished, they adapt according to the law of the place where the *res* is situated—the *lex situs*.[66] As a general rule, property rights are spatially determinate. This begs the question, if property rights are so intimately connected with areas of exclusive spatial authority, how can property rights be created, allocated and regulated in ABNJ.

When considering the potential for property rights in ABNJ, it is worth recalling that title is a relative concept. As Lord Diplock pointed out in *Ocean Estates Ltd v. Pinder*:

> At common law [. . .] there is no such thing as an "absolute title". Where questions of title to land arise in litigation the court is concerned only with the relative strengths of the titles proved by the rival claimants. If party A can prove a better title than party B he is entitled to succeed notwithstanding that C may have a better title than A, if C is neither a party to the action, nor a person by whose authority B is in possession or occupation of the land.[67]

---

[64] P.J. Fitzgerald *Salmond on Jurisprudence* (Sweet and Maxwell, London: 1966) at 331.

[65] See Judge Huber in the *Islands of Palmas* case (Netherlands v. United States) [1928] 2 RIAA 829 at 838.

[66] In *Winkworth* v. *Christie Manson & Woods* [1980] 1 Ch. 496, a painting stolen in England and sold in Italy gave the purchaser good title because the paining was purchased *bona fides*. *Luthor* v. *Sagor* [1921] 3 KB 532 confirms the application of this rule to property expropriated abroad. Cf *Kuwait Airways Corporation* v. *Iraqi Airways Company* [2002] UKHL 19, where the House of Lords refused to apply the *lex situs* (Iraq) concerning the unlawful expropriation of Kuwaiti aircraft. In general, see A. Briggs *The Conflict of Laws* (Clarendon Press, Oxford: 2002) at 205–211. The principal exception to this is intangible moveable property. Debts and the like are considered akin to contractual rights for jurisdictional purposes. Intellectual property is generally governed by the *lex protectionis*. See *ibid.*, 211–213.

[67] *Ocean Estates Ltd v. Pinder* [1969] 2 AC 16 at 24–25.

International tribunals follow this relative approach to title.[68] So although we are concerned with title and rights effective against the world, in most instances the determination of those rights is limited to the parties to a case and the wider effects are left alone. If property rights arise in ABNJ, and this only affects a limited number of persons, then it may be that a relatively weak title is sufficient for practical purposes. This is important in respect of potential rights-based fishing entitlements in RFMOs. When fishing is limited to a discrete number of participants, then it may be that any title only needs to be recognized between those parties to work in practice.[69]

Returning to the issue of moral excludability. Above, I noted that there are a range of general philosophical justifications for property.[70] First, occupation allocates a thing to the first person to take possession or control of it. Its use is restricted to unowned things. Occupation must be manifest physically rather than merely claimed, and the scope of what may be owned is limited to that which is occupied. As a general justification for property, this approach is generally rejected because it does not explain why property exists.[71] It merely explains how property is allocated once the permissibility of property is accepted. Despite this, it retains a powerful resonance. In fisheries it explains rights of capture. It also seems to justify initial allocations of quota rights on the basis of historical catch records.

The labor/desert justification provides that property rights will accrue to persons producing socially worthwhile goods through their art, intelligence and industry. This approach is rooted in the natural rights theories of Locke, but has received more recent attention from property scholars such as Munzer.[72] It provides a powerful justification for property because it rewards socially productive activities, accords each some return for his/her own work, and allows a degree of social control over property, in the sense that society determines the extent of socially productive activities. For example, property in this tradition is generally subject to limits that prevent waste, spoiling or accruals beyond one's needs.[73] In the context of fisheries regulation, 'labor/desert' reinforces the idea of ownership of fish or other resources upon capture.

---

[68] I. Brownlie *Principles of Public International Law* 6th ed. (Oxford University Press, Oxford: 1998) at 154–155.

[69] See further section 3 infra.

[70] Here I proceed on the assumption that property systems are pluralist, that there is no single unifying justification for property. Rather, property in general and particular property rights may have several mutually exclusive justifications.

[71] See L.C. Becker *Property Rights* (Routledge and Kegan Paul, London: 1977) at 24–31.

[72] S. Munzer *A Theory of Property* (Cambridge University Press, New York: 1990) at 256ff.

[73] *Ibid.*, 284.

A number of arguments in favor of private property derive from liberty. The central idea here is that ownership of things gives people material independence, which in turn facilitates moral or political independence. Any dependence upon others for material needs will in some way render people beholden to others and so unable to exercise true independence in their actions. Although this approach is weakened by the absence of a universally accepted account of liberty, it remains influential. For example, it infuses much of the discourse shaping the notion of the common heritage of mankind. Property in this tradition also seeks to provide some minimum level of holding to ensure material needs can be met.

Utilitarian justifications of property admit forms of property that result in a net increase in human welfare. This generally means that property is designed to maximize the productive capacity of resources and security of expectations.[74] Contemporary accounts of utility focus on the maximization of preference and dovetail with economic justifications of property, as discussed above.[75] Utilitarian approaches tend to preserve certain core entitlements to essential goods in order to avoid social disutility, thereby limiting the scope of exclusive rights.

A final justification of property accords to each person that which is proper or appropriate.[76] According to the justification of property derived from propriety, property entails not only rights and privileges, but certain responsibilities to the wider community as well. It may even result in collective interests taking priority over private interests in order to ensure that certain fundamental public needs or goals are met. Property in this tradition can be used to explain concepts such as the trust and stewardship.[77] However, property in this tradition is also subject to a similar criticism as liberal accounts of property; it depends on some contestable notion of good order. Arguably this justification of property influenced the development of the EEZ, and the idea that the coastal States were best situated to regulate fishing activities in littoral waters.

This brief review of justifications shows that there are strong reasons for limiting property rights in order to meet certain public interests, or when certain conditions for their justification are not met. For example, property may be

[74] J. Bentham "Principles of the Civil Code" in C.K. Ogden (ed.) *Jeremy Bentham: The Theory of Legislation* (Kegan Paul, London: 1931) chapter III. Also, D. Hume *Treatise of Human Nature* (ed.) Selby-Bigge (Clarendon Press, Oxford: 1955) at 484–516.

[75] C.M. Rose *Property and Persuasion: Essays on the History, Theory and Rhetoric of Ownership* (Westview Press, Boulder: 1994) 3 ff.

[76] *Ibid.*, 59.

[77] See e.g. C. Redgwell *Intergenerational trusts and environmental protection* (Manchester University Press, Manchester: 1999).

denied in the absence of worthwhile labor, or where accumulations of property impede liberty, or when it fails to maximize preferences, or when it fails to secure order. We can also expect limits to be placed upon property rights to ensure their coherence with some or all of the above justifications. These are important considerations, because if we heedlessly strengthen private property rights to ensure they function at an economically optimum level, then this may result in other meaningful social goals being discounted. In the present context, if we accept the immediate benefits of property rights-based instruments to regulate resources in ABNJ, either conceptually in order to define States' interests, or directly, so as to create directly enforceable entitlements for individual fishermen, then we must do so in a way that is compatible with these moral limits.

Whilst there are significant differences between economic rights and legal rights, it is important to note that strong economic rights will depend upon their proper articulation and protection by law.[78] This has a number of implications. Foremost is the fact that whilst economists may advocate particular forms of property, this is contingent on law being able to deliver the property right in a particular form. Furthermore, values other than efficiency will feed into the legal system that dictates that form and operation of a property right. The influence of complex physical, legal and moral factors on the form of property rights can be illustrated by reference to biodiversity concerns. In law, biodiversity is defined as the:

> variability among living organisms from all sources including, *inter alia*, terrestrial, marine and other aquatic ecosystems and the ecological complexes of which they are part; this includes diversity within species, between species and of ecosystems.[79]

Biodiversity is a non-exclusive attribute rather than the actual physical resource itself, although the latter remains an important component of biodiversity.[80] The individual component of biodiversity may be subject to exclusive control. However, the wider community retains a legal interest in regulating certain aspects of the good to ensure the protection of vital needs, or resource potential. This may require use restrictions to be placed on the holder of a

---

[78] As Barzel comments, "[e]conomic rights are the end (that is, what people see), whereas legal rights are a means to achieve that end." In: Y. Barzel *Economic Analysis of Property Rights* (Cambridge University Press, Cambridge: 1989) 3.

[79] Article 2 of the CBD (Convention on Biological Diversity of 5 June 1992 ((1992) 31 ILM 818)).

[80] See further, C. de Klemm and C. Shine *Biological Diversity Conservation and the Law: Legal Mechanisms for Conserving Species and Ecosystems* (IUCN, Gland: 1993); W.J. Snape *Biodiversity and the Law* (Island Press, Washington: 1996) 16–24.

right, or to provide that certain uses are controlled by the State or other agencies. More than this, biodiversity measures may require positive acts of cooperation between holders and other agencies. In short, the facilitation of biodiversity may require quite complex forms of holding to be prescribed. This will require carefully drafted regimes for the control and regulation of marine living resources in ABNJ. These observations are important because they indicate that the full bundle of ownership rights in a thing will invariably be restricted in the public interest. This may result in sub-optimal forms of holding, as far as the economist is concerned. For the lawyer, it points to the need for sophisticated and carefully calibrated legal regimes that prescribe and ensure the functioning of the property rights in accordance with a plurality of values.

To summarize, property as a legal institution has three essential features. Firstly, there is an actual property right, or rather a bundle of entitlements that define the holder's rights in respect of the use of a particular resource. Secondly, there is the body of property rules, being the rules under which a particular property entitlement is exercised. These two facets presuppose the existence of a third feature of a property system—a supporting legal structure. This is generally domestic law, although international law can have both a direct and indirect influence on specific forms of property. This is important because property rights are never purely abstract or economic rights; they are legal rights, infused with the values of the community that shape the legal system. Property rights take a variety of forms, and this is influenced by the diverse ideologies and value systems that hold sway in different societies. However, as Waldron notes, "[n]o society, whatever its ideological predilections, can avoid the fact that some resources are more amenable to some types of property rule than others".[81] More specifically, the application of property rules to resources is contingent upon its excludability, either physically, legally or morally. It follows that the potential for property rights in resources located in ABNJ are contingent upon the existence first of legal structures capable of supporting property rights, and then upon how physical, legal and moral factors may shape the excludability of resources.

The potential for international law to utilize property rights is now considered, first through a conceptual application of property models to State-based entitlements, and then as a means of creating entitlements for individuals directly.

[81] Waldron, note 54 at 45.

3. *Property Rights in High Seas Fisheries*

The continental shelf and EEZ indicate the importance of exclusive control in natural resources regimes. This has allowed coastal States to establish complex management regimes for fisheries that utilize domestic legal mechanisms for the prescription and enforcement of fishing and mineral activities. In theory, the exclusive control over such areas also vests coastal States with an 'owner's' interest in conserving and managing the resources therein because the zones form part of the State's natural resource base. Even if this has not always resulted in the successful conservation and management of domestic fisheries and other resources, there is little doubt that the creation of exclusive maritime zones was a necessary step towards more effective regulation of natural resources.

ABNJ are characterized by the absence of exclusivity. This has rendered high seas fisheries regulation much more difficult than domestic fisheries. RFMOs are the principal vehicle for coordinating and managing fisheries regulation on the high seas. Unfortunately, they have a mixed record of preventing over-capacity and over-exploitation of fish stocks.[82] Some problems arise from widespread IUU fishing. Others result from the failure of States to participate in cooperative management regimes. And yet others may be attributed the predominant use of input controls to restrict fishing effort. The High Seas Task Force (HSTF) has made a number of suggestions as to how States and RFMOs might improve upon their track record. Although the HSTF touches upon the use of quotas, it stops short of advocating stronger property rights-based mechanisms.[83]

Under Article 116 of the LOS Convention, States enjoy the freedom to fish on the high seas. This is subject to their treaty obligations, the rights and interests of coastal States, and the provisions of Articles 117–120. Article 117 requires States to take action, alone or in cooperation with other States, to ensure the conservation and management of the living resources of the high seas. More specifically, Article 118 requires States to cooperate towards establishing regional fisheries organizations to this end. Whilst the convention emphasizes cooperation, it does not preclude fishing on the high seas where cooperative measures are not taken or where regional fisheries organizations are not established. Where RFMOs are established, the scope of their powers

[82] High Seas Task Force *Closing the net: Stopping illegal fishing on the high seas* (Sadag SA, Bellegarde: 2006).

[83] *Ibid.*, 107. Some commentators have been more direct in their advocacy of stronger property rights-based entitlements. See R. Quentin Grafton *et al.* "The Economics of Allocation in Tuna Regional Fisheries Management Organisations" (2006) *ANU Economics and Environment Network Working Paper* EEN0612.

depends on their constituent treaty. A number of RFMOs adopt quota-based systems, whereby members are allocated a share of the TAC on an annual basis for the stock(s) in question. Such allocations do not generally comprise the kind of strong property rights-based entitlements that we have been discussing so far. However, it remains theoretically possible that instead of a mere annual allocation of a share of the TAC, States could receive an exclusive, durable (permanent) and transferable share of the TAC. This seems to be desirable from the point of view of improving the management of high seas fisheries. It would, in theory, vest States with a stronger interest in the conservation and management of the resource, and facilitate more efficient fishing by allowing for the transfer of these entitlements to States with the most efficient fishing operations.[84] However, it requires us to consider whether such permanent and exclusive entitlements are permissible under international law.

It seems that the principal objection is whether or not such *permanent* and *exclusive* entitlements can be allocated to States. Clearly, this would seriously challenge the long-standing common property nature of the high seas, and there appear to be obstacles to any such development. Article 89 of the LOS Convention protects the common property aspects of the high seas, by invalidating claims of sovereignty over the high seas. This would appear to preclude allocations of entitlements which effectively amount to a permanent *de facto* appropriation of components of the high seas.[85] Arguably, the well-established freedom to fish on the high seas would be effectively negated if RFMOs excluded access through the allocation of permanent and exclusive fishing rights. The response to this is that what is being allocated is merely a use right, akin to a *profit a prendre*, rather than a stronger form of sovereign appropriation. Similar use rights already exist on the high seas and only sovereign claims are prohibited. Of course, fishing through the operation of exclusive use

[84] Admittedly, this is contingent on the State's willingness to aggregate fishing entitlements having any correlation to the efficiency of its domestic fishing fleet. All that can be claimed here is that States with efficient domestic fishing fleets may generate more economic rent, which may be utilised to finance the acquisition of new fishing entitlements. It must be acknowledged that States may wish to accumulate fishing entitlements for other reasons, such as the protection of domestic fishing industries, and which have no relevance to efficiency.

[85] This appears to be consistent with the award in the *Behring Fur Seals Arbitration* (1893) RIAA, Vol. XXVIII 263, which rejected the United States right of property or protection in fur seals outside the ordinary three-nautical mile (nm) limit. Notably, both the United States and Great Britain engaged in a full-ranging debate as to the nature and extent to which property could exist in high seas areas. However, the precise reason for this decision is not entirely clear, although Lauterpacht notes that the majority of arbiters considered the freedom of the seas to warrant the exclusion of other juridical considerations (H. Lauterpacht, *Private Law Sources and Analogies of International Law* (Longmans, Green & Co, London: 1927) 226). Moreover, it seems reasonable to concede that a strict application of the freedom of the high seas is no longer tenable.

rights under an RFMO, rather than under a residual freedom of the high seas infers that that ultimate title to (or sovereignty over) the resource vests with the RFMO or other managing agency. The only defense to this is to suggest that the RFMO measures amount to an *inter se* limitation of an entitlement, rather than the creation of a positive use right.[86] This raises the question of the effectiveness of such an approach against third States. Although the freedom to fish on the high seas is qualified, it is not at all clear that it can be subject to the absolute condition that it may only be exercised via the machinery of an RFMO.[87] In practice, open membership of RFMOs may mitigate the problem of non-member participation by ensuring non-discriminatory entrance requirements. Thus, as long as States are happy to join or comply with RFMO measures then they may participate in the fishery. However, willingness to submit to RFMO measures cannot be assumed, and, in light of the problems associated with flags of convenience, it may only take a few States to remain outside the regime to jeopardize its effectiveness.

If this issue can be overcome, there remains the problem of new entrants. Although the number of potential participants in a regime may be limited to States with a 'real interest', this requirement is one imposed under the Fish Stocks Agreement,[88] and not under general international law. This leaves it open for non-parties to the Fish Stocks Agreement to seek entry to an RFMO managed fisheries, without the degree of interest as defined by the Fish Stocks Agreement.[89] In any event, regardless of questions of membership criteria, it is clear that each new entrant will require a downwards revision of existing quota allocations held by existing members. Any revised allocations, in the form of a reduced share, would effectively be subtracted from existing members' shares and so deny them security of expectation desired in a limited entry rights-based management system.[90] It is also likely that any downward revision of TAC shares will generate resistance to new entrants.

---

[86] This means that exclusive rights are created through a system of mutual restrictions on a pre-existing liberty. Subsequent reference to entitlement or rights in this context does not ignore this nuance. They are simply used for convenience.

[87] Cf. R.G. Rayfuse, *Non-Flag State Enforcement in High Seas Fisheries* (Martinus Nijhoff, Leiden: 2004) at 357.

[88] Agreement for the Implementation of the Provisions of the United Nations Convention on the Law of the Sea of 10 December 1982 relating to the Conservation and Management of Straddling Fish Stocks and Highly Migratory Fish Stocks (1995) 34 *ILM* 1542.

[89] See Article 8(3). It also opens the door to any State petitioning to join an RFMO and claiming a share of the fishery, and then immediately transferring this for gain. If such "abuses" are to be prevented, then this will require carefully calibrated rules on participation being imposed under general international law.

[90] It should be noted that whilst there is no security of expectation under the traditional (open access) freedom of the high seas, this position is modified where an RFMO exercises exclusive authority to regulate a fishery.

It is generally desirable for rights-based entitlements to be transferable. A recent review of RFMO provisions indicates that there is no objection in principle to quotas being transferred.[91] It also indicates that several RFMOs provide for transferable rights, and that limited trading takes place in practice. What may be more problematic is ensuring that the consequences of transfer are fully appreciated and controlled. If we consider the form of domestic property rights-based entitlements, we can see that they usually have two components: a permanent share of the TAC and an annual catch entitlement (ACE). The ACE represents the actual amount of fish that can be caught under a quota in any given year. This can usually be subdivided and transferred, with the advantage that the permanent entitlement is not lost. Whilst transfer of the ACE may not pose too many problems, the transfer of the permanent quota share is more significant because it will amount to the State relinquishing any right to fish in the RFMO area, or in other words cede its freedom to fish in a particular area of the high seas, or for a particular species. This will require the development of rules that permit and control how States cede a partial exercise of their freedom to fish.[92] Of course, it may be observed that States are unlikely to transfer their permanent share in the TAC. As a consequence of this, the potential optimization of holdings through the transfer of rights to the most efficient operators is unlikely to arise.

Although strengthening the proprietary characteristics of States' fishing rights in RFMOs seems to provide a means of harnessing the benefits of rights-based mechanisms, it is important to note some general problems with this approach. Firstly, it might be regarded as a form of creeping jurisdiction through the grant of *de facto* permanent and exclusive rights over fisheries on the high seas. This much seems to be politically objectionable. Secondly, operation of any such *de jure* entitlement will be undermined unless it can be upheld against non-members of the RFMO (or non-members that agree to be bound by the fisheries management rules). The Fish Stocks Agreement makes some inroads into the exclusivity of flag State jurisdiction, but these are concerned with matters of port State control and consent to boarding and inspection measures. Thirdly, the success of any property rights-based entitlement depends not just upon the ability of holders to secure their interests

[91] See A. Serdy "Trading of Fishery Commission Quota under International Law" (2007) 21 *Ocean Yearbook* 265–288.

[92] In such a system, it would be theoretically possible for a State to buy its way back into a fishery by purchasing another State's quota, or share thereof. This raises the interesting spectre of States trading their sovereign rights in a way like ordinary commodities.

against other persons, but for third parties to ensure that the holders act in accordance with the terms of their holding. For example, most property systems, and certainly some domestic rights-based fisheries, have rules which cancel entitlements when the conditions for holding them are breached. At the very least there needs to be a system of sanctions or penalties in place to ensure that holders act in accordance with the terms of any exclusive harvesting right. Here it may be argued that it may be easier to regulate individual entitlements, rather than State-held entitlements, as it seems easier to cancel individual fishermen's quotas than relieve States of their entitlements. For these reasons, it may ultimately be more beneficial to focus on the creation of individual rather than State entitlements in RFMOs. Of course, this would represent something of a revolution in international fisheries law, and cannot be considered lightly.

Finally, this approach falls short of establishing individual entitlements, although it does not preclude such measures being further implemented by States. ITQs are designed to encourage individuals to conduct themselves in a particular way. States may possess exclusive rights over a thing but this does not entail that individual fishermen receiving fishing entitlements from the State will act other than in their own self-interest. Indeed, in the absence of a stake in the resource they are likely to perpetuate the tragedy of the commons within the exclusive ambit of the RFMO in the same way that has occurred within EEZs. If the benefits of rights-based fisheries are to be realized, then this requires some form of individual property rights-based entitlement to run on from the State's entitlement. Of course, when this next step is taken, this may result in a duality and incompatibility of regimes. For example, States are likely to place limits on how individuals utilize their entitlements, not just to protect domestic public interests (i.e. to ensure that certain conservation goals are met), but to protect the State's exclusive entitlement, for example by prohibiting transfers into foreign ownership. This may inhibit the attainment of optimal efficiency or reduce the value of the individual entitlement, thereby weakening the holder's interest in sustaining the fishery or desire to comply with fishing rules.

Although the extension of coastal State authority through the continental shelf and EEZ indicates the importance of exclusive control over natural resources, this is not in itself sufficient to prevent overfishing. The experience of domestic fisheries management regimes shows the need for exclusive rights to be taken a stage further, and to be made operational at the level of individuals. Exclusive State rights over living resources are a necessary but insufficient condition for better resource management. For this reason, consideration should be given to the more radical possibility of individual fishing rights being directly created and enforced through RFMOs.

4. *Incidents of Individual Property Rights in Areas Beyond National Jurisdiction*

So far it has been shown that a case exists for the creation of rights-based entitlements, such as an ITQ, for individuals directly under international law. Here some international mechanism, such as an RFMO, establishes the scope and form of the holding, allocates it to individuals and manages its operation in practice. This is done without first allocating sovereign rights to regulate the quota system to a domestic regime.[93] This presents some novel challenges to traditional perceptions of international law, as law between and for States. Indeed most international lawyers would discount the operation of right-based entitlements directly under international law, viewing the question of 'private' rights and obligation as the exclusive domain of domestic law. Notably the Fish Stocks Agreement does not prohibit such measures, indicating only a series of general principles that should govern conservation and management measures.[94] Arguably, where ITQs satisfy these general conditions, then their use is permitted by international law.

The traditional position reflects a positivist, State-centric, view of law rather than one that recognizes the possibility of rights derived from natural law. In this legal tradition Bentham,[95] Hobbes,[96] Hume,[97] and Rousseau[98] have all claimed that property is the result of law and civil society; a view that finds some resonance in contemporary international legal doctrine in the writings of Oppenheim and Brownlie.[99] However, this view has not always been univer-

---

[93] However, it is conceded that some domestic machinery will be necessary at an operational level. Such machinery is dedicated to protecting the measures adopted by the RFMO.

[94] Article 5.

[95] "[T]here is no such thing as natural property [...] it is entirely the work of law [...]. Property and law are born together, and die together. Before laws were made there was no property; take away laws, and property ceases" (Bentham, note 74 at 111–113).

[96] T. Hobbes *Leviathan* J.C.A. Gaskin (ed.) (OUP, New York: 1996) 164.

[97] "Property is nothing but those goods, whose constant possession is established by the laws of society; that is, by the laws of justice [...] Tis very preposterous, therefore, to imagine, that we can have any idea of property, without fully comprehending the nature of justice, and shewing its origin in the artifice and contrivance of man" (Hume, note 74, part 2, § 2 at 491).

[98] J.-J. Rousseau "Discourse on the Origin and Foundation of Inequality Among Men" reprinted in J.-J. Rousseau *The Social Contract and Discourse on the Origin of Inequality* L.G. Crocker (ed.) (Washington Square Press, New York: 1967) 211.

[99] Both assert that only States may claim title to territory, thereby excluding the establishing of property rights outside of the State system. Lauterpacht, H. *Oppenheim's International Law* 6th ed. (Longmans, London: 1947) 507; Brownlie, note 68 at 168. According to Singer, property imposes rights on the owner and responsibilities on non-owners, which are enforced by the government. Therefore private property cannot exist without a government to enforce the system (J.W. Singer "Sovereignty and Property" (1991) *Northwestern University Law Review* 1–56 at 47).

sally accepted, at least historically.[100] Under the natural law tradition, property rights are derived from nature, not the State, and so do not depend on States for their viability, and were often viewed as a bulwark against the arbitrary exercise of power by the State. In the natural law tradition, property rights arise under a different set of circumstances and for differing reasons.[101] Indeed, if individual property rights-based entitlements are established by RFMOs then they might be more directly shaped by the values and interests of the international community, rather than the States through which they are ordinarily facilitated. If this is the case, then the form and allocation of a property right emerging under international law may differ from property rights within domestic legal orders.

The spread of territorial sovereignty is so extensive that there has been little scope for the operation of property rights out with States' domestic legal systems. However, such rights have emerged for consideration as a matter of positive international law in a number of ABNJ, including *terra nullius*, Antarctica, Outer Space and the Deep Seabed.

4.1. *Terra Nullius*

In 1927, the United States pursued a claim for the recognition of the ownership of two fox farms on Jan Mayen on behalf of the American-based Polarfront Company against Norway for rights that had been claimed before Norway obtained sovereignty over the territory.[102] The United States Department of State had expressed the view that this right could only be secured to the owner under the authority of the Government exercising sovereignty with relation to the island.[103] However, it was also unwilling to deny that Polarfront lacked proprietary rights in the absence of a territorial sovereign. In a similar dispute, the Norwegian Supreme Court held that the Government was obliged to uphold

---

[100] See J. Locke *Two Treatises of Government* (1690) P. Laslett (ed.) (Cambridge University Press, Cambridge: 1960) 342–343 and 378; E. de Vattel *The Law of Nations* (1797) Kapossy (ed.) (Liberty Fund, Indianapolis: 2008) 170; H. Grotius *De Jure Belli ac Pacis Libri Tres* (1625) trans. F.W. Kelsey (Oxford University Press, Oxford: 1925) 295; S. Puffendorf *De Jure Naturae et Gentium Libri Octo* (1688) trans. Oldfather (Clarendon Press, Oxford: 1934) 555–556; C. Wolff, *Jus Gentium Methodo Scientifica Pertractatum* trans. Drake (Clarendon Press, Oxford: 1934) 50–51; J. Westlake *Chapters on the Principles of International Law* (Cambridge University Press, Cambridge: 1894) 11.

[101] See L.B. Ederington "Property as a Natural Institution. The Separation of Property from Sovereignty in International Law" (1997) 13 *American University International Law Review* 263–332 at 265–266.

[102] G.H. Hackworth 1 *Digest of International Law* (U.S. Government Printing Office, Washington, D.C.: 1927) 475–476.

[103] Letter from the Department of State to Mr. Ekerold, Feb. 16, 1927. Quoted in Hackworth, *ibid.*

a proprietary claim arising in the territory of Jan Mayen that pre-dated Norwegian sovereignty over the islands.[104] Although this suggests that the court accepted that private property rights could exist independent of a domestic legal system, this was not explicit in the court's judgment. Around the turn of the 20th century, commercially exploitable deposits of coal were discovered on the Spitsbergen archipelago, and companies from a number of countries, including the United States, Russia, Germany, Norway, and the United Kingdom, were encouraged to stake claims and carry out mining activities.[105] In order to resolve the conflicting private claims in territory regarded as *terra nullius*, the interested nations adopted the Treaty concerning the Archipelago of Spitsbergen.[106] This recognized Norwegian sovereignty, subject to the recognition of "the acquired rights of nationals of the High Contracting parties", and their expropriation only with "proper compensation".[107] The negotiating parties made it clear that any solution that recognized property rights without first establishing a sovereign authority was unworkable.[108] In order to mediate any conflicting property claims, a tribunal was founded, and its decisions ultimately led to Norway recognizing a number of pre-existing ownership claims.[109]

In each of these cases the emphasis was on securing recognition of pre-existing proprietary claims in *terra nullius* by the subsequent sovereign agent, suggesting that such rights were dependent on Norway's domestic legal order for their effectiveness. This approach is echoed in the opinion of a number of leading authorities, such as Lauterpacht and Brownlie, who are also skeptical as to the existence of property claims without the sanction of States.[110] Of course, this leaves aside the possibility that States may exercise diplomatic protection over their nationals whose rights appear to have been infringed by another State. Such an approach appears to be advanced by Goldie, who argues that the prior rights of the private mining companies were mere personal

---

[104] *Jacobsen v. Norwegian Government* [1933] Norske Retstidende 511 reproduced in 7 ILR 109.

[105] See generally, L.F.E. Goldie "A General International Law Doctrine for Seabed Regimes" (1973) 7 *International Lawyer* 796–824 at 807–811.

[106] Treaty concerning the Archipelago of Spitsbergen, done in Paris 9 February 1920, in force 14 August 1925 (2 LNTS 7).

[107] Articles 6 and 7.

[108] F.K. Nielsen "The Solution of the Spitsbergen Question" (1920) 14 *American Journal of International Law* 232–235 at 233. Also R. Lansing "A Unique International Problem" (1917) 11 *American Journal of International Law* 763–771 at 770–771.

[109] These are noted in M.F. Lindley *The Acquisition and Government of Backward Territory in International Law* (Longmans, Green and Co., London: 1926) 320.

[110] Lauterpacht, note 99; Brownlie, note 68. Cf. P. Guggenheim *Traité de Droit International Public* (Georg, Geneva: 1954) 456–457.

usufructory rights.[111] As such they could be vested through mutual recognition and States' personal jurisdiction over the miners. However, whilst Goldie's approach avoids the complications arising from the accrual of real rights in *terra nullius*, it does not accurately reflect the nature of the mining claims. Also, it adopts the idea of 'mutual recognition' as a means for securing the elements of the claim that are qualitatively real—that is to say valid against the world—and so tries to invest the usufructory rights with stronger proprietary qualities through the backdoor.

In 1854, two United States citizens established guano mining facilities on the barren, unoccupied Los Monjes Islands which are located approximately 40 kilometers off the Guajira Peninsula coast of Venezuela. In 1855, Venezuela asserted jurisdiction over the islands and the miners, seized the miner's property and ordered them to leave the islands. As with Jan Mayen and Spitsbergen, property rights already established on the islands were given subsequent recognition upon the assumption of sovereignty by Venezuela. An arbitral commission established to deal with the expropriation of United States citizens' property on the islands held that Venezuela was bound to compensate the individuals for the seizure of their property and expulsion from the islands.[112] As the United States-Venezuela Claims Commission stated, "the claimants have an equity to be reimbursed for their outlay in taking possession of what was apparently derelict and abandoned property".[113] The Commission relied upon the labor as the basis of their right, and did not regard the existence of a sovereign as crucial to the emergence of their property rights.[114] A similar dispute arose between the United States and Venezuela in 1854 in respect of Aves Island when the latter asserted sovereignty over the island. United States citizens had been mining guano deposits and were evicted by Venezuelan military forces. Prior to the dispute, the island had not been subject to any recognized claim of sovereignty. The United States adopted the position that the island was derelict. Notably, despite the precise status of the islands being unclear, the two States reached an agreement requiring Venezuela to pay $ 130,000 dollars to

[111] L.F.E. Goldie "Title and Use (Usufruct)—An Ancient Distinction Oft Forgot" (1985) 79 *American Journal of International Law* 689–714.

[112] *John E. Gowen and Franklin Copeland v. Venezuela* [1890] in J.B. Moore *History and Digest of the International Arbitrations to Which the United States has been a Party* (1898) 3354–3359. Although hinting that the islands were not subject to any conclusive claim of sovereignty, the Commission put aside the question of the validity of Venezuela's claim of sovereignty as being too serious and far reaching in its consequences. Moreover, it was subject to arbitration pending between Venezuela and Colombia.

[113] *Ibid.*, 3359.

[114] J.B. Moore *A Digest of International Law* vol. 1 (Government printing, Washington: 1906) 576.

the victims.[115] This seems to support the idea that property rights (i.e. claims for expropriation) may exist despite uncertainty as to the sovereignty of the territory. Indeed, this success encouraged the United States to pass the Guano Islands Act in 1865.[116] This extended protection to United States citizens who discovered guano deposits on other islands that were "not within the lawful jurisdiction of any other government and not occupied by the citizens of any other government, and [who] shall take peaceful possession thereof".[117] The Act also extended United States criminal law to the islands as if such crime were committed on the high seas. In 1890, a United States citizen, Henry Jones, was prosecuted for a murder that occurred on one such guano island, Navassa.[118] In its ruling, the Supreme Court noted that

> '[b]y the law of nations, when citizens or subjects of one nation, in its name and by its authority or with its assent, take and hold actual, continuous and useful possession (although only for the purpose of carrying on a particular business, such as catching and curing fish, or working mines) of territory unoccupied by any other government or its citizens, the nation to which they belong may exercise such jurisdiction and for such period as it sees fit over territory so acquired'.[119]

Given the passing of the Guano Act, it is doubtful whether these later claims can truly be regarded as supporting property rights in *terra nullius*.

There is other evidence that property rights could exist beyond the confines of the positive law of a State in the territories of 'uncivilized nations'.[120] However, this view became marginalized during the 18th century, particularly under the influence of Vattel.[121] Despite considering such territories as *terra nullius*, States tended to recognize property claims arising before the sovereignty of the 'civilized' State arose. Thus, Lindley notes that property

[115] *Ibid.*, 571. It should be noted that the United States agreed to refrain from future claims to the island, and so the underlying settlement is more complex that a simple recognition of property rights in a vacuum.

[116] An Act to Authorize Protection to be Given to Citizens of the United States who may Discover Deposits of Guano (1856) 11 Stat. 119; 48 USC §§ 1411–1419.

[117] *Ibid.*, § 1411.

[118] *Jones* v. *United* States [1890] 137 US Supreme Court 202.

[119] *Ibid.*

[120] This possibility was recognised by de Vitoria. See F. de Vitoria *De Indis et de Iure Belli Relectiones* (1557) trans. E. Nys (Carnegie Institute, Washington: 1917) 128. For a commentary on this and the subsequent claims advanced on behalf of Spanish title to territory see J.S. Davidson "The Rights of Indigenous Peoples in Early International Law" (1994) 5 *Canterbury Law Review* 391–423.

[121] E. de Vattel *Le Droit des Gens* (1758) trans. Fenwick (Clarendon Press, Oxford: 1916) 37–38. Jennings notes that territory was considered as inhabited by communities that were not organised as a State, and that such inhabitation was not an obstacle to the acquisition of that territory. See R.Y. Jennings *The Acquisition of Territory in International Law* (Manchester University Press, Manchester: 1963) 20.

rights acquired in such territories remained unimpaired through the accretion of sovereignty by the colonial State.[122] In the *Burt case*, decided by the British American Claims Tribunal, it was held that Britain had to respect the property title of an American citizen acquired from a native chief prior to British annexation of the Fiji Islands in 1874.[123] The United States was also quick to demand recognition of American citizens' property rights in the Gilbert, Solomon and Marshall groups of islands, despite acknowledging their *terra nullius* status.[124] Such claims were subsequently recognized by Great Britain and Germany.[125] Ultimately, this practice was entrenched in Article 35 of the Final Act of the 1885 Conference of Berlin, which provided for the protection of 'existing rights (*droits acquis*)'.[126]

Although there may well have been a time when property rights in *terra nullius* could exist, the value of this approach seems to be limited today, except perhaps in the exceptional circumstances when new lands emerge from volcanic activities in ocean spaces beyond national jurisdiction. The *Western Sahara case* and the *Case Concerning the Territorial Dispute (Libya v. Chad)* have confirmed that territory inhabited by people cannot be *terra nullius*.[127]

More recently, Australia has addressed the matter of ownership claims pre-dating the annexation of Australian territory and the extension of the common law thereto.[128] In the case of *Milirrpum* v. *Nabalco Pty Ltd*, the Supreme Court of the Northern Territory rejected the plaintiff's claim that they possessed some form of native title predating the settlement of the lands by the Crown.[129] However, the decision turned on the fact that there was no doctrine of communal native title in the common law, and so no basis for recognizing the plaintiff's claims.[130] In *Mabo* v. *Queensland (No. 2)*, the High Court of Australia recognized certain pre-existing claims to land.[131] The Court rejected the argument that the acquisition of sovereignty, through whatever

[122] Lindley, note 109 at 316. See also, Ederington, note 101 at 292.

[123] George Rodney Burt (U.S.) v. Great Britain in F.K. Nielsen *Report on American and British Claims Arbitration under Agreement of August 8, 1910* (GPO, Washington: 1926) 588 at 598.

[124] Cable from United States Secretary of State Bayard to Mr. Pendleton (Feb. 27, 1886), reproduced in Moore, note 114 at 422.

[125] *Ibid.*, 424–425.

[126] Final Act of the Conference of Berlin of 26 February 1885 (165 Consolidated Treaty Series 485).

[127] *Western Sahara case* [1975] ICJ Reports 12 at 39 paras 79–80. *Case Concerning the Territorial Dispute* (Libya v. Chad) [1994] ICJ Reports 6 at 54–55.

[128] See R. Van Krieken "From *Milirrpum* to *Mabo*: The High Court, *Terra nullius* and Moral Entrepreneurship" (2000) 23 *University of New South Wales Law Journal* 63–77.

[129] *Milirrpum* v. *Nabalco Pty Ltd* [1971] 17 FLR 141.

[130] *Ibid.*, 262.

[131] *Mabo* v. *Queensland (No. 2)* [1992] 175 CLR 1.

means, automatically resulted in the extinction of native title.[132] Underpinning this was a finding that the territory was subject to some form of native legal system, even if it was incomparable to the common law. In justifying this position, Brennan observed that if international law had rejected the idea that inhabited land could form *terra nullius*, then the common law could not retain an antiquated view of other legal cultures, ignoring peoples 'low in the scale of social organization'.[133] As such *Mabo* sidestepped the possibility of property rights in a legal vacuum, a matter which remains problematic.

These examples demonstrate the difficulty of asserting proprietary claims in the absence of some *lex situs* or supporting legal system. Ederington argues that these examples amount to recognition of a natural rights-vision of property.[134] This may well be the case, but this is not the same as admitting a legally valid claim of ownership. In each case, the point of the litigation was to secure the apparently inchoate proprietary claims under the operative domestic legal regime. The examples do show how States have sought to protect rights acquired in accordance with fundamental moral precepts. There seems to be recognition of claims based upon first appropriation, and claims based upon natural rights or propriety, such as rewarding the acts of the individual in putting land and resources to productive use. However, one must be careful about over-relying on such moral justifications because their particular influence on the legal process of claim and recognition is difficult to discern. Such explanations are often an *ex post facto* rationalization of events that are just as likely to have been influenced by other factors such as comity, cooperation, and security. Less controvertible is the fact that where property rights are claimed in a legal vacuum, States and tribunals have sought to subsume claims to title, or property rights, within positive legal structures so as to provide certainty and security of the rights. At this point the property rights lose any external source of authority other than domestic law, and, at best, one can argue that moral justifications have played a role in the initial allocation and recognition of a claim to property in *terra nullius*.

4.2. *Antarctica*

Antarctica is subject to the provisions of the 1959 Antarctic Treaty,[135] which establishes its marine, land and ice-covered areas as a scientific reserve, and dedicates it to peaceful purposes. Antarctica is subject to a moratorium on

---

[132] *Ibid.* Brennan J., paragraph 53.

[133] *Ibid.*, paras 41–43.

[134] Ederington, note 101 at 280–289.

[135] Antarctic Treaty of 1 December 1959 (402 UNTS 71).

sovereign claims, placing it beyond the exclusive spatial sovereignty of a single State.[136] The regime established was intended to declare the status of Antarctica generally, and regardless of whether one considers treaties binding on non-parties, it is generally agreed that the rules embodied in the treaty are binding on all States.[137] In order that activities in Antarctica can take place in an ordered manner, the Treaty provides that activities are to be controlled according to the nationality principle.[138] Where questions relating to the exercise of jurisdiction arise, they are to be resolved at meetings of the consultative parties 'with a view to reaching a mutually acceptable solution'.[139] However, no decisions or agreements have tackled this issue directly, and the juridical status of Antarctica remains complex and unresolved.[140] We can distinguish between two forms of property in Antarctica. There is the 'allocated' property that States and individuals bring into Antarctica, such as research stations and equipment, and there is the 'unallocated' property that forms part of Antarctica *per se*, namely its natural resources.

Although Article VIII of the Treaty provides for the application of jurisdiction under the nationality principle to Antarctica, does such jurisdiction provide a firm basis for the regulation of property rights? Theoretically, if property rights are perceived merely as rights between persons in respect of a thing, then it is possible to conceive of how States could exercise control of the property of their nationals according to the nationality principle by virtue of its power to govern those individuals. However, this ignores the *in rem* function of property rights. The nationality principle can guarantee rights as against other nationals, but not against nationals of third States. It also runs counter to the general rule that property rights are determined by the *lex situs*.[141] Moreover, jurisdiction based upon nationality is usually subordinate to territorial jurisdiction.[142] The rationale for this is that certainty and security are paramount concerns in

---

[136] *Ibid.*, Article IV.

[137] See Brownlie, note 68 at 262.

[138] Article VIII(1).

[139] Article VIII(2).

[140] See for example C.J. Joyner and E.R. Theis "The United States and Antarctica: Rethinking the Interplay of Law and Interests" (1987) *Cornell International Law Journal* 65–102 at 75; G.D. Triggs, "The Antarctic Treaty System: some jurisdictional problems" in G.D. Triggs (ed.) *The Antarctic Treaty Regime. Law Environment and Resources* (Cambridge University Press, Cambridge: 1987) 88.

[141] Note 66 and accompanying text.

[142] In general States respect territorial limitations over legislative and enforcement jurisdiction, and are unwilling to give effect to extra-territorial measures by other States. Exceptions to this tend to arise only in respect of serious crimes, or where the vital interest of the State are concerned. Thus, the United Kingdom only seeks to try nationals over very serious offences committed abroad, such as murder or treason. See the Offences Against the Person Act 1861, ss. 9, 57.

respect of property and this is best guaranteed by reference to the *lex situs*. The practical value of this approach is most apparent when considering how to deal with property transactions between nationals of different States in Antarctica. However, the difficulty is that other than the general provisions of the 1959 Treaty and subsequent agreements, there is very little by way of Antarctic property law that could form the basis of a *lex situs* in this respect.

There are no conflicts of law provisions in respect of Antarctica, and even if there were, they would have difficulty in determining applicable rules of property given the centrality of the *lex situs* rule. However, despite these objections to the application of the nationality principle, some transactions involving allocated property rights are not too controversial and may be overcome in two ways. Firstly, States may waive overlapping jurisdictional competence. There appears to be some evidence of this happening, although such an *ad hoc* approach does not provide a secure basis for the determination and application of property rules.[143] As Antarctic activities become more commonplace, a more systematic set of property-type rules will become necessary. Secondly, one may treat the situation as analogous to ships on the high seas. According to this approach the law of the flag (nationality principle) will apply, unless two or more differently flagged vessels are involved, in which case the jurisdiction properly seized of the matter may apply its own law.[144] This may be consistent with the spirit of comity and cooperation that suffuses the Antarctic regime. However, given the *ad hoc* nature of the approach and the acute possibility of conflict between domestic rules on jurisdiction and substantive law, the absence of unifying general principles may undermine the certainty and security needed for effective property rules. More importantly, such approaches will not work for unallocated property rights in Antarctic natural resources.

Technical studies have revealed that exploitation of the mineral resources of Antarctica is unlikely to take place in the near future.[145] However, it was believed that the prospective creation of a regime for mineral exploration and exploitation would pre-empt future conflicts and encourage broader participation within the Antarctic Treaty System (ATS).[146] The development of a

[143] F. Orrego Vicuña *Antarctic mineral exploitation. The emerging legal framework* (Cambridge University Press, Cambridge: 1988) 103.

[144] In common law jurisdictions torts committed on the high seas outside a ship, i.e. a collision, are governed by the *lex fori*. See *The Zollverein* Reports of cases decided in the High Court of Admiralty of England, and on appeal to the Privy Council (M.C. Merttins Swabey (ed.)) 96; *The Esso Malaysia* [1978] QB 198; *The Tubantia* [Hague Court Reports (New York, 1932), p. 78. In the United States, this is covered by the Restatement of Conflict of Laws (1934) § 410(b).

[145] G. Pontecorvo "The economics of the resources of Antarctica" in J.I. Charney (ed.) *The New Nationalism and Use of Common Spaces* (ASIL, Allanheld Osmun: 1982) 155 at 158.

[146] See A. Watts "Antarctic Mineral Resources: Negotiations for a Mineral Resources Regime" in Triggs, note 140, 164 at 166.

mineral regime occurred through a series of Special Consultative Meetings, which operated in a manner akin to the consensus-based negotiating system utilized at the Third United Nations Conference on the Law of the Sea (UNCLOS III).[147] This allowed collective interests to develop via consensus to produce hard legal outcomes. For the most part, the negotiations took place behind a weak sort of Rawlsian veil of ignorance. Without firm knowledge of existence of minerals, or their location, the negotiations tended to be speculative and the principles of the eventual regime were formulated on the basis of general considerations. The participation of non-claimant States as Consultative Parties increased to the point where they outnumbered the claimant States, thereby reducing the influence of territorial-based arrangements. Crucially, negotiations took place against a growing world-wide concern for the environment.[148] This was complemented by growing antipathy towards any mineral regime, which was viewed by developing States as a 'rich States' club.[149] The result was the inclusion of a wider range of concerns into the mineral regime than would have otherwise occurred if a regime was developed by a closed group of States. Although the 1988 Convention on the Regulation of Antarctic Mineral Resources (CRAMRA) has not entered into force, and is unlikely to enter into force, principally because international opinion favored a complete ban on mineral exploitation, it merits consideration because it is illustrative of how proprietary concerns are dealt with in international mechanisms for resource regulation.[150]

Although prospecting does not generate any right to mineral resources, intellectual property rights may arise over the resultant scientific data. As a general rule, the results of scientific research are, to the greatest extent feasible and practicable, to be made freely available within the ATS.[151] However, this would wholly undermine the commercial rationale for prospecting, and so Article 16 of the CRAMRA provides that data from prospecting may be

---

147 The key features of the negotiating process were: flexibility, allowing the use of *ad hoc* meetings, groups better suited to the exigencies of the situation, informality and privacy, which allowed candid interchange of views, and the use of reports to generate dialogue and consensus. See Orrego Vicuña note 143 at 187–189. For a commentary on UNCLOS III negotiating process see B. Buzan "Negotiating by Consensus: developments in technique at the United Nations Conference on the Law of the Sea" (1981) 75 *American Journal of International Law* 324–348.

148 A.D. Watts *International Law and the Antarctic Treaty System* (Grotius, Cambridge: 1992) 223.

149 *Ibid.*, 224.

150 Convention on the Regulation of Antarctic Mineral Resource Activities, Wellington, 2 June 1988, not into force (1988) 27 ILM 868. It has been superseded by the Protocol on Environment Protection to the Antarctic Treaty of 4 October 1991 ((1991) 30 ILM 1455). However, this contains no provisions on mineral rights.

151 Antarctic Treaty, Article III(1)(c).

retained by the Operator in accordance with Article 37, which allows the data to be exclusively retained whilst it has a commercial value. The CRAMRA is silent on the extent of the Operator's rights over such data, and there is nothing to prevent its transfer on the open market if the CRAMRA became operative. As no prior permission for prospecting is necessary, it is subject to the primary control of the Sponsoring State, rather than the institutional mechanisms of the CRAMRA. Accordingly, proprietary data-rights are allocated on the basis of discovery, and are regulated by the domestic law of the Sponsoring State.

The CRAMRA purports to vest authority to regulate mineral activities in two international bodies: the Commission and the Regulatory Committee. Thus, competence to determine the allocation of any mineral rights would be taken out of the hands of individual States. Exploration and development was intended to operate via a permit system.[152] This would operate within a Management Scheme, which sets out the specific terms and conditions for the exploration for and development of mineral deposits. As the Regulatory Committee shall have recourse to the Sponsoring State and any relevant Claimant States in determining the Management Scheme, this would, as Watts notes conceal "what is likely in reality to be in most cases a mini-negotiation" between the Sponsoring State and the Claimant States.[153] This would also ensure a strong degree of control over exploration and development applications by Claimant States, who would possess an effective veto over the terms of the Management Scheme.[154] Notably, permits under the CRAMRA regime are subject to a number of conditions, requiring all stages of resource activity to be consistent with the Antarctic Treaty, to give overriding priority to the protection of the environment, to protect scientific research, to use the area exclusively for peaceful purposes, to promote the fair and effective participation of all parties, and to take into account the interests of the international community as a whole.[155]

The CRAMRA recognizes that for any resource-rights to be effective they must be secure and exclusive. According to Article 3, mineral activities are prohibited outside the convention regime. Thus the right to determine title is annexed to the regime.[156] Arguably, the model for this approach was the regime of contracts or concessions for the offshore development of oil. In such

[152] Article 45.

[153] Watts, note 148 at 244.

[154] Article 48 requires a two-thirds majority of the Committee.

[155] Recommendation XI-1 (1981) sets out the essential principles for this regime.

[156] This raises important questions about the *pacta tertiis* rule, in that treaty obligations are generally only binding upon parties to the treaty. This is considered in section 5 infra.

cases ownership of the resource *in situ* rests with the State until the point of recovery at which time it transfers to the developer. Thus the exploitation can take place without necessarily reaching any conclusion about who has title to the resources *in situ*.

The CRAMRA demonstrates that the inclusion of certain values, particularly the protection of the environment, may be more crucial to the success of resource systems than sophisticated institutional provisions. Indeed, the perception that a minerals regime was incompatible with the preservation of the Antarctic environment contributed to the failure of the CRAMRA. It also demonstrates that the need for certainty in the underlying regime is crucial. Rich notes that from a commercial perspective, when profit margins are small there will be a commensurate increase in the need for certainty of title and the associated rights to explore and exploit.[157] This works against any new international institutions as the basis for regulation, and produces a bias towards proven mechanisms based upon exclusive territorial sovereignty.[158]

The unique context of the Antarctic minerals regime makes it difficult to draw too many lessons for the application of property rights in ABNJ. Clearly, the influence of underlying territorial claims remains influential. The CRAMRA, at least superficially, attempts to establish a regulatory system dealing with general rights and duties, and not questions of ownership. This suggests that a system of private ownership can only emerge once questions about the underlying status of a regime have been resolved. However, some of the concepts of control set forth in the CRAMRA have distinctly proprietary attributes. Thus, permits may be held by Operators (legal persons established in States parties), who obtain exclusive control over resources, or at least a *profit a prendre*, which transforms into ownership upon capture. Despite the CRAMRA permit system purporting to allocate resources fairly, there is no guarantee of an even distribution of wealth. As mineral-activity permits are allocated upon application, this would result in the allocation of permits on a first-come, first-serve basis. It would also produce a bias towards States with the actual capacity to exploit resources.

The 1980 Convention on the Conservation of Antarctic Marine Living Resources (CCAMLR) is the principal instrument for the conservation and utilization of marine living resources in Antarctica.[159] Central to the CCAMLR

---

[157] R. Rich "A Minerals Regime for Antarctica" (1982) 31 *International and Comparative Law Quarterly* 709–725 at 711.

[158] Rich later points out that mineral resource exploitation is not internationalised anywhere else in the world and so falls under territorial sovereignty. *Ibid.*, 719.

[159] Convention on the Conservation of Antarctic Marine Living Resources of 20 May 1980 (13 UNTS 47).

is the ecosystem approach to resource conservation and management.[160] This, along with other management principles, is developed in Article II. Beyond these, the CCAMLR contains no operational conservation or management provisions, instead relying for such measures on initiatives taken by the Commission for the Conservation of Antarctic Marine Living Resources (Commission).[161] The Commission has opted for a traditional regulatory approach to resource management, relying upon the setting of TACs and adopting various input controls.[162] Thereafter the actual control of fishing is largely left to flag States.[163]

Given that the problems facing Antarctic fisheries are the same as other fisheries, why have property rights-based systems not been developed within CCAMLR?[164] Arguably, the ecosystem approach has impeded the development of certain modes of regulation. It is not yet fully developed, and has been undermined by the uncertain scientific basis for policy decisions and the inherent politicization of the scientific process within CCAMLR.[165] In recent years, a number of important initiatives have been taken within CCAMLR that advance an ecosystem approach to fisheries, including the development of precautionary limits to catches, management regimes that take into account the impact of fishing on dependent species and an ecosystem monitoring program.[166] As Scheiber notes, the complexity of the ecosystem approach inevitably creates its own difficulties as it tries to reconcile competing social values as well as varied scientific imperatives.[167] CCAMLR's particular, and laudable, attachment to this approach clearly requires more sophisticated management and regulatory controls. In the context of property rights-based measures, an ecosystem approach will require that certain checks and balances are

[160] M. Howard "The Convention on the Conservation of Antarctic Marine Living Resources: A Five-Year Review" (1989) 38 *International and Comparative Law Quarterly* 104–150.

[161] Articles VII–XIII.

[162] Current regulations available at the website of the Commission (available at ⟨http://www.ccamlr.org⟩).

[163] See Article XXI of the CCAMLR.

[164] Gulland notes that the regulatory issues in the Southern Ocean (the Convention area) arise from the same root causes as in fisheries elsewhere, namely the unmanaged exploitation of a common property, open-access resource. J.A. Gulland "The Antarctic Treaty system as a resource management mechanism" in Triggs, note 140 at 116.

[165] C. Redgwell "Protection of Ecosystems under International Law: Lessons from Antarctica" in A. Boyle and D. Freestone (eds) *International Law and Sustainable Development* (Oxford University Press, Oxford: 1999) 205–224 at 216 and 223.

[166] See A. Fabra and V. Gascón "The Convention on the Conservation of Antarctic Marine Living Resources (CCAMLR) and the Ecosystem Approach" (2008) 23 *International Journal of Marine and Coastal Law* 567–598 at 575–581.

[167] H.N. Scheiber "From Science to Law to Politics: An Historical View of the Ecosystem Idea and its Effect on Resource Management" (1997) 24 *Ecology Law Quarterly* 631–651 at 651.

built into fishing entitlements to ensure that holders do not exercise their entitlements in a manner that detrimentally impacts upon other components of the ecosystem. The effectiveness of such complex management systems may be undermined by a lack of institutional sophistication and security in the Commission. Although the Commission has a central role in developing conservation and management measures, the CCAMLR adopts a largely decentralized regulatory structure, whereby primary responsibility for implementing and enforcing such measures remains with the Contracting Parties.[168] This may obstruct the adoption of property rights-based measures because such measures generally require a high degree of centralized authority, at least to determine, allocate and enforce the property rights. This facilitates a uniform and consistent approach to the substantive rights. In practice, the Commission faces considerable problems with non-parties' participation, flags of convenience, implementation and enforcement. Although estimates of IUU fishing are declining, IUU fishing remains problematic in the region.[169] These issues have taken priority in CCAMLR bodies. However, the only means of addressing them is through flag State control. The result is that various national laws and policies are applied to the regulation of vessels and fishing activities. This reinforces a decentralization of authority, which militates against adoption of property rights-based measures.

A number of lessons are to be taken from the Antarctic experience. Firstly, cooperative regimes in international areas require the underlying claims to sovereignty to be addressed, if not resolved; otherwise these will destabilize the future success of the regime. Secondly, States are generally reluctant to provide an institution with the exclusive and extensive competence necessary to regulate property rights. Thirdly, any commitment to an ecosystem approach requires much more complex management regimes. These need to be carefully considered before property rights-based systems can be implemented. Finally, in ABNJ, the predominance of the nationality principle or flag State jurisdiction undermines the potential for property rights because it does not allow the rights to be secured against the world. They may only be secured against other nationals of the same State as the rights holders.

---

[168] For example, under Article XXI, compliance and sanctions for violations are the responsibility of Contracting Parties, rather than any institutional body. Similarly, monitoring mechanisms (Article XXIV) and dispute settlement procedures (Article XXV) are in the hands of Contracting Parties.

[169] Commission for the Conservation of Antarctic Marine Living Resources *Report of the Twenty-Seventh Meeting of the* Commission (Hobart Australia 27th October – 7 November 2008).

4.3. *Outer Space*

Outer space and its resources are principally regulated by the 1967 Outer Space Treaty and the 1979 Moon Treaty.[170] Article 2 of the Outer Space Treaty provides in no uncertain terms that:

> Outer space including the Moon and other celestial bodies, is not subject to national appropriation by claim of sovereignty, by means of use or occupation, or by any other means.

This is reiterated and developed in the Moon Treaty, which specifically precludes the Moon from becoming the "property of any State, international intergovernmental or non-governmental organization, national organization or non-governmental entity or of any natural person."[171] The ban on proprietary claims does not prevent resources from being exploited and a system of equitable resource sharing is set forth.[172] However, in the absence of exclusive authority, control may only develop through international agreement between States. Crucially, the lack of realistic and immediate prospects for the commercial exploitation of space means that States have had no reason to claim exclusive control over its resources, so, at a political level it has been much easier to imbue the regime with idealistic, cooperative principles. In general, most forms of private property in extra-terrestrial resources are incompatible with the current legal regime for outer space. This reflects the impracticability of carving up space into 'national' allocations, and the important role of inclusive, 'common denominator' principles in cooperative agreements. This may be contrasted with principles drawn from pure self-interest that are more common in other resource regimes.

By way of qualification it must be noted that the exclusion of private ownership rights over outer space and celestial objects is not absolute. There is an exception in the Moon Treaty that permits the collection of samples of the moon to be removed.[173] The legal status of such samples is not mentioned, although they remain at the disposal of the collecting State. Presumably they are taken out of the *res communis*, reduced to the ownership of the State that has collected them and henceforth subject to its domestic law of property. Also, States retain ownership rights over objects launched into

---

[170] The Treaty on Principles Governing the Activities of States in the Exploration and Use of Outer Space Including the Moon and Other Celestial Bodies (Outer Space Treaty) of 27 January 1967 (610 UNTS 205); Agreement Governing the Activities of States on the Moon and Other Celestial Bodies (Moon Treaty) of 18 December 1979 ((1979) 18 ILM 1434) Article 11(3).

[171] Article 11(3).

[172] Article 11(7).

[173] Article 6.

space.[174] The mere presence of any object in space or its return to Earth outside the territorial jurisdiction of the launching State does not affect the ownership of the object.[175] The obvious analogy here is with the control that States retain over ships flying their flag on the high seas.

4.4. *The Deep Seabed*

Although the existence of mineral resources on the deep seabed has been documented for over a century, their exploitation remains a distant prospect. Historically, the deep seabed formed part of the high seas, which put developed States with the technology to exploit its resources in a favorable position. The potential inequity of this position prompted developing States to push for the establishment of an international regime that would have powers to regulate exploitation, prevent the inevitable 'land grab' and protect developing States from any adverse effects on their terrestrial mining operations. Despite disagreements over the precise nature of the regime for the deep seabed, States were able to agree to the adoption of a series of UN General Assembly Resolutions that put in place a broad framework of principles for the deep seabed.[176] The key principles of these resolutions define the deep seabed and its resources as the common heritage of mankind, prohibit sovereign claims, dedicate it to peaceful use, and subject the activities in the area to a dedicated international regime.[177]

This regime is found in Part XI of the LOS Convention and the 1994 Implementation Agreement.[178] Article 136 of the LOS Convention defines the Area and its resources as the 'common heritage of mankind' (CHM). This principle has four key attributes. Firstly, there is a prohibition on acts of appropriation by States.[179] This extends to the Area and any part thereof. This does not prohibit mining except when done in a manner that brings a part of the Area under the exclusive control of a State, or where it is done in a

---

[174] Article 8 of the Outer Space Treaty provides that States parties "shall retain jurisdiction and control over such an object, and over any personnel thereof, while in outer space or on a celestial body".

[175] See Article 5 of the Agreement on the Rescue of Astronauts, the Return of Astronauts and the Return of Objects Launched into Outer Space 22 April 1968 ((1969) 63 AJIL 382).

[176] See United Nations General Assembly Resolution 2574 of 15 December 1969 ((1970) 9 ILM 419); Declaration of Principles Governing the Sea Bed and Ocean Floor, and the Subsoil Thereof, beyond the Limits of National Jurisdiction of 17 December 1970 ((1971) 10 ILM 220).

[177] See Declaration of Principles, note 176 at paras 1–5.

[178] Agreement relating to the Implementation of the Part XI of the United Nations Convention on the Law of the Sea of 10 December 1982 of 28 July 1994 ((1994) 33 ILM 1309).

[179] See Article 137(1).

manner that breaches other provisions of Part XI of the LOS Convention and the 1994 Implementation Agreement. Also, some extraction of resources must be permitted under Article 143 on marine scientific research (MSR), if this provision is to have any practical effect.

The principle of non-harmful use has two aspects: the reservation of the Area for peaceful uses, and the obligation to protect the marine environment. Article 141 requires that the "Area shall be open to use exclusively for peaceful purposes by all States".[180] The precise scope of the peaceful use requirement is not at all certain.[181] However, what is crucial is that this responsibility is devolved to individual States, thereby decentralizing some of the use rights in the Area. Article 145 requires measures to be taken to ensure the protection of the marine environment from the harmful effects of activities in the Area.[182] The text of Article 145 suggests that the International Seabed Authority (ISA) is primarily responsible for this, through the adoption of appropriate rules, standards regulations and procedures. However, this does not preclude States taking such action independently.

The third facet of the CHM concerns the equitable sharing of benefits. It requires activities in the Area to be carried out for the benefit of mankind as a whole. As a result of the United States holding out on accession to the LOS Convention, States were forced to compromise on a number of substantive provisions that embodied equity and benefit sharing. Through the 1994 Implementation Agreement this resulted in operative provisions that were more sensitive to commercial needs and the market-based ideology of developed States, such as the removal of provisions on mandatory technology transfer and production limits.[183] Indeed, production policy is to be in accordance with free market principles, and access is now on a first-come, first-serve basis, as opposed to being subject to rigorous qualification rules.[184] Clearly, this favors those States that possess the capacity

---

[180] Also Article 138, which requires the Area to be used in accordance with principles embodied in the UN Charter.

[181] For example, Vukas concludes that it has not been fully demilitarised (B. Vukas "Peaceful Uses of the Sea, Denuclearisation and Disarmament" in J.-M. Dupuy and D. Vignes (eds) *A Handbook on the New Law of the Sea* (Martinus Nijhoff, Dordrecht: 1991) 1233 at 1295–1296. Cf. Oude Elferink, who notes a potentially wider reservation for peaceful purposes under Article 141 (A.G. Oude Elferink "The Regime of the Area: Delineating the Scope of Application of the Common Heritage Principle and the Freedom of the High Seas" (2007) 22 *International Journal of Marine and Coastal Law* 143–176 at 156).

[182] Similarly, Article 146 requires that measures are taken to ensure the protection of human life.

[183] 1994 Implementation Agreement, Annex, section 5, para. 1(b) and section 6 respectively.

[184] Section 6, para. 7 removes the original requirements set out in Article 161.

to prospect, designate areas for development, and develop seabed mineral resources at an earlier stage. The effectiveness of the above provisions is closely tied to final aspect of the CHM—the existence of an international management regime.

The fourth facet of the CHM is the requirement for some form of international administration. This is necessary to achieve the other aspects of the CHM. In the case of the Area, this function is provided for by the ISA. Although the ISA has been relatively successful in managing the current pre-mining situation, engaging in the development of draft mining codes and contracts, as well as other training and development initiatives, the scope of its original authority was curtailed in the 1994 Implementation Agreement to accommodate the interests of developed States. For example, its decision-making procedures were redrawn to make the regime more acceptable to developed States.[185] The locus of decision-making power was shifted from the one-State, one-vote Assembly, to the Council, with its membership limited to 'interested States'.[186] At an operational level, the Enterprise, the mining arm of the ISA, is now subject to the same obligations as private contractors.[187] It is to conduct initial operations on a joint-venture basis, that accord with sound commercial principles.[188] As such, the ISA as a vehicle for development is much reduced.

Wolfrum points out that there is an absence of sovereign authority in the Austinian sense.[189] This observation is important as it alludes to the typical need for resource regimes to have teeth—the authority of States behind them. In the case of the Area, it seems that compliance with the law is not to be ensured through legal sanctions ordinarily understood, but rather through the pull exerted by the perceived legitimacy of substantive rules. It is notable that most States have rejected the status of the Area as *res nullius*, and either ignored or refuted private claims to its resources.[190] The effectiveness of the prohibition on sovereign claims suggests that State 'ownership' or exclusive sovereignty is no longer considered to be a pre-requisite to any exploitation

---

185 On the voting procedure see B. Oxman "Law of the Sea Forum: The 1994 Agreement on the Implementation of the Seabed Provisions of the Convention on the Law of the Sea. The 1994 Agreement and the Convention" (1994) 88 *American Journal of International Law* 687–696 at 689ff.

186 Section 3, paras 1 and 4.

187 Section 2, para. 4.

188 Section 2, para. 2.

189 R. Wolfrum "The Principle of the Common Heritage of Mankind" (1983) *Heidelberg Journal of International Law* 312–337 at 316–319.

190 See for example the claims made by Deepsea Ventures in the mid 1970s. J. Barkenbus *Deep Seabed Resources* (Free Press, New York: 1979) at 37ff.

regime.[191] However, it is clear that there needs to be some controlling agency, otherwise a free-for-all would result. As such the operation of the prohibition of sovereign appropriation is closely linked to the existence of a regime which facilitates access and use.

Some reference to the CHM principle remains in respect of the collection and distribution of payments made to the Authority by commercial operators and the Enterprise. The means of such sharing is not stipulated exactly, although it must be equitable.[192] There will be some preferential treatment of developing State land-based producers through the provision of economic assistance.[193] However, such payments will be determined by the ISA, and the distribution of such payment may fall foul of entrenched interests under the complicated voting system.

As long as an international agency has exclusive authority to regulate mining activities, the possibility of property rights originating directly under international law exists. At this point what becomes crucial is the nature and content of the principles and rules that govern the proprietary interests. This brief review indicates that the detailed mining rules fall far short of the ideals found in the CHM principle. The original regime was suffused with a strong proprietary element, whereby equitable access to resources, centralized management and benefit distribution would contribute to international order. It was also intended to mitigate a powerful liberal/first appropriation basis of entitlement, whereby only those States with the mining technology could 'labor' so as to capture the resources. As a result of the 1994 Implementation Agreement, only the prohibition on sovereign claims and the requirement of peaceful use of the seabed remain intact. This shows how the distributional values that emerge through international law are still susceptible to the self-interests of States. Although no exploitation of the Area has yet taken place, it is quite clear that many of the redistributionary and protectionist measures that were designed to inform the CHM regime have been modified to allow for a free-market approach to exploitation.[194]

---

[191] Thus Dolman stresses that the key consideration is access rather than ownership (A.J. Dolman "The Common Heritage of Mankind and Global Reform" in A.J. Dolman (ed) *Resources, Regimes, World Order* (Pergamon Press, New York: 1981) 223 at 247–252).

[192] See Article 140 of the LOS Convention.

[193] 1994 Agreement, Annex, section 7.

[194] See for example, A.A. Saguirian "Excision of the Deep Seabed Mining Provisions from the 1982 Law of the Convention: Reappraising the Principle of a Treaty's Integrity under the New Realities" in J.M. van Dyke, D. Zaelke and G. Hewison (eds) *Freedom of the Seas for the 21st Century* (Island Press, Washington: 1983) 375–387 at 382. Cf. Nelson, who considers the regime to remain true to the fundamental principles that inform the regime (L.D.M. Nelson "The New Deep Sea-Bed Mining Regime" (1995) 10 *International Journal of Marine and Coastal Law* 189–203 at 203).

The development of detailed mining rules by the ISA shows the potential for complex resource regimes to operate directly through international institutions.[195] The debate about access to deep seabed resources has now refocused upon the question of genetic resources located on deep seabed mounts and other locations in the Area.[196] It is notable that already there is a divided opinion as to whether such resources fall within the scope of the CHM principle, and so are subject to some equitable use restrictions and international management, or whether they are subject to the freedom of the high seas and subject to far weaker use constraints.

4.5. *Summary Remarks*

Property rights in *terra nullius* tend to collapse into property rights under the inheriting sovereign. Private property rights in resources *in situ* cannot be said to exist in Antarctica or outer space. Here property rights in resources *in situ* are incompatible with the moratorium on sovereign claims and the absence of operational institutional regimes for the determination of property rights. However, both regimes appear to provide strong support for cooperative and equitable institutions governing the use of natural resources. These requirements have arisen through a combination of factors: the absence of unilateral regulatory authority, the subsequent rejection of extensions of national appropriation or sovereignty, the development of law through agreement rather than State practice, the influence of developing States' interests in the prescriptive process, the difficulty or inability to actually exploit the resources, and finally the influence of legal developments in other global commons. Given that practice in such areas is scarce, law has necessarily drawn inspiration from practice and jurisprudence in other areas. The development of the CHM principle in respect of the deep seabed has clearly been influential in this respect. However, even in this elaborate regime there is clear evidence of the subversion of cooperative and equitable arrangements in favor of strong free-market principles and the extension of self-interest-type rights.

5. *Supporting Legal Mechanisms*

If property rights in pre-capture resources are to exist in ABNJ, there needs to be some institutional framework capable of supporting the rights. Indeed, in the absence of any such structure, claims could only survive through the

---

195 Eg, the draft mining code and instruments (available at ⟨http://www.isa.org⟩).

196 See A.G. Oude Elferink, note 181 at 162–166.

creeping spatial sovereignty of coastal States over the area and their reduction into property rights under that State's domestic legal order. At the present time there is no purely international regime that directly engages in the regulation of resource activities via property rights-based mechanisms. The ISA does not yet regulate actual commercial mining activities and whilst some RFMOs allow for members to adopt property rights-based measures to regulate quotas allocated by RFMOs, this still relies upon domestic law to give effect to the individual entitlements. As indicated in section 3 of this paper, property concepts can also be applied to the fishing quotas that are granted to States in RFMOs. Indeed, this approach seems the most likely way in which property rights-based approaches will develop. However, these approaches suffer from crucial limitations. Firstly, the former requires dual levels of regulation. If different States adopt different domestic regimes to regulate the entitlements they are granted by RFMOs, then different and incompatible mechanisms may regulate the individual components of the same resource-base. The latter do not necessarily generate incentives for individual fishermen to change their fishing practices, unless the State adopts individual rights-based entitlements. In both cases, their success depends upon the RFMO rules having objective effect.

In the case of either exclusive State-based entitlements or individually held property rights, the legal framework must possess the following attributes for the introduction of property rights: there must be a single exclusive legal regime for the determination, operation and enforcement of any rights in pre-capture resources; the regime must be effective *in rem*, and capable of dealing with the rights and responsibilities of non-State actors; and the regime must be spatially determinate. In addition, the regime must be consistent with any principles of international law that govern the use of resources in the area to which the regime pertains. This latter requirement involves questions of who may hold an entitlement and what limits are placed on the holding to ensure that community interests are taken into account. It is suggested that any regime utilizing property rights for the regulation of natural resources in ABNJ must be a creature of treaty for only a treaty is able to meet the above requirements. Only a treaty is able to stipulate the precise rules necessary for property-type holdings. However, as a general rule, treaties do not have objective legal effects. This is due to the *pacta tertiis* principle, which provides that treaties cannot establish rights and obligations binding on non-parties without their consent.[197]

---

[197] See Article 34 of the Vienna Convention on the Law of Treaties (Vienna Convention) of 23 May 1969 (1155 UNTS 331). The principle is widely regarded as fundamental. See R. Roxburgh *International Conventions and Third States* (Longmans, Green & Co., London: 1917) at 29; Sir I. Sinclair *The Vienna Convention on the Law of Treaties*, 2nd ed. (Manchester University Press, Manchester, 1984) at 98; Brownlie, note 68 at 628; A.C. McNair *Law of Treaties* (Clarendon, Oxford: 1961) at 309.

This may fundamentally limit the usefulness of treaties in sustaining property rights-based regimes. All is not lost here. There are two potential exceptions to the *pacta tertiis* principle. The first looks to the role of custom in making rules of treaty applicable to non-parties. The second possibility, that of objective regimes, renders the treaty applicable to third parties by virtue of the quality of the rules embodied in the treaty.

Although customary international law cannot provide the requisite structures of governance necessary for resource activities, a subtle alternative is advanced by Rayfuse, who argues for a rule of custom that compels States to exercise their pre-existing liberties through cooperation with regional fisheries organizations.[198] In the context of fisheries, Rayfuse argues that the obligation to cooperate in the utilization of high seas fisheries in Articles 117–119 of the LOS Convention, and as institutionalized in the Fish Stocks Agreement, means that States cannot fish for high seas fisheries except on the terms laid down by a regional fisheries organization. They must either refrain from fishing or comply with conservation measures established by the regional fisheries organization. There is some merit in this approach, not least because it avoids the problem of qualifying a most fundamental norm of treaty law. It suggests an evolution of the principle of freedom of the high seas which may indeed have come about. However, until the Fish Stocks Agreement gains widespread ratification, one should be cautious about accepting a significant modification of a fundamental principle of the law of the sea. Although there is practice to support this argument, this is primarily limited to the parties to regional agreements, or explicable on the basis of port State control or the consent of the third State.[199] The acid test of this approach will be whether or not non-parties accept the full exclusive regulatory authority of RFMOs. There is also another problem with this approach. It commits third States to regional fisheries treaty regimes without any consideration of whether or not the treaty regime actually advances the conservation and management of a fishery. It presumes that the cooperative mechanism will meet conservation and management objectives. By way of contrast, the binding nature of an objective regime depends on whether or not it actually advances a general interest. This, at least, retains a strong focus on the reason why States may be compelled without their specific consent.

---

[198] Rayfuse, note 87 esp. at 373. Cf Molenaar, who suggests that a duty to cooperate may take many forms and does not necessarily translate into a duty to participate in or establish an RFMO or arrangement. E.J. Molenaar "The Concept of 'Real Interest' and Other Aspects of Co-operation through Regional Fisheries Management Mechanisms" (2000) 15 *International Journal of Marine and Coastal Law* 475–532, at 482 et seq.

[199] Rayfuse, note 87 at chapter 8.

The *pacta tertiis* rule is fundamental, but not absolute. Indeed, the Vienna Convention mitigates its strict application in Articles 35–36 and 38 which provide for the binding effect of rights and obligations through the consent of the affected party, and the subsequent development of custom. Further exceptions to the scope of the principle were considered by the ILC in the drafting process, although they did not find a place in the final text.[200] These latter exceptions, which have been characterized as objective regimes, have received some support from commentators.[201] However, it must be stressed that the category of objective regimes is by no means generally accepted. The concept has attracted sharp criticism, particular from those adopting a view of international law strongly rooted in the notion of consent.[202] What we can observe is that if treaty regimes can bind third States, then this would potentially overcome the limits on the creation of effective property rights-based instruments in international agreements pertaining to ABNJ.

In his systematic study of objective regimes, Klein sets out four criteria for an objective regime. Firstly, such regimes are not to be presumed and the intention to create such a regime must be clear.[203] The requirement of intent is uncontroversial and generally agreed upon by commentators.[204] A relevant example of this is Article 8(4) of the Fish Stocks Agreement, which provides that:

> only those States which are members of such an organization or participants in such an arrangement, or which agree to apply the conservation and management measures established by such organization or arrangement, shall have access to the fishery resources to which those measures apply.[205]

---

[200] See Fitzmaurice, who noted that such exceptions "constitute in the aggregate a considerable gloss on the *pacta tertiis* rule" (International Law Commission *Yearbook of the International Law Commission 1960* vol. II (United Nations, New York: 1961) at 73). Waldock's report to the ILC contained a draft Article on treaties providing for objective regimes, and a comprehensive commentary: International Law Commission *Yearbook of the International Law Commission 1964* vol. II (United Nations, New York: 1965) at 26ff.

[201] The most thorough treatment of the concept is by E. Klein *Staatsvertäge im Völkerrecht* (Springer, Berlin: 1980). Some support can be found in the work of C. Chinkin *Third Parties in International Law* (Clarendon Press, Oxford: 1993). Also, R. Barnes "Objective Regimes Revisited" (2000) 9 *Asian Yearbook of International Law* 97–145.

[202] The orthodox position is held by Brownlie, note 68 at 289 who regards consent as crucial to the prescriptive process.

[203] See the *Free Zones Case*, where the Permanent Court of International Justice (PCIJ) noted that "stipulations *pour autrui* are not to be lightly presumed" (1932 PCIJ Ser. A/B, No 4 at 147–148). See also the *North Sea Continental Shelf* cases (Federal Republic of Germany v. Denmark; Federal Republic of Germany v. The Netherlands) [1969] ICJ Reports 3 at 25–26.

[204] S.P. Subedi "The Doctrine of Objective Regimes in International Law and the Competence of the United Nations to Impose Territorial or Peace Settlements on States" (1994) 37 *German Yearbook of International Law* 162–205 at 194–195. Also, Klein note 201 at 352; Waldock *Yearbook of the International Law Commission 1964* vol. II at 26ff.

[205] See also Arts. 5, 17(1), 17(2), 18 and 33(2), which impact on the position of third States, and vessels flying their flag.

The clear aim of this provision is to limit the right to fish to States that comply with conservation and management measures thereby ending the problem of the free rider.[206] Whilst this might be construed as an extension of the conservation and management requirements of Article 117 of the LOS Convention, it goes considerably beyond this because it requires States to conform to conservation measures that have been agreed by other States, i.e. RFMO members, rather than conservation measures taken unilaterally. Article 117 provides States with an option between taking cooperative and independent conservation measures for their nationals fishing on the high seas. Such unilateral conservation measures are not provided for in Article 8(4) of the Fish Stocks Agreement, although one must reasonably ask whether it is possible in practice for individual States to unilaterally assume conservation measures for stocks that may be exploited by several States. Moreover, the provision is phrased so as to establish a general rule, rather than an obligation *inter se*.[207] A literal and contextual reading of the provisions suggest that the *ratione personae* is not limited to States parties, and it is arguable that the Fish Stocks Agreement is intended to have objective effect.[208]

Secondly, such regimes must relate to the status or use of territory.[209] This serves to distinguish them from general law-making treaties or purely institutional regimes, such as the United Nations Charter. It would be untenable

[206] See E. de Lone "Improving the Management of the Atlantic Tuna: The Duty to Strengthen the ICCAT in Light of the 1995 Straddling Stocks Agreement" (1998) 6 *New York University Environmental Law Journal* 656–673 at 663–664.

[207] It may be argued that the obligation to adhere to regional arrangements only applies to States Parties to the Fish Stocks Agreement. See, e.g. D. Freestone and Z. Makuch "The New International Environmental Law of Fisheries: The 1995 United Nations Straddling Stocks Agreement" (1996) 7 *Yearbook of International Environmental Law* 3–51 at 34. Thus the States become bound by subsequent fisheries treaties by virtue of their consent to the Agreement. Cf. Franckx, who argues that because this provision is neither objective nor customary, it is ineffective (E. Franckx, *Pacta Tertiis and the Agreement for the Implementation of the Provisions of the United Nations Convention on the Law of the Sea of 10 December 1982 relating to the Conservation & Management of Straddling Fish Stocks and Highly Migratory Fish Stocks* (FAO Legal Papers Online #8, Rome: July 2000)).

[208] This is supported by statements in the *travaux préparatoires*. Thus Australia and the EU supported measures against third State vessels acting contrary to regional arrangements, as long as this is consistent with international law (doc. A/CONF.164/L.19 and 20, respectively). Also paragraph 109 of the Background Paper of 8 July 1993 suggests an increased role for regional arrangements in the supervision and enforcement of standards (doc. A/CONF. 164/INF/6).

[209] Commentators on such regimes have emphasised the essential requirement that they be territorial regimes. See for example McNair, note 197, at 255 ff.; J. Kunz "Austria's Permanent Neutrality" (1956) 50 *American Journal of International Law* 418–425; H. Mosler "The International Society as a Legal Community" (1974-IV) 150 *Recueil des Cours* 11 at 152; Klein, note 201 at 352.

to admit that a group of States could legislate for States generally without restriction, and institutional regimes are dealt with under the rules on legal personality.[210]

Thirdly, the parties to an objective regime must have a particular competence to act or a particular interest in the regime.[211] Ordinarily, this requires States having territorial sovereignty over the territory in question, and this would preclude objective regimes in ABNJ.[212] However, at least for arrangements which straddle international and domestic areas—such as many fisheries regimes—this may not be an insurmountable problem. Certain provisions of the Fish Stocks Agreement purport to have objective effect and these are based upon a combination of territorial competence, preferential rights[213] and the 'compatibility principle'.[214] Where coastal States, or States with a real interest in the fishery, participate in regional arrangements, this would seem to satisfy this condition for an objective regime.

Finally, an objective regime must serve the general interests of the international community.[215] This requirement is crucial because it justifies the adjustment of the legal position of third States. As Lauterpacht argues, "as international society is transformed into an integrated community, departure from the principle [of *pacta tertiis*] becomes unavoidable, in particular in the sphere of international peace and security."[216] Such general interests may comprise fundamental norms of international law such as *jus cogens* or '*ordre public*'. International peace and security, fundamental human rights and the conservation of vital natural resources arguably constitute the core of such interests and justify the imposition of duties on third States. Clearly, it may be difficult to discern whether or not a general interest exists. However, given the general acceptance of categories of peremptory norms, this should not prove to be critical. Although it might be suggested that the general interest is the source of the

---

210 See Brownlie, note 68 chap. XXX.

211 Klein, note 201 at 21.

212 See Waldock, note 200.

213 Orrego Vicuña notes that Chile and the United States have put forward such claims when fish stocks are at risk (F. Orrego Vicuña *The Changing International Law of High Seas Fisheries*, (Cambridge University Press, Cambridge: 1999) at 121). Canada and the Russian Federation adopted a similar position during the negotiation of the Fish Stocks Agreement. See the Letter dated 27th July from the alternative chairman of the Russian Federation, A/CONF.164/L.27, and the List of Issues of 4th June 1993, A/CONF. 164/L. 5 respectively.

214 Article 7(2) of the Fish Stocks Agreement states that: "Conservation and management measures established for the high seas and those adopted for areas under national jurisdiction shall be *compatible* in order to ensure the conservation and management of straddling fish stocks and highly migratory fish stocks in their entirety". Emphasis added.

215 See Klein, note 201 at 352.

216 H. Lauterpacht *Oppenheim's International Law* 8th ed. (Longman, Green & Co., London: 1955) at 528.

obligation, rather than the objective regime, it is clear that the open texture of a general interest frequently requires a degree of refinement before it becomes legally operative. As such, objective regimes may have a role to play in articulating general interests in the form of meaningful, particular obligations. This actualization of objective rules is illustrated by Davies and Redgwell:

> The future law of high seas fisheries will be governed by three levels of largely mutually compatible and reinforcing treaty obligations, ranging from the general provisions of the [LOS Convention] through the [Fish Stocks Agreement] to the RF[M]Os. In practice these will not operate as three separate and conflicting sources of treaty law, since the principles contained at each level may be viewed as simply steps in the concretization of general norms of conservation, management and enforcement.[217]

This approach depends on a high degree of consistency between the general and particular treaty regimes. The key then is not the consent of States to a 'new' rule but the quality of the overarching general interest and its coherent transposition into a particular form.

Objective regimes are not merely an academic concept. There is a body of State practice and jurisprudence that lends support to the existence of objective regimes. This includes both territorial and extra-territorial neutrality and demilitarization agreements that establish benefits for third parties.[218] The Antarctic Treaty system is often claimed to be an objective regime.[219] Arguably, certain provisions of the LOS Convention and 1994 Implementation Agreement demonstrate an intention to establish a regime for the Area that is binding upon all States.[220] Although this objective status is often rejected, it is clear that any regulation of the Area will impact on third States.[221]

---

[217] P.G.G. Davies and C. Redgwell "The International Regulation of Straddling Fish Stocks" (1996) 67 *British Yearbook of International Law* 199–274 at 272.

[218] See Subedi, note 204. Even Roxburgh, who tows the orthodox line, claims that neutrality settlements should be respected by non-party States. Roxburgh, note 197 at 58.

[219] See Waldock, note 200 at 30; R.D. Hayton "The Antarctic Settlement of 1959" (1960) 54 *American Journal of International Law* 349–371. Boczek notes that a majority of Soviet writers support the conclusion that the Antarctic Treaty establishes an objective regime (Boczek "The Soviet Union and the Antarctic Regime" (1984) 78 *American Journal of International Law* 834–858 at 856). However, there are equally strong rejections of this position. See I. Brownlie "Legal Status of Natural Resources" (1979-I) 162 *Recueil des Cours* 245–318; J. Hannesian "The Antarctic Treaty 1959" (1960) 9 *International and Comparative law Quarterly* 436–480. Mouton tries to reconcile these positions, suggesting the Antarctic Treaty may be considered objective law if it is recognised as representing general international law, and thus enforceable *erga omnes* (M.W. Mouton "The International Regime of the Polar Regions" (1962-III) 107 *Recueil des Cours* 174 at 258).

[220] See section 4.4 above. The provisions on the Area are necessarily of a general nature, and not merely binding on contracting parties *inter se*.

[221] See S. Vascianne "Part XI of the Law of the Sea Convention and Third States: Some General Observations" (1989) 48 *Cambridge Law Review* 85–97; D. Arrow "Seabeds, Sovereignty and Objective Regimes" (1984) 7 *Fordham Journal of International Law* 169–243.

The pathways provided both by Rayfuse's evolution of a customary principle and objective regimes proceed in the same direction towards the objectification of conservation and management obligations in regional fisheries instruments. This much seems necessary if either the general conservation and management goals of RFMOs are to succeed or if property rights-based approaches to resource regulation are adopted. The virtue of Rayfuse's approach is its general orthodoxy: it relies upon consent, as manifest in State practice showing a change in a general customary rule, to act as a proxy for the consent needed to make RFMOs effective against third Sates. This is also its weakness. It seems to commit States unquestioningly to any regional fisheries instrument, regardless of its substantive provisions. Objective regimes directly challenge the consensual nature of international law, but only when there is a clear advancement of a general interest in a particular context.[222] It does not change the general rule. Thus any RFMO, as an objective regime, is open to challenge on the grounds that it does not advance general conservation and management goals.

It is clear that proving the objective qualities of an RFMO is a challenge to the effectiveness of both high seas fisheries management and the potential adoption of property rights-based entitlements. However, this should not deter us. There is good reason for accepting the conservation and management provisions as being in the general interest. Many States participated in the negotiation and development of the Fish Stocks Agreement. There has been a high level of support for the rules and standards formulated therein, and this suggests a positive outlook for the Fish Stocks Agreement.[223] The Fish Stocks Agreement is strongly supported by international organizations with a particular interest and influence in fishing matters, such as the FAO, UNCED, and the UN General Assembly. It has also received widespread approval among expert commentators, suggesting that it is consistent with internationally recognized standards.[224] Finally, there is as yet no direct opposition to the rules and provisions of the Fish Stocks Agreement and this would seem to imply that its provisions are generally acceptable. More difficult is the task of showing that individual RFMOs possess the same degree of support. It should be noted that many RFMOs have been subject to criticisms concerning the effectiveness

[222] As objective regimes are spatial or territorial regimes, they usually take the form of regional arrangements.

[223] The Fish Stocks Agreement has 75 Parties as of February 2009.

[224] See for example M. Hayashi "The 1995 Agreement on the conservation and management of straddling and highly migratory fish stocks: significance for the Law of the Sea Convention" (1995) 29 *Ocean and Coastal Management* 51–69; D.A. Balton "Strengthening the Law of the Sea: The New Agreement on Straddling Fish Stocks and Highly Migratory Fish Stocks" (1996) 27 *Ocean Development and International Law* 125–151.

of their conservation and management measures.[225] Moreover, there is a general recognition that the accountability of RFMOs needs to be improved.[226] Addressing these concerns is central to the future success of RFMOs. However, if the objective effects of the Fish Stocks Agreement and the legitimacy of measures adopted by regional organizations or arrangements can be sustained, then this would open the way for the adoption of stronger property rights-based entitlements.

6. *Some Observations on the Allocation of Entitlements under International Law*

From the outline of property rights-based measures so far, I would like to make some brief observations on the form and allocation of entitlements as they might occur under international law. The common starting point is that the worst-case scenario for resource regulation is one where there are no rules. The absence of exclusive rights of control, either by States, regional arrangements, or individuals is likely to perpetuate a tragedy of the commons. Secondly, there is good evidence from domestic fishery regimes that property rights-based measures can result in the improved conservation and management of marine living resources. Whilst the benefits are primarily in respect of encouraging more efficient resource use, there is evidence of conservation gains from reduced fishing capacity, placing an economic value on the resource and vesting individuals with an interest in sustaining the resource base. The expansion of property rights-based systems under domestic law, and the interest shown by RFMOs in such measures, is indicative of the future potential of this approach. On the other hand, the lessons from domestic fisheries regimes and the distributive consequences of this approach, particularly in ABNJ, need to be carefully considered. If we are to follow the advice of economists, and adopt exclusive property rights-based measures to regulate fisheries, we need to do so in a way that ensures that use restrictions are in place to protect non-exclusive interests, such as the ecosystem and biodiversity, and to ensure that distributive concerns are met. We must also ensure that allocations are made in accordance with the fundamental interests of the international legal community.

---

[225] See K. Gjerde "High Seas Fisheries Management under the LOSC" in D. Freestone, R. Barnes and D. Ong (ed.) *Law of the Sea. Progress and Prospects* (OUP, Oxford: 2006) at 281.

[226] *Ibid*., at 298; M.W. Lodge and S.N. Nandan "Some Suggestions Towards Better Implementation of the United Nations Agreement on Straddling Fish Stocks and Highly Migratory Fish Stocks of 1995" (2005) 20 *International Journal of Marine and Coastal Law* 345–380 at 357–359; E.J. Molenaar, "Addressing Regulatory Gaps in High Seas Fisheries" (2005) 20 *International Journal of Marine and Coastal Law* 533–570 at 551 et seq.

The content of any legal norm is shaped by a wide range of social, economic, political, cultural and ideological values that drives its host legal system, or by the particular systemic procedures that generate the legal norm. This applies to property rules as it does to any other legal norm. It means that the form and allocation of any property right will be determined by the underlying structure and values of the legal system that sustain the property right. In ABNJ, the absence of territorial sovereignty and the inadequacy of nationality-based regulation inhibit the development of property rights as usually conceived of under domestic law. However, the possibility of property rights-based entitlements arising directly under international law remains, for example through RFMOs or other international institutions. Sections 3 and 4 above indicate how this might take place, either through State-based entitlements structured round property rights or through individual property rights-based entitlements, such as ITQs. However, significant obstacles must be overcome first. Principally these relate to the enforcement of such measures against third parties.

If such obstacles can be overcome and rights-based approaches were to be adopted, then it is useful to consider what factors will shape the form and allocation of such entitlements. Here I would emphasize that the absence of effective legal sanctions under international law to ensure adherence to the measures so established means that compliance will largely turn on the perceived legitimacy of the rules. This serves to reinforce the role of general or moral factors in the operation of exclusive use rights and property in ABNJ. However, it also means that allocative rules will have to be determined in accordance with the interests of those most directly concerned with the actual exploitation of a resource, rather than those parties unable to access the resource, or without a strong voice in the prescriptive process. If the experience of domestic fisheries is replicated, this will result in allocations to fishing interests according to the *status quo*, as evidenced by historic fishing practices.

As indicated above, the form and allocation of property is fundamentally shaped by physical, legal and moral factors. First, legal rules must accord with the physical qualities of the resources that they regulate. Such physical factors represent absolutes to which any legal system must adapt. This is particularly important to the regulation of living resources in ABNJ. For example, the fungible and unascertained nature of wild fish demands the adoption of access rights or quotas because pre-capture rights in *ferae naturae* are not practicable. Furthermore, for common pool resources, the law must take into account the high costs of excluding access and overuse. As indicated above, this supports the creation of some form of exclusive use right. The law must also appreciate the potentially high costs and risks of recovering resources. These factors reinforce the need for strong degrees of exclusive control and security of title as preconditions for the commercial investment in harvesting activities. The legal regime must be sensitive to the capacity of living resources to renew themselves. If the continued existence of the resource is desirable, then this will require rules that restrict the capacity of owners or users to alienate the resource, and rules that ensure the sustainable use of the resource. Legal regimes must also account for the contribution of fisheries and other natural resources to vital needs, such as food supply. This reinforces the need for rules to ensure that levels of harvesting are sustainable and, perhaps, that post capture distribution of resources meet subsistence and food supply needs.[227] These latter two factors appear to require some public machinery to control or supervise the management of resources to ensure that individual self-interests in maximal economic exploitation are balanced against wider community interests.

In addition to these factors, I want to emphasis the important contribution of marine resources to biodiversity, and the need to protect marine habitats and ecosystems. As a result of the fluid, interconnected nature of the marine environment and commonly used fishing techniques, exploitation of marine living resources may significantly affect the ecosystem within which they are located. Such concerns can be exacerbated because of the uncertain consequences of many exploitation activities. The protection of biodiversity is also important because it manifests a coming together of physical and legal imperatives. Thus under international law there is an obligation to protect biodiversity. Crucially, this vests the wider community with an interest in the physical components of a marine resource that cannot be satisfactorily regulated in a system based purely upon exclusive control. The diffuse nature of biodiversity entails that the holder or exploiters of the components of biodiversity have to be aware of the more complex patterns of use which affect their use of the natural resources or the systems within which they are located. For example, it might not be contrary to the CBD for States to permit a single fisherman at a local level to exhaust a particular species in a particular area. As long as the stock can recover, no harm may be done to biodiversity at the species level. However, if all fishermen for the same species adopted the same approach at the same time, then this may cause the collapse of the fishery, and the potential extinction of the species. Preventing such scenarios entails coordination of resource exploitation activities. Individual owners of natural resources must bear some responsibility to ensure that resource degradation does not occur, rather than purely

[227] Although such concerns may be regarded as moral limits on resource use, it is clear that the physical attributes of a resource determine its relevance to these moral goals. For example, grain supplies are likely to be more important to food supply networks than truffles, and so subject to stronger public regulation.

pursuing their private interests. Obligations to protect ecosystems and biodiversity place important limits on the extent to which exclusive control of resources through property rights can be granted to individuals, and may require States to retain significant management responsibilities in privately held individual entitlements.

International law places a number of legal limits on the exclusive use and allocation of resources. In general, it appears to place considerable emphasis on equity and fairness in the allocation of resources. This much is evident from the above consideration of resources in international commons. Especially relevant is the principle of 'equitable utilization'.[228] This requires States to manage and utilize resources in "a way that other States can also use them as well or at least obtain a reasonable and equitable share".[229] The principle has a primary role to play in the regulation of international watercourses, and has been extended to cover other shared natural resources, such as fisheries and shared petroleum deposits. It is clear that what is equitable is highly contextual, and depends upon the nature of the resource, its location, the way in which it can be used and the parties concerned with its use. It may also require account to be taken of a wide range of complex phenomena, such as need, opportunity, fairness or merit. At a minimum the principle requires a consideration of all the relevant factors and a balancing of interests concerning the use of things. Crucially, it will require some degree of cooperation between States in determining how to manage and use natural resources.

More specifically, it can be considered in terms of substantive fairness and procedural fairness.[230] The former concerns the basic principles that govern the allocation of resources, and may include recognition of formal equality and allocation according to need and so on. In most societies it is necessary to have in place procedures that regulate transactions in holdings. It is also desirable to have in place procedures that permit principles of substantive equity to be revised in light of changed circumstances. As such transactions or changes will alter any initial allocations, and may result in accumulations of wealth that run counter to original notions of substantive equity. Unless strict control over allocations is maintained, or things are periodically restored to a position of formal equality of holdings, then the procedures for change must also possess some agreed upon qualities of fairness, thereby legitimizing any subsequent changes in allocation of holdings. This will require quite sophisticated

[228] See O. Schachter *Sharing the World's Resources* (Columbia University Press, New York: 1977) at 64 ff.; N. Schrijver *Sovereignty over Natural Resources* (Cambridge University Press, Cambridge: 1997) at 243–244 and 276–278.

[229] Schrijver, note 228 at 243.

[230] T.M. Franck *Fairness in International Law and Institutions* (Clarendon, Oxford: 1995) at 7–9.

institutional mechanisms that are sufficiently independent and strong enough to carry out their functions and advance principles of equitable use. At this point it seems clear that the generality of the principle of equity and its context specificity mean that more is to be gained from considering it in context, for example as it pertains to the CHM in the deep seabed or fisheries covered by an RFMO. As indicated in section 4.4, the initial regime for the Area was characterized by a high degree of equitability. Although the broad principles that shape the resource regime remain in place, it is clear that they have been watered down at an operational level and entitlement to the resource is largely predicated upon the technical capacity of operators to actually explore and exploit mineral deposits. Although some limits on the conduct of mining operations can be imposed under the LOS Convention, indicating the importance of balancing rights and responsibilities, the key provisions on benefit distribution are somewhat muted. Notably, production policies are now based upon 'sound commercial principles'.[231] This indicates that international institutions are vulnerable to the typical, preference maximizing rationales that influence many property regimes.

The Fish Stocks Agreement is also concerned with the allocation of entitlements. Under Article 8(3), the participation of States in fisheries managed by an RFMO is based upon the existence of a real interest in the fishery. Although this notion of a real interest is primarily linked to participation in RFMOs or arrangements, it seems difficult to separate the initial matter of participation in a fishery from the secondary issue of the nature and extent of participatory rights for new members or participants as detailed under Article 11.[232] Article 11 lists six criteria to be taken into account: the state of stocks and existing fishing levels; the interests and fishing patterns of new and existing members or participants; contributions to conservation and management measures; the needs of dependent coastal fishing communities; the needs of coastal States whose economies are highly dependent upon fishing; and the interests of developing States. Notably, Molenaar points out that although these factors pertain to the participatory rights once a real interest has been established, he is careful not rule out the influence of these factors in verifying a real interest at the initial stage of determining membership or participation.[233] There are clearly important issues of principle and practice at stake here, issues that are compounded by the fact that the precise meaning of 'real interest', and,

---

[231] See section 6.1 of the Annex to the 1994 Implementation Agreement.

[232] For example, Henriksen *et al* suggest that it imposes restrictions on entitlement (T. Henriksen, G. Hønneland and A. Sydnes *Law and Politics in Ocean Governance. The UN Fish Stocks Agreement and Regional Fisheries Management Regimes* (Martinus Nijhoff, Leiden: 2005) at 21).

[233] Molenaar, note 198 at 494.

ultimately, its impact upon entitlement is open to debate.[234] In practice, it is suggested that historical, actual and intended fishing levels will have a significant bearing upon participation in RFMO managed fisheries per se, and upon the subsequent extent of those participatory rights when allocations are determined according to Article 11. The factors listed under Article 11 are not exclusively limited to fishing levels, and could permit the involvement of States with an interest in advancing community interests in conservation and management. However, no particular weight is given to these criteria, nor are they exhaustive. This leaves considerable discretion in the hands of the RFMO or arrangement concerning the extent of participatory rights.[235] In practice, it is suggested two factors: existing fishing practices and zonal attachment, i.e. geographic distribution of a stock, are most likely to be determinative because they can be more readily identified. Arguably, they can be objectively quantified and so are more transparent and easier to use.[236] Ultimately, this is likely to reinforce any status quo in access, thereby protecting established users' interests and making any reallocation on the basis of more equitable considerations difficult. This is compounded because distributive considerations, such as the needs of developing States are very much open to interpretation and so provide an unspecific and contentious basis for the allocation of participatory rights. As in the case of the Area, this reaffirms the susceptibility of international resource regimes to pragmatic considerations rather than distributive ideals.

Our experience with international resource management regimes suggests that the influence of general obligations to distribute resources in accordance with equitable principles tends to dissipate when the actual exploitation of a resource becomes a commercial reality. In domestic property systems, the State generally assumes responsibility for ensuring that certain public functions of property are protected. These include meeting those common minimal requirements that justifications of property require (e.g. ensuring minimal subsistence needs and the protection of agency). It also includes ensuring that the exercise of private property rights does not run counter to fundamental goals of proper social order. The reason for this State assumption of control over property is that holders of private rights cannot always be expected to act

---

[234] See Freestone and Makuch, note 207 at 29. See generally Molenaar, note 198.

[235] Here we can note how the Northwest Atlantic Fisheries Organization (NAFO) adopted a resolution indicating that although it is an open organization, as stocks managed by NAFO are fully allocated, fishing opportunities for new members are likely to be limited, for instance, to new fisheries. NAFO "Resolution to Guide the Expectations of Future New Members with Regard to Fishing Opportunities in the NAFO Regulatory Area" in *NAFO Annual Report 1999* (NAFO, Darthmouth: 1999) paras 1 and 2 at 62.

[236] See A.H. Hoel and I. Kvalvik "The allocation of scarce natural resources: The case of fisheries" (2006) 30 *Marine Policy* 347–356.

altruistically or act to their detriment. This suggests that strong institutional structures are essential to the articulation and protection of public interest limits on resource use, because it is often the case that achieving certain public ends means restricting private rights or freedoms to act.

In the context of international resource regimes this is critical because the absence of strong 'public' regulatory machinery renders any such public interest, such as the protection of non-target species or marine habitats more generally, vulnerable to the private self-interested desires of individual States. Although there are pressures to establish property type rules for natural resources in ABNJ, international law struggles to provide the degree of institutional and legal support necessary for this. This stems from a fundamental political resistance to ceding authority over natural resources to independent regulatory agencies. Of course, the risk here is that if international law cannot regulate property through international regimes, then domestic legal systems are likely to expand to fill the gap. If this occurs, then the hard fought concessions to equitable use obligations, benefit sharing and, potentially, the opportunity for international collaboration to protect ecosystems and biodiversity may be lost.

COMMENTARY: PROPERTY RIGHTS IN AREAS BEYOND NATIONAL JURISDICTION—NOT TOO LATE FOR A PROPER DEBATE?

Andrew Serdy*

Introduction

As a quasi-record of the proceedings in the relevant session of the Symposium, this contribution does not seek to take issue with Barnes's excellent paper but merely to add a few pertinent and, it is hoped, provocative observations. Because of space constraints, the reader's familiarity with the basic legal framework applicable to international fisheries under Articles 63, 64 and 116–119 of the United Nations Convention on the Law of the Sea (LOS Convention)[1] is assumed.[2]

The first thing one notices in any discussion of property rights in areas beyond national jurisdiction (ABNJ) is a conceptual obstacle: the lack, in public international law, of any law of property as such. States do buy and sell commodities to each other, extend loans to each other and so on, but these are essentially commercial transactions that are either embodied in treaties,[3] or the transaction is conducted under the system of domestic law of one of the parties[4] or sometimes a third State. The closest that traditional international

* School of Law, University of Southampton, United Kingdom.

[1] Adopted on 10 December 1982; 1833 UNTS 3.

[2] For a fine account of that framework see W.T. Burke *The New International Law of Fisheries: UNCLOS 1982 and Beyond* (Clarendon Press, Oxford: 1994) 82–150 (chapter 3 on high seas fisheries) and 199–254 (chapter 5 on highly migratory species).

[3] One of the better known examples is the post-war line of credit of $ 3.75 billion extended by the United States to the United Kingdom (Financial Agreement between the Governments of the United States of America and the United Kingdom of Great Britain and Northern Ireland of 6 December 1945 (126 UNTS 13)). Although not a loan, the reparations of 132 billion gold marks quantified by the Reparation Commission under Article 233 of the Versailles Treaty (Treaty of Peace with Germany of 28 June 1919 (1919) 13 AJIL Supplement 151) afford another illustration of how a debt from one State to another can be incurred and given recognition in a treaty.

[4] For example, in the *Norwegian Loans* case ([1957] ICJ Reports 9), the bonds issued by Norway and purchased by French investors were governed by Norwegian, not international law. The International Court of Justice (ICJ) found that it had no jurisdiction to decide the case. There

Alex G. Oude Elferink and Erik J. Molenaar (eds.), *The International Legal Regime of Areas beyond National Jurisdiction: Current and Future Developments*, pp. 143–158.

law comes to a regime of property independent of national legal systems concerns the law on the acquisition of territory. More recently, however, the recognition of the tragedy of the commons at the heart of certain global-scale problems has produced on the international plane some tentative steps towards property-like solutions. The most prominent of these is the creation of an emissions trading system envisaged under the Kyoto Protocol to the Framework Convention on Climate Change,[5] but this is both very complex and still at an early stage of development, 2008 having been the first year in which a significant number of transactions took place.[6]

On the face of it, the freedom of fishing on the high seas seems a more formidable barrier to creation of property rights in fisheries than in the case of harmful emissions, since under Article 116 of the LOS Convention fishing is a positive right subject to certain qualifications, whereas there is no such freedom to pollute the atmosphere. Rather, since the *Trail Smelter* arbitration as long ago as 1941 established the wrongfulness of cross-border air pollution,[7] in this instance from a point source, the problem has been one of proving causation in the form of relative contributions to damage by multiple polluters or diffuse sources: even if there is scientific consensus that the cause of damage suffered by a low-lying State from, say, rising sea-levels is anthropogenic global warming, this will be of no avail to that State.

The shift in thinking that is nonetheless beginning to make property rights seem possible can best be traced in the evolution of the views of one of the law of the sea greats, Judge Oda. At the start of his career he was doubtful as to whether extending exclusive coastal State jurisdiction even to twelve nautical miles from the territorial sea baseline (as the Second United Nations

---

is a great deal of practice and case law on compensation for expropriation of property of foreign nationals, but the character of the assets as property is still rooted in the domestic law of the expropriating State.

[5] United Nations Framework Convention on Climate Change of 9 May 1992 (1771 UNTS 107) and the Protocol to the Framework Convention on Climate Change (Kyoto Protocol) of 11 December 1997 (2303 UNTS 162); see "Decision 12/CMP.1, Guidance relating to registry systems under Article 7, paragraph 4 of the Kyoto Protocol" and "Decision 13/CMP.1, Modalities for the accounting of assigned amounts under Article 7, paragraph 4 of the Kyoto Protocol" *Report of the Conference of the Parties serving as the meeting of the Parties to the Kyoto Protocol in its first session* (30 March 2006) UN Doc FCCC/KP/CMP/2005/8/Add. 2 (available at ⟨http://unfccc.int⟩) 21 and 23 respectively.

[6] See "Table 3, Transaction volume for the international transaction log" *Annual report of the administrator of the international transaction log under the Kyoto Protocol: Note by the secretariat* (27 November 2008) UN Doc FCCC/KP/CMP/2008/7 (available at ⟨http://unfccc.int⟩) 10, indicating that of the 12,049 transactions that took place from November 2007 to October 2008, more than three quarters were in a single month (October 2008).

[7] *Trail Smelter* (United States v. Canada) (1941) 3 Reports of International Arbitral Awards 1905, reprinted in (1941) 35 AJIL 684.

Conference on the Law of the Sea narrowly failed to do) was needed,[8] and stoutly advocated the superiority of the 'free competition' model on the high seas (that is, one that does not rule out States acting jointly to regulate or limit their catch of fish, but applies any limit equally to vessels of all flags—what is now termed an Olympic fishery).[9] Even to modern eyes this phrase remains rhetorically seductive—but only until we remember, as Barnes's paper sets out, that in the absence of property rights this dooms high seas fisheries management efforts to failure through the tragedy of the commons.[10] Soon afterwards, Oda's growing awareness of the flaw in this model was crystallised in his admission of defeat at an early conference of the Law of the Sea Institute by the problem of allocation when new entrants emerge in an existing fishery.[11] That even such an eminent jurist could confess himself unable to resolve it is not surprising because, in terms of the classical principles of international law, notably the high seas freedom of fishing, it does indeed appear to be insuperable in substance—an archetypal who-gets-what, i.e. political, question.[12] Restated in economic terms, the problem stems from the open-access nature of high seas fisheries, which the residual character that the legal freedom has since acquired does nothing to alter. The growing number of exclusive economic zones (EEZs) in the 1970s and 1980s and the continued depletion of fish stocks within them means that the share of the world's fish catch taken on the high seas is likely to have grown beyond the 8–10 % estimated by the Food and Agriculture Organization of the United Nations (FAO) in 1994 for the United Nations Conference on Straddling Fish Stocks and Highly Migratory Fish Stocks (Fish Stocks Conference),[13] a figure that itself had risen from less than 1 % on 1972 catch data.[14] Finally, in the context of more general criticisms of the drafting of the fisheries provisions of the LOS Convention, Judge Oda speculated a quarter of a century ago on the consequence of their failure to deal with the question of allocation.

---

[8] S. Oda *International Control of Sea Resources* (A.W. Sijthoff, Leiden: 1963) 139.

[9] See e.g. *ibid.*, 60, 63–64 and 80.

[10] Paper by R. Barnes in this volume at 87 ff, esp. at 89.

[11] S. Oda "Distribution of Fish Resources of the High Seas: Free Competition or Artificial Quota?" in L.M. Alexander (ed) *The Law of the Sea: The Future of the Sea's Resources: Proceedings of the Second Annual Conference of the Law of the Sea Institute* (University of Rhode Island, Kingston: 1968) 29.

[12] This is not, however, to say that law simply disappears from the picture. Procedurally, through the availability—where it exists—of compulsory dispute settlement, law has an important role to play in giving competing parties an incentive to reach political agreement.

[13] "Some High Seas Fisheries Aspects relating to Straddling Fish Stocks and Highly Migratory Fish Stocks" (15 June 1993) UN Doc A/CONF.164/INF/4 in J.-P. Lévy and G. Schram *United Nations Conference on Straddling Fish Stocks and Highly Migratory Fish Stocks: Selected Documents* (Martinus Nijhoff Publishers, Boston: 1996) 377–396 at 378, paragraph 4.

[14] J. Gulland "Letter to the editor: How much of the world's fisheries lies within EEZs?" (1984) 8 *Marine Policy* 359.

This, he thought, was that sooner or later high seas fisheries would have to be brought under the same type of regime as Part XI of the LOS Convention had just instituted for the mineral resources of the deep sea-bed:

> Surely, discussions similar to those now taking place on seabed mineral resources will eventually be held on the new concept of the common heritage of mankind as applicable to ocean fishing.[15]

This presupposes unification of ownership or at least management of the resource by an international authority in which States pool their rights in respect of the stock. As there is no single organisation competent to administer international fisheries,[16] the intermediate solution adopted in the Fish Stocks Agreement[17] is to strengthen the role of regional fisheries management commissions, by requiring States fishing for the stocks covered either to join them or to cooperate with their management measures. Despite the drawback that, under Article 34 of the Vienna Convention on the Law of Treaties,[18] this rule applies only among the parties to the Agreement, it is possible that the qualification on its general applicability has been resolved if Rayfuse's argument on the customary status of Article 8, paragraphs 3 and 4 is correct. For her review of State practice shows that fisheries commissions all now "demand either membership, cooperation or abstention [from fishing] from non-members" who in turn have in several ways "acquiesced in these assertions of jurisdiction".[19] Be that as it may, tension is likely to remain between the proprietorial attitude towards quota exhibited by existing participants who wish to exclude

---

[15] S. Oda "Fisheries under the United Nations Convention on the Law of the Sea" (1983) 77 *AJIL* 739–755 at 755. Hayashi, however, has more recently come to the opposite conclusion: M. Hayashi "Three Decades' Progress in High Seas Fisheries Governance: Towards a Common Heritage Regime?" in M.H. Nordquist, J. Norton Moore and S. Mahmoudi (eds) *The Stockholm Declaration and Law of the Marine Environment* (Martinus Nijhoff Publishers, The Hague, London and New York: 2003) 375–398 at 392.

[16] An early chance to create one offered by the International Law Commission (ILC) was missed (see notes 22-26 infra and accompanying text). Note, however, the suggestions made by speakers at the 2005 Conference on the Governance of High Seas Fisheries and the Fish Stocks Agreement that the FAO or the UN General Assembly should act as a residual body able to step in to impose emergency conservation measures on States concerned when there is no existing organisation covering the fishery in question on the high seas with the competence to do so: M.W. Lodge and S.N. Nandan "Some Suggestions Towards Better Implementation of the United Nations Agreement on Straddling Fish Stocks and Highly Migratory Fish Stocks of 1995" (2005) 20 *International Journal of Marine and Coastal Law* 345–380 at 373 and E.J. Molenaar "Addressing Regulatory Gaps in High Seas Fisheries" *ibid.*, 533–570 at 551.

[17] Agreement for the Implementation of the Provisions of the United Nations Convention on the Law of the Sea of 10 December 1982 Relating to the Conservation and Management of Straddling Fish Stocks and Highly Migratory Fish Stocks of 4 August 1995 (2167 UNTS 3).

[18] Vienna Convention on the Law of Treaties of 23 May 1969 (1155 UNTS 331).

[19] R.G. Rayfuse *Non-Flag State Enforcement in High Seas Fisheries* (Leiden/Boston, Martinus Nijhoff Publishers: 2004) at 373.

outsiders to the extent possible,[20] and those outsiders who resist this as a solution to global overcapacity. Not wishing to be arbitrarily deprived of any future benefit from a fishery which they had no part in depleting, they prefer a solution much closer to a *tabula rasa* approach in which the existing investments in the fishery count for nothing.

Solutions to the Tragedy of the Commons

If absence of property rights is the problem at the root of the tragedy of the commons, then according to classical economics there are two possible ways to solve it by introducing such rights.[21] One is to retain the commons but impose restrictions on its use, including limitation and regulation of access. This entails imposition of control by some central entity over the right to enter, and a system of allocation designed to ensure that the carrying capacity of the commons is not exceeded. For fisheries, in theory, an international organisation could be established with power to regulate access to high seas fisheries. In economic parlance the organisation acts as a 'single owner'; provided that political considerations do not prevent it from rationally maximising the return from the fishery, it will have a natural incentive to conserve the resource.

In fact something similar was originally proposed by the International Law Commission (ILC) in the 1950s for any fisheries on which Governments could not agree. In its 1951 Draft Articles on the Continental Shelf and Related Subjects, article 2 on 'Resources of the Sea' was in the following terms:

> Competence should be conferred on a permanent international body to conduct continuous investigations of the world's fisheries and the methods employed in exploiting them. Such body should also be empowered to make regulations for conservatory measures to be applied by the States whose nationals are engaged in fishing in any particular area where the States concerned are unable to agree among themselves.[22]

Paragraph 3 of the accompanying commentary stated that:

---

[20] An initial allocation of quota only to existing participants implicitly recognises their property rights: G.R. Morgan "Optimal fisheries quota allocation under a transferable quota management system" (1995) 19 *Marine Policy* 379–390 at 380.

[21] H.G. Knight *Managing the Sea's Living Resources: Legal and Political Aspects of High Seas Fisheries* (Lexington Books, Lexington MA and Toronto: 1977) 3–4.

[22] Draft Articles on the Continental Shelf and Related Subjects, Annex to the Report of the International Law Commission covering the work of its third session in *Yearbook of the International Law Commission 1951, Vol II* (United Nations, New York: 1957) 143. The history of the ILC's work on the law of the sea is related by Oda, note 8 supra, at 83–89.

> This system [i.e. of regulation being left to the States concerned] might prove ineffective if the interested States were unable to reach agreement. The best way of overcoming the difficulty would be to set up a permanent body which, in the event of disagreement, would be competent to submit rules which the States would be required to observe in respect of fishing activities by their nationals in the waters in question. This matter would seem to lie within the general competence of the United Nations Food and Agriculture Organization.[23]

In the ILC's 1953 report the text of draft article 3, as it had by then become, read:

> States shall be under a duty to accept, as binding upon their nationals, any system of regulation of fisheries in any area of the high seas which an international authority, to be created within the framework of the United Nations, shall prescribe as being essential for the purpose of protecting the fishing resources of that area against waste or extermination. Such international authority shall act at the request of any interested State.[24]

Hard though it is to imagine a similar reaction today, the only opposition to this came from a minority within the ILC who "contended that the proposal to give an international authority power to issue regulations binding on the nationals of States was in conflict with the basic principles of international law"; it elicited not even a single objection from any Government:

> [I]t is significant of the present state of opinion and of the widely felt need for the removal of what is considered by many to be a condition approaching anarchy, that in the replies sent by governments, no opposition was voiced against the proposals then advanced by the Commission.[25]

In its comprehensive overhaul of the draft articles in the wake of the 1955 International Technical Conference on the Living Resources of the Sea (Rome Conference),[26] however, the ILC abandoned the idea of an international organisation in favour of compulsory arbitration.

---

[23] *Ibid.*, 143.

[24] Report of the International Law Commission covering the work of its fifth session in *Yearbook of the International Law Commission 1953, Vol II* (United Nations, New York: 1959) 218.

[25] *Ibid.*, paras 97 and 99; see also at 241–269 of Annex II to the 1953 report "Comments by Governments on the draft articles on the continental shelf and related subjects prepared by the International Law Commission at its third session in 1951".

[26] The Conference was convened by the UN General Assembly in its Resolution 900 (IX) of 14 December 1954 in order to "study the problem of the international conservation of the living resources of the sea and to make appropriate scientific and technical recommendations." Based on this report, García Amador, a Cuban member of the ILC who had been Deputy Chairman of the Rome Conference, submitted to the ILC's 1955 session new draft articles which were adopted with minor amendments: Report of the International Law Commission covering the work of its seventh session reprinted in *Yearbook of the International Law Commission 1955, Vol II* (United Nations, New York: 1960) 29–31; see also Oda, note 8 at 86.

The other solution is to establish private property rights, but, since the high seas are not subject to appropriation,[27] this option has for the moment no equivalent in international fisheries. Yet it is not as novel as one might think. In the view of Knight, writing in the 1970s at the time of the Third United Nations Conference on the Law of the Sea (UNCLOS III), the fishery commissions of the day, though imperfect, had by and large achieved their objectives for a time, but in the past decade unrestrained increases in fishing effort had:

> seriously reduced certain fish stocks in spite of the conservation regulations. It seems abundantly clear that some new device is needed—a means of controlling fishing effort and effectively enforcing regulations on all those fishing common resources.[28]

As to what that means might be, Knight discerned an evolutionary process applying to the whole law of the sea, moving through four phases: (1) unrestricted and unregulated freedom; (2) reasonable use; (3) regulated use; (4) establishment of property rights,[29] but appeared unsure of what stage the process had reached.[30] He saw that, when overcrowding begins to result in conflict or economic waste, and regulation is insufficient or unattainable, property rights would be required for rational and efficient management. Allocation of harvesting rights among participating States would be a theoretical solution to the open access problem, Knight wrote, and there were instances on record where States had accepted the need to establish quotas and done so by negotiation, each pressing "within the context of its own national priorities for the maximum allocation of the stocks in which it has the greatest interest". There was, however, no legal barrier to entry of new States to the fishery, which "usually renders ineffective the conservation and allocation system agreed on by the parties". He correctly foresaw that:

> the problem of the new entrant is likely to become more severe in the next two decades as a result of developing countries' emphasis on fishery industries coupled with technical assistance from F.A.O. and other organizations.[31]

The enclosure of the EEZ was a necessary though not sufficient condition for controlling fishing effort, bringing with it some if not all of the advantages of property rights, and assisting the creation of the latter by coastal States that were so minded. Acknowledging the EEZ as a major step in this direction, Knight nonetheless doubted whether isolated property systems would be

---

[27] Article 89 of the LOS Convention provides that "No State may validly purport to subject any part of the high seas to its sovereignty."

[28] Knight, note 21 at 48.

[29] *Ibid.*, 27.

[30] *Ibid.*, 28 (just entering the third phase) and 95 ("well into" the fourth phase).

[31] *Ibid.*, 42–44.

sufficient without some interlinking set of international standards to govern the national regulation of activities within each zone.[32] This doubt continues to be particularly apposite for straddling and highly migratory fish stocks, which move back and forth between EEZs and the high seas. As a result of the relative neglect of high seas fisheries at UNCLOS III, the change of most practical significance—the marked reduction in the area of the high seas—was in fact merely consequential on the creation of the EEZ. Within that reduced area the applicable law was little affected and thus the tragedy of the commons continued unabated.

The fundamentally economic nature of the problem has meant that it has not escaped the attention of the Organisation for Economic Co-operation and Development (OECD). From the empirical evidence it gathered for its 1997 study of the issue, the OECD concluded that:

> management regimes which limit the total catch, or the number of fishing vessels, or which restrict the efficiency of the harvesting sector, including technical measures [...], have generally yielded poor results when used in isolation [...]. The main reason [...] is that these regimes do not give the fisher the incentive to account for all the costs of his fishing activity.[33]

The findings of the study supported the introduction of "rights-based management systems" such as individual quotas, despite the added burden on governments through having to establish and maintain a legal framework for the rights, with a possible increase in administrative costs and the possibility of "structural adjustment consequences, including lower employment opportunities and distributional conflicts."[34] The recommended objective of regulation was to create economic incentives or legal sanctions to reduce externalities.[35]

The OECD elaborated:

> From an economic point of view, the basic reason why government regulations of the use of living marine resource [*sic*] are needed is that, in an unregulated fishery, the decisions made by individual fishers and groups of fishers result in economic overexploitation. [...] [B]ecause each fisher does not [...] pay for the resource he uses, he tends to use them to the point at which additional use would be of no additional value to him. This excludes higher valued uses by others, including the protection of the future abundance and productivity of the resource.[36]

---

[32] *Ibid.*, 29.

[33] OECD, *Towards Sustainable Fisheries: Economic Aspects of the Management of Living Resources* (OECD, Paris: 1997) 9–10.

[34] *Ibid.*, 10.

[35] *Ibid.*, 12. Where costs can be imposed on others, they are known in economic terms as 'externalities'. In this case they are imposed on other fishing operators, the rest of society and the environment: *ibid.*, at 11.

[36] *Ibid.*, 62.

As an alternative to property-like rights for States to participate in high seas fisheries, i.e. a permanent but alienable share of the total allowable catch (TAC) or effort, it is conceivable that allocation could be made directly by the fishery commission to individuals or companies sponsored by its member States, which ideally would guarantee their performance (a motivation to choose wisely whom they sponsor). Despite the precedent for this solution in the LOS Convention's provisions on deep sea-bed mining, notably Annex III, for the foreseeable future it remains unlikely that States will voluntarily relinquish their role as middlemen. Nor has there been any detectable enthusiasm for the similar proposal of Crothers and Nelson, namely the creation of a series of regional ocean organisations which become beneficial owners of the high seas resources by transforming the high seas freedom to fish of the States who are their members into a right to a share of the profits.[37] Barnes rightly points to the difficulties that would arise if States remain the allocation holders,[38] e.g. it would make it very cumbersome for quotas to be traded from one national system into another, and without elaborately negotiated rules, one could expect there to be substantial confusion, at least initially, as to how and to whom an operator holding quota from more than one State, or a State having parted with its quota midway through a season, should account for its catch. On the other hand, Crothers and Nelson do not clearly state what under their scheme would become of existing fisheries commissions whose mandate extends to the high seas.

Ironically, while from an economic point of view it does not matter who is the 'owner'—a high seas equivalent of the International Seabed Authority which can manage the living resources on a common heritage basis on behalf of its member States and subject to their direction, or empowering fisheries commissions to carve up catch shares among individual owners, be they States or operators—each will be opposed on ideological grounds by different blocs of States. All that can be ventured is an educated guess: that a sudden crisis in the

---

[37] G.T. Crothers and L. Nelson "High Seas Fisheries Governance: A Framework for the Future?" (2006) 21 *Marine Resource Economics* 341–354. A similar idea was considered a third of a century earlier by A.W. Koers, *International Regulation of Marine Fisheries: A Study of Regional Fisheries Organizations* (Fishing News Books Ltd, West Byfleet and London: 1973) 253–258, but he concluded that it:

> would be required to function within an extra-legal context which would be largely unforeseeable at the time of its creation and [...] would have a virtual monopoly, the price of the organization's failure could be disaster. This also explains why States will be extremely reluctant to create such an organization (*ibid.*, 257).

This made it "at best a blueprint for a remote future, although not necessarily [...] for utopia." (*ibid.*, 258).

[38] Paper by R. Barnes in this volume at 107 and 128.

form of, say, the near-simultaneous collapse of multiple fisheries may generate a surge of support for a common heritage regime, but in any other case the slow drift towards transferable rights is likely to continue. Yet, to the extent that this movement may in large part be unwitting, it may well not survive attention being drawn to it, since the concept of property rights continues to be resisted by States even while they use arguments relying at bottom on notions of vested rights to justify maintaining their existing catch shares. Once this contradiction is brought out into the open, it is not clear whether States will drop their rhetoric hostile to property rights so as to match their actions, or cease taking actions that are at odds with their rhetoric.

Saying One Thing, Doing Another?

With discussion of the issue happening already in a number of commissions, its progress is less likely to encounter the sorts of objections enumerated by the OECD,[39] which are not automatically translatable to the international level. Firstly, there is no reason to expect resistance from current members, even those whose fisheries are less profitable than those of potential new entrants, as the choice to retain or sell all or part of their national allocation will remain one for them alone.[40] If a member considers that it receives significant non-monetary benefits from participating in the fishery, such as satisfying a social imperative to maintain employment in economically depressed fishing villages, it can be expected and is entitled to resist offers. Secondly, while the wider concerns about the fairness of reserving an open-access resource for a privileged few with capital investment in the fishery and excluding all others have more substance, these can be met with two arguments: (a) at the international level those wanting to enter the fishery will most likely have made their investments already, and in any event there are few international fisheries in a healthy enough state for new investment in them to be encouraged; (b) their exclusion, if such it is, comes about not merely as a result of any action by the fisheries commission, but by the effect on that action of a parallel development: the putative elaboration of the customary rule of cooperation in international fisheries law into a requirement that non-members abide by non-discriminatory rules of a commission if they are to fish. This test should be

---

[39] OECD, note 33 at 79.

[40] This is not to say that such resistance if it occurs would be surprising; one reason for it might be that, to the extent that the initial allocation is made on the basis of past declared catch, it would effectively penalise underreporting: R. Falloon (with the assistance of T.M. Berthold) "Individual Transferable Quotas: the New Zealand Case" in OECD, *The Use of Individual Quotas in Fisheries Management* (OECD, Paris: 1993) 43–62 at 46.

met by a commission that is open to new entrants to join, by either becoming a full member of the commission or subscribing to any formal cooperation mechanism that it operates, thus becoming eligible to purchase quota from existing members.

In the longer term, the commission may well be able to capture some of the resource rent generated and distribute it among the commission members; ideally, non-members, even those not interested in fishing at all, should be able to become eligible for a modest share of this surplus by joining the cooperation mechanism, in effect trading any residual high seas freedom of fishing for this revenue stream.[41] Beyond that, it is possible to imagine a future legal rule in which monetary or other payments would be a way of compensating States for their compulsory exclusion from a share of the maximum sustainable yield,[42] though the question of how to calculate the quantum of compensation is likely to remain vexed for many years and delay the emergence of any such rule.

Few predictions can be ventured with confidence, but if one proceeds from the reasonable assumption that the prevalence of anti-property-rights rhetoric reflects a continuing sentimental attachment to the freedom of fishing, then open calls to end it are not likely to be heeded any time soon, though more subtle prescriptions stand a better chance of success.[43] Such calls also disregard the very significant change in State practice concerning new entrants over the last 50 years. One has only to contrast the failure of the arguments advanced by the United States in the 1950s to convince the world to adopt its abstention

[41] See the discussion of the Crothers and Nelson proposal above. It is suggested, however, that an overt creation of property rights at a stroke would be more likely to provoke opposition than the gradual development of them by the existing commissions themselves, particularly through trading, as it may not be until years later that a 'Molière moment' occurs, in the way that Monsieur Jourdain resisted the idea of employing prose, only to discover that this was precisely what he had been doing all his life: "Par ma foi! il y a plus de quarante ans que je dis de la prose sans que j'en susse rien, et je vous suis le plus obligé du monde de m'avoir appris cela." (Molière, *Le Bourgeois Gentilhomme* (1670) Act II, Scene 4).

[42] Having rejected a related idea, Koers instead proposed transferable rights of access to fully exploited stocks and levies for fishing them (as agent of the world community), which would be set at a level that made it equally attractive to fish or simply collect revenue, but adjusting this for the risks of fishing, so that the average fishing return should be somewhat higher (Koers, note 37, at 301–303). This revenue Koers would have distributed under a formula basing a State's share on a 'reverse' relationship with its share in total world catch and *per capita* national income. Nonetheless, it was "crucial" that any limitation of entry be effected at the global level, because "[...] it should not be left to fishing nations alone to decide to what extent non-fishing States would have access to the wealth of the sea's living resources" (*ibid.*, 311).

[43] See e.g. the attenuated form in which this call is reflected in the first of the ten principles adopted by the International Union for the Conservation of Nature (IUCN) at its October 2008 Barcelona congress (available at ⟨www.iucn.org⟩) which includes the statement that enjoyment of high seas freedoms should become "condition[ed] [...] on the implementation [...] of the duties" set out in the LOS Convention.

doctrine with the silence in response to the neo-abstentionist resolutions of the two North Atlantic non-tuna fisheries commissions advising new entrants to expect allocations only of newly exploited or still unallocated stocks. The Northwest Atlantic Fisheries Organization (NAFO)[44] adopted the following resolution at its 21st annual meeting in 1999:

1. NAFO is an open organization. Non-members may join the organization by depositing an instrument of accession in accordance with Article XXII of the Convention. In accordance with Article IV of the Convention, all Contracting Parties are Members of the General Council.
2. Should any new member of NAFO obtain membership in the Fisheries Commission, in accordance with Article XIII(1) of the Convention, such a new member should be aware that presently, and for the foreseeable future, stocks managed by NAFO are fully allocated, and fishing opportunities for new members are likely to be limited, for instance, to new fisheries (stocks not currently allocated by TAC/quota or effort control), and the "Others" category under the NAFO Quota Allocation Table.[45]

More recently the North-East Atlantic Fisheries Commission (NEAFC),[46] at its 22nd Annual Meeting in 2003 adopted a document entitled "Guidelines for the expectation of future new Contracting Parties with regard to fishing opportunities in the NEAFC Regulatory Area" whose operative paragraphs are reproduced below:

> Non Contracting Parties of NEAFC should be aware that presently and for the foreseeable future, stocks regulated by NEAFC are fully allocated, and fishing opportunities for new members likely to be limited to new fisheries (stocks not currently allocated),
>
> New Contracting Parties will participate, on the same basis as existing Contracting Parties, in future allocations of stocks which are unregulated at the time when the application is made,
>
> New Contracting Parties who were previously Cooperating Non Contracting Parties may request an allocation of a part of the relevant Co-operative quota. Such allocations will be done on a case by case basis.[47]

---

[44] Created by the Convention on Future Multilateral Cooperation in the Northwest Atlantic Fisheries of 24 October 1978 (1135 UNTS 369).

[45] NAFO "Resolution to Guide the Expectations of Future New Members with Regard to Fishing Opportunities in the NAFO Regulatory Area" in NAFO *Annual Report 1999* (NAFO, Dartmouth: 1999) (available at ⟨www.nafo.int⟩) 62. The Convention referred to is that in the previous footnote. Article XIII(1) limits membership of the Fishery Commission to those parties who either participate in the fisheries of the Regulatory Area defined in Article I(1) and (2), or satisfy the General Council at an annual meeting that they expect to do so in that or the next year.

[46] Created by the Convention on Future Multilateral Cooperation in the Northeast Atlantic Fisheries of 18 November 1980 (1285 UNTS 129).

[47] See NEAFC *Report of the 22nd Annual Meeting of the NEAFC, Vol. I, Main Report* (10–

These conditions are extremely restrictive, coming very close to a suggestion from Norway that "The message to new entrants should be: future members cannot have a share in stocks that are already regulated."[48] In essence, new members that were previously cooperating non-contracting parties are restricted to part of the relevant cooperative quota which is subtracted from that quota for this purpose, leaving even less for future new entrants. In other words, "to be blunt, a just and reasonable share of the TACs for new entrants is interpreted largely as being what is left over."[49] But not even this goes as far as the proposal of several unidentified NAFO Members not to share the benefits of the access to the stocks even if they recover, "in recognition of their [Members'] restraints and contributions to conservation",[50] which rightly provoked Molenaar's scorn: "irresponsible management in the past thereby provides a justification for minimising allocations to new participants in the present and future."[51]

Attitudes such as these when adopted by commissions would seem on the face of it to make it improbable that they would be accepted as legitimately advancing the general interest rather than just their own—as would be necessary, Barnes explains, if their regulations are to take on any sort of objective status binding on all comers.[52] Remarkably, however, there is no evidence of any State objecting to its exclusion from a share of the catch in the NAFO and NEAFC fisheries on the basis of the documents quoted above. The likeliest explanation is that, by comparison with the 1950s, a much larger number of States now have a stake in one international fishery or another and see on

14 November 2003) (available at ⟨archive.neafc.org⟩) 26–27. The Guidelines are not included in the report of the 2003 Annual Meeting, but are also available on the NEAFC website.

[48] See NEAFC *Draft Summary Records, Meeting of the Working Group on the Future of the North-East Atlantic Fisheries Commission* (NEAFC, London: 2003) (available at ⟨archive.neafc.org⟩) 3, part of an informative discussion of the issue reported *in extenso* at 1–4.

[49] G. Munro, A. van Houtte and R. Willmann "The Conservation and Management of Shared Fish Stocks: Legal and Economic Aspects" (2004) *FAO Fisheries Technical Paper* no. 465 47.

[50] NAFO *Report of the Working Group on Allocation of Fishing Rights to Contracting Parties of NAFO and Chartering of Vessels Between Contracting Parties* (NAFO, Halifax: 13–15 April 1999) NAFO/GC Doc. 99/4 (unpublished, copy supplied by NAFO Secretariat on file with author) 4, opposing the original United States proposal *ibid.*, which envisaged broader sharing should the stocks recover; see also E.J. Molenaar, "The Concept of "Real Interest" and Other Aspects of Co-operation through Regional Fisheries Management Mechanisms" (2000) 15 *International Journal of Marine and Coastal Law* 515–516.

[51] Molenaar, note 50, at 516. Molenaar contrasts the position in the International Commission for the Conservation of Atlantic Tunas (ICCAT), where those States apt to be excluded by such a policy were already in the commission and thus able to mount the obvious arguments to counter it (*ibid.*, 520). The authors of FAO Fisheries Technical Paper 465, note 49, however, would argue that only in this way can existing participants have sufficient incentive to limit their catches to allow the stocks' recovery at all.

[52] Paper by R. Barnes in this volume at 134.

balance more benefit from shoring up their position by excluding newcomers from those, even at the price of their own exclusion from fisheries they have not themselves yet entered. Applebaum may therefore have been ahead of his time in treating abstention as custom (without using the word) where a fishery is managed by a commission.[53]

Yet, while it is one thing to object to locking-up of a high seas fishery by its first exploiters, it is another to find an alternative mechanism by which the tragedy of the commons can be averted. If new entrants cannot be excluded from a fisheries commission, the situation is:

> uncomfortably close to that of a fishery wholly confined to coastal state waters in which the coastal state authorities establish and enforce a TAC, but exert no control over fleet size.[54]

Although 'abstention' is a word for which one searches in vain in modern fisheries commission meeting reports and papers from the Fish Stocks Conference, objectively it is the inspiration for the 'real interest' requirement in Article 8, paragraph 3 of the Fish Stocks Agreement which is the new entrant's *entrée* card to the relevant fisheries commission.[55] The true character of the "fully subscribed" argument becomes apparent when these non-members join the commissions or avail themselves of the increasingly formalised procedures for cooperation with them that Article 8 has inspired.[56] For, in the words of

---

[53] R. Applebaum "The Straddling Stocks Problem: The Northwest Atlantic Situation, International Law, and Options for Coastal State Action" in A.H.A. Soons (ed), *Implementation of the Law of the Sea Convention through International Organizations: Proceedings of the 23rd Annual Conference of the Law of the Sea Institute, June 12–15, 1989, Noordwijk aan Zee, The Netherlands* (Honolulu, Law of the Sea Institute, University of Hawaii: 1990) 282–317 at 303.

[54] V. Kaitala and G.R. Munro "The Management of High Seas Fisheries" (1993) 8 *Marine Resource Economics* 313–329 at 320.

[55] Text following note 17. Nevertheless, it is submitted that to equate the cumulative effect of the pertinent provisions of the Fish Stocks Agreement itself with abstention, as does Y. Tsuru "Rethinking the Principle of Abstention: The North Pacific and Beyond" (2004) 28 *Marine Policy* 541–552 at 542 and 548, is an oversimplification. They do not close the door to new entrants, but subject their entry to the requirement of cooperation with existing participants through the relevant commission. Leaving aside the uncertain definition of 'real interest', however, it cannot be that abstaining from entering a fishery altogether is the only way to cooperate with the existing participants.

[56] Such formalised procedures exist in ICCAT "Resolution by ICCAT on Becoming a Cooperating Party, Entity or Fishing Entity" (Annex 5–17 to *Report of the Fifteenth Regular Meeting of the Commission* (14–21 November 1997) Madrid, Spain) in ICCAT *Report for Biennial Period 1996–1997 Part II—Vol. 1* (1997) 79, as well as in the Commission for the Conservation of Southern Bluefin Tuna (CCSBT) "Resolution to Establish the Status of Co-operating Non-Member of the Extended Commission and the Extended Scientific Committee" (Attachment 7 to *Report of the Extended Commission of the Tenth Annual Meeting of the Commission* (7–10 October 2003) Christchurch, New Zealand) (available at ⟨http://www.ccsbt.org⟩) and the Commission for the Conservation and Management of Highly Migratory Fish Stocks in the Western and Central

Butterworth and Penney,[57] this simply transforms what has hitherto been a 'non-member problem' into a 'new member problem', namely how 'old' members can retain their existing shares of the catch if its absolute level cannot rise to accommodate newcomers because there is no surplus. Coastal States are grudgingly admitted by virtue of their geographical location to have a real interest, and in the International Commission for the Conservation of Atlantic Tunas (ICCAT) at least the visible result of this to date is the 2001 Criteria for Allocation of Fishing Opportunities and the allocation Recommendations based on it,[58] but other new members without a catch history from the relevant stock are told that they lack a real interest and therefore have no business fishing it in future. In this way limited entry to the fishery is achieved on the international plane, but only by depriving some potential new entrants of the possibility of even acquiring a "real interest".

Let the Debate Begin

To conclude, we now seem to be poised at a delicate moment in the history of international fisheries law, where the consequences of the divergence between States' rhetoric and their concrete actions could take us in one of two directions. To those favouring creation of property rights irrespective of the past responsibility of the holder for overfishing, the continuation of current trends is a good thing—but if that depends on States continuing to be able to bring them about under a cloak of anti-property-rights rhetoric, then pragmatically the subject is best left alone and this contribution has done a disservice to the cause by casting light on it. Surely, however, the other direction is preferable—there is no case for property rights unless one is confident that they will pay their way, and that includes proper compensation for those who lose access to fish stocks by such a development. The present commentator is not opposed to the institution of property rights as a solution to the tragedy of the commons afflicting high seas fisheries, but only to the current state of affairs in which

Pacific Ocean (WCPFC) has its "Conservation and Management Measure 2004-02, Cooperating Non-Members" (WCPFC, Pohnpei: 2004) (available at ⟨www.wcpfc.int⟩). The same status in NEAFC is applied for via Article 34 of its 2008 Scheme of Control and Enforcement (available at ⟨www.neafc.org⟩) the latest in a succession of instruments containing such a provision.

[57] D.S. Butterworth and A.J. Penney "Allocation in high seas fisheries: avoiding meltdown" in A. Payne, C. O'Brien and S. Rogers (eds) *Management of Shared Fish Stocks* (Blackwell Publishing Ltd, Oxford: 2003) 165–189 at 170.

[58] ICCAT "ICCAT Criteria for the Allocation of Fishing Possibilities" (Annex 8 to *Proceedings of the 17th Regular Meeting of the International Commission for the Conservation of Atlantic Tunas* (12–19 November 2001) Murcia, Spain) in ICCAT *Report for biennial period 2000–2001 Part II (2001)—Vol. 1* 211.

property rights are being unsystematically and fitfully consolidated through the collective hypocrisy of fishing States, who are not being held to account to the generality of States for their past over-exploitation, and with no prospect of compensation for those States affected by the loss of freedom of fishing. It is only marginally less objectionable if one believes that fishing States are acting this way because they do not realise the appropriative nature of this process in which they are engaged, though if this is true, then at least a debate would show whether they are willing to change course if it is pointed out to them. Since international law often ends up with second-best solutions, and the LOS Convention is replete with them, perhaps there is no reason to expect on this issue that things will be any different. In particular, if the States that on the foregoing analysis are the losers from this development fail to react, that can be taken as evidence that they put only a low value on their lost rights. But it should not be too much to hope that, if the economic gains from restoring fisheries to maximum sustainable yield through property rights live up to their proponents' advocacy of them, then such rights should be openly adopted by a conscious decision of the relevant international bodies after full debate, and with proper compensation for those who lose by it. By contrast, where the gains in a given international fishery do not easily outweigh the compensation due, that should give grounds for second thoughts about the wisdom of pressing ahead. The Barnes paper is to be welcomed as a thought-provoking point of departure for participants in such a debate.

ENTITLEMENTS TO MARINE LIVING RESOURCES—COMMENTARY ON RICHARD BARNES

Louise A. de La Fayette*

The amount of research underlying this report is truly impressive. However, one cannot help thinking that it is largely misplaced. In my view, the concept of 'property rights' is not a useful way to approach the increasingly serious problem of over-exploitation and even depletion of marine living resources on the high seas. Conceptually, fisheries resources on the high seas belong collectively to the international community. States have the right for their nationals to fish on the high seas, but they also have the responsibility to conserve and manage those fisheries by controlling their nationals and by cooperating with other states to ensure that the fisheries are exploited sustainably. Many States, perhaps most, have not fulfilled their responsibilities, with the catastrophic consequences we see today. Some scientists have predicted that, if drastic measures are not taken, all the world's fisheries will collapse by 2050.[1] The rapidly deteriorating condition of international fisheries must be addressed with utmost urgency.

The granting of property rights over fish, or individual transferable quotas (ITQs) to fishing vessels has been proposed as a solution to this problem. ITQs have been used, with mixed results, in a few jurisdictions. Yet, even within national jurisdiction, where a coastal State theoretically has absolute control over fishing, certain grave limitations of this 'tool' have been observed. Economists theorise that if individual fishers, companies or vessels are given 'property rights' over a certain amount of fish, or percentage of fishing opportunities in a certain area, they will have an interest in ensuring that the stock remains healthy and will fish in a sustainable manner. There is little evidence that this is the case.

Two sources of over-fishing are over-capacity (too many boats chasing too few fish) and the use of an 'Olympic fishery' approach. An Olympic fishery is a race among fishing vessels to catch as many fish as possible before the catch limit is reached. An authority will set a total allowable catch (TAC), and

* Visiting Professor, Maritime Institute, University of Greenwich, London.

[1] B. Worm *et al.* "Impacts of Biodiversity Loss on Ocean Ecosystem Services" (3 November 2006) 314 *Science* No. 5800 787–790.

Alex G. Oude Elferink and Erik J. Molenaar (eds.), *The International Legal Regime of Areas beyond National Jurisdiction: Current and Future Developments*, pp. 159–162.

a possibly unlimited[2] number of boats rush out to take as many fish as possible until the authority calls a halt to the fishing, on the basis that the reported catch has reached the TAC. Economists argue that giving a limited number of vessels an absolute right to take a certain number of fish (individual quotas) will eliminate over-fishing. The fishing boats will take the authorised amount of fish and then stop. They will do so, because they 'own' (have a property right in) their quotas and will wish to ensure that there is no over-fishing, so that they can continue to fish their quotas the following year(s). At least, that is the theory.

However, the reality is quite different and rather more complex. Giving a limited number of ships a right to take a specific amount of fish each can certainly help to reduce over-capacity as well as to reduce the amount of fish taken by legally licensed vessels, provided that they do not over-fish their quotas. However, this measure is not a panacea and in reality may not prevent over-exploitation or even depletion of the fishery. There are a number of defects in the ITQ system and a considerable number of problems causing the depletion of international fisheries are not even addressed. Furthermore, the idea that economists have the solution to every problem is an idealistic fantasy. Economists are not the solution; most often, they are the problem, as evinced by the current global economic crisis. Real life is more complicated and chaotic than they imagine. Unfortunately, most human beings are irrational and short-sighted, and fishermen find it difficult to accept that the conservation of fisheries is in their best interests.

The first problem not addressed by the ITQ system is the setting of the TACs above the limits recommended by scientists. The main source of over-exploitation is the politicians' propensity to ignore scientific advice and to set TACs that are far too high. This happens regularly every year in many parts of the world, despite abundant evidence that the result will be a disaster. For example, every year the EU fisheries ministers adopt TACs that are higher than those advised by scientists and the European Commission, not only for European fisheries, but also for those abroad regulated by regional fisheries management organisations (RFMOs). Therefore, even with individual quotas and if all fishermen kept to their quotas, over-fishing would result. Politicians adopt these disastrous decisions because of pressure from fishermen who focus only on the current year's fishing.

Second, even with ITQs, there would still be a problem of abuse. Many people abuse and over-use their own property. During the negotiations for the

[2] Under some regimes, for example the Commission for the Conservation of Antarctic Marine Living Resources (CCAMLR), the number of vessels may also be limited, if only due to administrative requirements (information provided by E.J. Molenaar).

United Nations Convention on the Law of the Sea (LOS Convention),[3] it was believed that if coastal States were given sovereign rights over fisheries within their Exclusive Economic Zones (EEZs), they would manage the fisheries responsibly and sustainably. This did not happen. Judge Treves also made this point. *Vide* the formerly great Canadian Grand Banks cod and other fisheries in the Northwest Atlantic. Scientific advice was ignored, over-capacity was supported, and the fisheries collapsed. Almost twenty years later, they still have not recovered. Every year, this example is cited to EU fisheries ministers and every year, it is ignored. Like coastal States, fishermen cannot be expected to manage their fishing responsibly. History demonstrates that they will tend to abuse their rights and will over-fish and misreport, if they are not strictly controlled, which is the third point.

Third, even with ITQs, the quota limits would have to be strictly enforced, because fishermen will tend to over-fish, and to take the wrong kind of fish, either deliberately or inadvertently. They will also underreport and misreport. If they catch 20,000 tonnes of cod, they will report 10,000 tonnes of cod, or any number of tonnes of something else. Active monitoring, control and surveillance will still be necessary, as will observers, satellite tracking and port inspections. Fishermen cannot be trusted to control themselves. Strict enforcement would be required. Unfortunately, many States cannot or will not control their fishing vessels, which is the next point.

Fourth, there is the problem of States of non-compliance. Many States are unwilling or unable to control fishing vessels flying their flags and do not adequately enforce fishing regulations. ITQs will not address this problem.

Fifth, ITQs will not address the problem of bycatch and discards: the incidental catch of either fish outside the quota when another type of fish is targeted, or unwanted fish, mammals or birds caught in non-selective gear and thrown back into the sea dead or dying. These issues would have to be addressed by special measures.

Sixth, ITQs will not address the problems of over-capacity or illegal, unreported and unregulated (IUU) fishing and may even exacerbate them, if fishermen and fishing vessels formerly fishing legally are crowded out by ITQs and simply continue fishing illegally, either in the same sea area or elsewhere. Measures would have to be taken to remove the excess number of vessels from service and to find alternative employment for the fishermen. However, the existing IUU fishing problem supported by flags of non-compliance would remain and would have to be addressed by the sorts of measures now being adopted by the Food and Agriculture Organization (FAO) and RFMOs.

---

[3] Adopted on 10 December 1982; 1833 UNTS 396.

Seventh, ITQs will not solve the problem of third parties. Even if RFMOs authorise their members to adopt ITQs, non-members may still allow their vessels to fish in the relevant area outside the ITQ system.

Eighth, as they would apply to individual target species, ITQs would not address the issues of conservation of biodiversity and the protection of ecosystem functioning. These would have to be tackled separately by coastal States and RFMOs.

Finally, the 'transferable' element of ITQs is extremely problematic. Although individual quotas applied to fishing boats might address the problem of over-fishing caused by over-capacity and the Olympic fishery to a certain extent, the ability to transfer quotas might cause more problems than it would solve. Large, well-financed fishing companies could buy up quotas from smaller operators to create very large enterprises with considerable economic power even better able to withstand any regulations that flag States and RFMOs might wish to impose. Furthermore, the rich would get richer and the poor would get poorer, which would have serious socio-economic consequences.

In conclusion, while ITQs might reduce over-capacity and over-fishing to a certain extent, they are not a panacea: regulation and enforcement by flag States and RFMOs would still be necessary. Holders of ITQs would not be able to manage the fisheries themselves and could not be expected to fish responsibly without strict enforcement and control.

Therefore, I would argue for individual *non-transferable* quotas for fishing vessels administered by flag States within the quotas granted by RFMOs to replace the current Olympic fisheries, within the context of a science-based TAC, plus strong institutional control, a comprehensive set of regulations to address all the problems outlined above, compliance mechanisms to ensure that flag States fulfil their responsibilities, and strong enforcement measures applied to all fishing vessels.

PART FOUR

COMPLIANCE WITH INTERNATIONAL REGULATIONS: ADDRESSING ENFORCEMENT GAPS IN THE LEGAL REGIME FOR AREAS BEYOND NATIONAL JURISDICTION

THE ANTHROPOCENE, AUTOPOIESIS AND THE DISINGENUOUSNESS OF THE GENUINE LINK: ADDRESSING ENFORCEMENT GAPS IN THE LEGAL RÈGIME FOR AREAS BEYOND NATIONAL JURISDICTION

Rosemary Rayfuse*

1. *The Anthropocene and Areas beyond National Jurisdiction*

The Earth has entered the anthropocene era: the era in which human activities have begun to have a significant global impact on the Earth's climate and ecosystems. According to the International Geosphere-Biosphere Programme:

> human activities are now so pervasive and profound in their consequences that they affect the Earth at a global scale in complex, interactive and apparently accelerating ways; humans now have the capacity to alter the Earth System in ways that threaten the very processes and components, both biotic and abiotic, upon which the human species depends.[1]

Covering more than 60 percent of the Earth's surface, the oceans comprise a complex, dynamic and vast component of the Earth's ecological system, second in size only to the global atmosphere. The oceans are a major provider of ecosystem services, food, mineral and other resources, and a major medium for global transportation and communication. Nevertheless, while once thought inexhaustible, unlimited and capable of supporting any human activity or use, it is now clear that the oceans are exhaustible and that increasing and intensifying human activities and uses are pushing the oceans to the limits of their ecological carrying capacity.

The adverse effects of activities such as over-fishing and destructive fishing practices and pollution of the marine environment have been well documented. In the fisheries context, more than 75 percent of the world's fish stocks are reported as already fully exploited or over-exploited or depleted

* Professor of International Law, Faculty of Law, University of New South Wales, Sydney.

[1] W.L. Steffen *et al. Global Change and the Earth System: A Planet Under Pressure* (IGBP Global Change Series) (Springer-Verlag, Berlin/Heidelberg/New York: 2004) 1.

Alex G. Oude Elferink and Erik J. Molenaar (eds.), *The International Legal Regime of Areas beyond National Jurisdiction: Current and Future Developments*, pp. 165–190.

and recovering from depletion.[2] Inadequate management, destructive fishing practices such as bottom trawling, and illegal, unreported and unregulated (IUU) fishing are to blame for a whole range of adverse effects on fish stocks and dependent and associated species and ecosystems. Other existing and emerging ocean uses pose other known and unknown risks to the marine environment, for example, ship source pollution, marine debris and noise pollution, ocean fertilisation, CO_2 sequestration, acoustic thermometry, construction of artificial islands and pipelines, offshore oil and gas exploration, seabed mining, bioprospecting and marine scientific research.[3] Indeed, increasing numbers of marine species are being listed as threatened or endangered[4] while fears are increasingly being expressed for the overall health of the oceans and their continued ability to provide the ecosystem services so vital to the continuation of life on Earth.[5]

Anthropogenic activities are not confined to areas under national jurisdiction, but are increasingly, and in some cases exclusively, carried out in areas beyond national jurisdiction (ABNJ).[6] On the high seas all States are entitled to enjoy the freedoms of navigation, overflight, laying of submarine cables and pipelines, construction of artificial islands or installations, fishing and marine scientific research, subject only to the conditions laid down in the United Nations Convention on the law of the sea, 1982 (LOS Convention)[7] and other rules of international law. The central feature of the high seas regime is that it is a common property, open access regime with equal right of user, where vessels are subject only to the jurisdiction of the State whose flag they fly. The central failing of the high seas regime is that it has led inexorably and inevitably to a 'tragedy of the commons', a tragedy which reliance on the principle of flag State jurisdiction has been unable to halt.

---

[2] FAO, *The State of World Fisheries and Aquaculture 2006* (FAO, Rome: 2007) (available at ⟨www.fao.org⟩).

[3] IUCN, *Co-Chair's Summary Report of the Workshop on High Seas Governance for the 21st Century* (IUCN, Gland: 2008) (available at ⟨www.iucn.org⟩).

[4] IUCN, *2007 Red List of Threatened Species* (IUCN, Gland: 2007) (available at ⟨www.iucn redlist.org/⟩).

[5] See eg C. Nellemann, S. Hain and J. Alder (eds) *In Dead Water—Merging of Climate Change with Pollution, Over-Harvest, and Infestations on the World's Fishing Grounds* (United Nations Environmental Programme, GRID-Arendal, Norway: 2008); and B. Worm *et al.* "Impacts of Biodiversity Loss on Ocean Ecosystem Services" (2006) 314(5800) *Science* 787–790.

[6] ABNJ include the deep sea bed beyond the continental shelf of States. However, this paper focuses on the issue of enforcement gaps in the context of the water column of the high seas.

[7] Adopted on 10 December 1982; 1833 UNTS 296.

This paper examines developments aimed at addressing enforcement gaps in the legal regime for ABNJ with particular reference to the principle of flag State jurisdiction.[8] These developments relate to both the substantive content of flag State jurisdiction and the role that can be taken by other, non-flag, States in situations in which a flag State is unwilling or unable to effectively exercise its jurisdiction. Against the broad backdrop of autopoietic theory, it will be demonstrated that these developments are both consistent with and necessary to the law of the sea's continued ability to meet the challenges posed by the anthropocene and the increasing impacts of human activities on the oceans.

2. *Autopoiesis and the Law of the Sea*

The theory of autopoiesis has its origins in the attempts by biologists to characterise the nature of living systems.[9] An autopoietic system is one in which the elements of the system "interact with each other in such a way as to continually produce and maintain the elements and the relationships between them".[10] An autopoietic system seeks not to generate something other than itself, but rather to generate the elements of itself through processes internal to and shaped by it in order to maintain a stable organised State over a long period of time. In other words, an autopoietic system is both shaped by and shapes the environment in which it exists.

Autopoietic theory has been applied in the social sciences,[11] and a number of authors have suggested its application to legal systems.[12] In this context,

---

[8] The principle of flag State jurisdiction is a natural corollary of the principle of the freedom of the high seas. As noted by the Permanent Court of Justice in the *Lotus* case:

> Vessels on the high seas are subject to no authority except that of the State whose flag they fly. In virtue of the principle of the freedom of the seas, that is to say the absence of any territorial sovereignty upon the high seas, no state may exercise any kind of jurisdiction over foreign vessels upon them (*Lotus* case (France v. Turkey) [1927] PCIJ (Ser. A) No. 10 at 25).

[9] F.J. Varela, H.R. Manturana and R. Uribe "Auotpoiesis: the organisation of living systems, its characterisation and a model" (1974) 5 *Biosystems* 187–196 and H.R. Maturana and F. Varela "Autopoiesis and Cognition: Realisation of the Living" in R.S. Cohen and M.W. Wartofsky (eds) *Boston Studies in the Philosophy of Science* (D. Reidel Publishing Co, Dordrecht: 1980) 42.

[10] T. Quick "A short Introductory Overview of Autopoesis" (available at ⟨www.cs.ucl.ac.uk⟩).

[11] See eg F.F. Robb "Accounting—A Virtual Autopoietic System?" (1991) 4(3) *Systems Practice* 215–235; I. Livingstone *Between Science and Literature: An Introduction to Autopoietics* (University of Illinois Press: 2006); J. Mingers *Self-Producing Systems: Implications and Applications of Autopoiesis* (Springer: 1994); M. Zeleny (ed) *Autopoiesis: A Theory of Living Organisation* (Elsevier, New York: 1981); F.P. Bensaler, P.M. Hejl and W.K. Kock (eds) *Autopoiesis, communication and Society: The Theory of Autopoietic Systems in the Social Sciences* (Campus Verlag, Frankfurt: 1980).

[12] See eg G. Teubner *Law as an Autopoietic System* (Blackwell, Oxford: 1993); N. Luhmann

although it is sometimes mistakenly interpreted as requiring, or at any rate leading to, ossification, autopoietic theory more accurately posits that the law naturally changes and adapts to new realities and new contexts just as these realities and contexts must change and adapt to the new laws. In other words, the law is shaped by the context in which it operates while that context is shaped by the law which operates within and upon it. Thus, while self-referential in that existing law must be perpetuated, a legal system is also self-generating in that the law must, through the processes internal to it, evolve to meet the new realties of the contexts in which it exists and operates.

Autopoietic theory has also been applied to international law[13] where its application has been said to be particularly apposite.[14] As D'Amato puts it:

> Autopoiesis explains how a system such as the ILS [international legal system], in its interrelationship with its environment, can attain relative autonomy and flexible coherence. The system 'observes' claims issuing from the environment, describes or codes them in relation to its own internal constitutive structure, and then either assimilates them (thus affecting that internal structure—the way that a biological system takes in and assimilates food which then becomes part of itself)—or stores them in memory. Stored communications can later be retrieved and either assimilated, deleted, or modified.[15]

D'Amato identifies four 'bias filters' through which a claim must pass in determining whether it should be assimilated, deleted or modified: the self-preservation filter, the equality filter, the reciprocity filter, and the interdependence filter. Essentially, each of these filters is a manifestation of the overarching systemic goal of self-preservation which requires perpetuation of the adoption and maintenance of order-producing rules rather than anarchy-producing rules. Given its preference for order over anarchy, D'Amato accepts the natural bias of international law in favour of retaining existing rules. However, he notes that a new rule may emerge where it is seen to be "more stability producing than the norms closely connected to it in [existing international law]".[16]

In the law of the sea context, the LOS Convention establishes a legal order for the oceans which is intended to:

"The Autopoiesis of Social Systems" in F. Geyer and J. van der Zouwen (eds) *Sociocybernetics Complexity, Autopoiesis and Observation of Social Systems* (Greenwood Publishing Group, Westport: 2001); N. Luhmann "The Coding of the Legal System" in G. Teubner and A. Febbrajo (eds) *State, Law and Economy as Autopoietic Systems: Regulation and Autonomy in a New Perspective* (Dott. A. Giuffrè Editore, Milan: 1992); H. Baxter "Autopoiesis and the 'Relative Autonomy' of Law" (1998) 19 *Cardozo Law Review* 2087–2190.

[13] A. D'Amato "International Law as an Autopoietic System" in R. Wolfrum and V. Röben (eds) *Developments of International Law in Treaty Making* (Springer: 2005) 335–399.

[14] *Ibid.*, 351.

[15] *Ibid.*

[16] *Ibid.*, 369.

> facilitate international communication, [and] promote peaceful uses of the seas and oceans, the equitable and efficient utilisation of their resources, the conservation of their living resources, and the study, protection and preservation of the marine environment.[17]

Prima facie, the objective and focus of the existing law of the sea is to promote order on and among uses and users of the oceans. However, as noted above, the new reality of the context in which the law of the sea operates is one of increasing and increasingly unbridled human activity resulting in damage, both potential and real, from over-use, over-consumption and over-exploitation. This new reality has altered the fundamental balance between the context in which the law of the sea operates and the law of the sea itself.

As regards the high seas, it has now been recognised that the law of the sea regime is fragmented both sectorally and geographically, leaving a large range of governance, regulatory, substantive and implementation gaps which serve to limit its effectiveness in securing an orderly and sustainable future for the high seas and other ocean areas beyond national jurisdiction.[18] In the enforcement context, in particular, the legal regime for the high seas is undermined by major gaps resulting, inevitably, from the basic international law rules relating to treaty application by which a treaty is only binding on States party to it, and by adherence to the principle of flag State jurisdiction.[19] These recurring failures, now compounded by new challenges such as those posed by climate change, seriously threaten the realisation of the core objectives of the law of the sea and lead inexorably to calls for the law to develop by 'filling the gaps' in order to re-establish the equilibrium between the law and the changed context in which it is operating.[20]

---

[17] LOS Convention, preamble.

[18] See eg E.J. Molenaar "Addressing Regulatory Gaps in High Seas Fisheries" (2005) 20(3–4) *International Journal of Marine and Coastal Law* 533–570; K. Gjerde et al. "An Analysis of the Regulatory and Governance Gaps in the International Regime for the Conservation and Sustainable Use of Marine Biodiversity in Areas beyond National Jurisdiction" *IUCN Marine Law and Policy Paper No 1* (Gland, IUCN: 2008) (available at ⟨www.iucn.org⟩); and K. Gjerde et al. "Options for Addressing Regulatory and Governance Gaps in the International Regime for the Conservation and Sustainable Use of Marine Biodiversity in Areas beyond National Jurisdiction" *IUCN Marine Law and Policy Paper No 2* (Gland, IUCN: 2008) (available at ⟨www.iucn.org⟩).

[19] R. Rayfuse *Non-Flag State Enforcement in High Seas Fisheries* (Martinus Nijhoff Publishers, Leiden/Boston: 2004) 24–38.

[20] See eg D.D. Caron and H.N. Scheiber "Bringing New Law to Ocean Waters" in D.D. Caron and H.N. Scheiber (eds) *Bringing New Law to Ocean Waters* (Martinus Nijhoff Publishers, Leiden/Boston: 2004) 3–14; and R. Rayfuse and R. Warner "Securing a Sustainable Future for the Oceans Beyond National Jurisdiction: The Legal Basis for an Integrated Cross-Sectoral Regime for High Seas Governance for the 21st Century" (2008) 23(3) *International Journal of Marine and Coastal Law* 399–422.

As a general proposition, re-establishing equilibrium in the law of the sea requires careful consideration of the manner in which the law can more adequately bring order to the oceans and protect the interests of all members of the international community in the high seas and ABNJ. In the particular context of addressing enforcement gaps, what is needed is a new normative framework capable of ensuring that all States comply with their specific treaty obligations and other generally accepted international norms and one that addresses situations where a State is unwilling or unable to do so. Only thus can the law of the sea preserve itself as a viable, order-producing normative system, for the protection, conservation and management of the oceans.

As discussed in subsequent sections of this paper, the law of the sea appears to be moving towards a new enforcement paradigm premised on clearly articulated flag State responsibilities and a role for non-flag States in exercising jurisdiction where flag States are unable or unwilling to do so. Before examining and assessing the normative force of these developments, however, it is necessary to assess the efficacy and stability-producing nature of the existing, traditional rule of flag State jurisdiction. This, in turn, requires an analysis of the content of the requirement of the genuine link.

3. *The Disingenuousness of the Genuine Link*

As noted above, the legal framework for enforcement of international law in ABNJ is premised on the principle of flag State jurisdiction. The high seas are open to all States and every State has the right to sail ships flying its flag on the high seas.[21] While on the high seas ships are generally subject only to the jurisdiction of the State whose flag they fly.[22] The jurisdictional linkage between a flag State and ships flying its flag is governed by the rules on nationality of ships. These rules, originally justified on the basis of a public order function necessary to avoid chaos,[23] are premised on the notion of the 'genuine link'.

Originating in the work of the International Law Commission (ILC) and its Draft Articles on the Law of the Sea,[24] the concept of the genuine link was intended as a means of ensuring adequate and effective control and

[21] LOS Convention, Articles 87 and 90.

[22] *Ibid.*, Article 92(1).

[23] M.S. McDougal and W.T. Burke *The Public Order of the Oceans: A Contemporary International Law of the Sea* (Brill Academic Publishers, Leiden/Boston: 1987) at 794; M.S. McDougal, W.T. Burke and I.S. Vlasic "The Maintenance of Public Order at Sea and the Nationality of Ships" (1960) 59 *American Journal of International Law* 25–63.

[24] International Law Commission "Draft Articles on the Law of the Sea Convention" [1956] *ILC Yearbook* Vol. II.

supervision of ships by States whose flag they fly. Only States meeting certain internationally accepted requirements regarding the genuine link would be entitled to grant their flag and have that grant recognised by all other States.[25] Having first opted for an economic test on which to ascribe nationality,[26] the ILC, apparently influenced by the decision of the International Court of Justice (ICJ) in the *Nottebohm* case,[27] ultimately settled on a broad formulation of the genuine link.[28] Unfortunately, no definition of 'genuine link' was given; an omission which was not rectified in the LOS Convention, Article 91 of which merely requires registration and acquisition of appropriate documentation pursuant to the municipal law of a State as the only test of a ship's nationality.[29]

The rules on nationality of ships have been described as "an axis of the law of the sea", "a well-defended preserve of the sovereignty of states" and a fundamental rule on which "inter-state relations concerning activities at sea depend".[30] However, these rules, disingenuously call, on the one hand, for the existence of a genuine link yet, on the other hand, require no content to that link other than mere registration.[31] In doing so, they establish what is, arguably, the most significant enforcement gap in the legal regime for the high seas.

When coupled with the rule of flag State jurisdiction, this minimalist approach to the concept of a genuine link presents a vast range of difficulties for those seeking to attach legal requirements to, and consequences for, the granting of a flag beyond the mere requirement to provide a vessel with documents to the effect that flag has been granted.[32] In short, the genuine link requirement, as currently interpreted, provides no incentive for vessels to comply with internationally agreed rules and standards, no incentive for flag States to ensure their vessels comply with those international obligations, no guidance as to how this compliance can be effected or enforced, and no guidance as to the consequences for vessels and/or flag States in situations where a flag State is unwilling or unable to exercise its jurisdiction in respect of its vessels.

---

25 Rayfuse, note 19 at 28–29.

26 See Draft Article 5 of the International Law Commission "Draft Law of the Sea Convention" [1955] *ILC Yearbook* Vol. I at 22.

27 *Nottebohm* case (Guatemala v. Lichtenstein) [1955] ICJ Reports 4.

28 International Law Commission "Draft Article 29 of the 1956 Draft Law of the Sea Convention" [1956] *ILC Yearbook* Vol. II at 278.

29 LOS Convention Article 91(2) as confirmed by the *M/V "SAIGA" (No. 2)* case (Saint Vincent and the Grenadines v. Guinea) (1999) 38 ILM 1323 para. 63.

30 T. Treves "Flags of Convenience Before the Law of the Sea Tribunal" (2004–2005) 6 *San Diego International Law Journal* 179–189 at 189.

31 LOS Convention, Article 91.

32 See eg *Grand Prince* case (Belize v. France) case No. 8 [1999] 7 ITLOS 17 and the *M/V Saiga (No. 2)* case (St Vincent and the Grenadines v. Guinea) (1999) 38 ILM 1323.

In addition, while not actively encouraging it, the genuine link rule does nothing to discourage the practice of flagging ships to avoid the application of international obligations. Thus, ships may deliberately flag in a State not party to relevant treaty obligations. This practice has been well documented in the use of 'flags of convenience' to avoid controls relating to vessel source pollution or to avoid the application of conservation and management measures established by regional fisheries management organizations (RFMOs).[33] Even where a State is party to a relevant treaty, it may become a flag of choice as a 'flag of non-compliance' due to its failure to adequately implement its treaty obligations either through a lack of political will to regulate activity, a lack of financial and technical expertise or a lack of infrastructure to promote and, if necessary, enforce compliance. In short, the 'genuine link' has proven to be anything but.

4. *Developing Flag State Responsibilities— The Requirement of 'Effective Control'*

Given the disingenuousness of the genuine link requirement, attention has become focused less on the rules for the granting of nationality and the requirements of establishing the genuine link, and more on articulating the precise duties and responsibilities of 'effective control' incumbent on States who choose to grant their flag.

The requirement of effective control is a natural corollary of the rules on the nationality of ships. For every right there is a concomitant duty. While States may have the right to grant their flag, the public order of the oceans and the principles of equality of user and due regard[34] require the exercise of a reciprocal duty to effectively control their vessels and exercise jurisdiction over them in situations where the actions of their vessels interfere with the interests of other States. In theory, only those vessels over which the flag State is exercising effective control can enjoy the freedom of the high seas and its concomitant advantages. Where flag States fail in their duty to exercise their responsibility and jurisdiction effectively, then arguably they are internationally responsible to other States which then acquire a reciprocal right to rectify the situation.[35]

---

[33] The term RFMO is used here to include both regional fisheries organizations and regional fisheries management arrangements which are cooperative mechanisms established by two or more States, but which do not establish a formal organisation as an independent international legal person.

[34] LOS Convention Article 87.

[35] Rayfuse, note 19 at 364–372.

The first task, therefore, lies in determining the precise content of the requirement of effective control, or the content of the responsibilities incumbent on flag States.

Article 94 of the LOS Convention sets out the duties of flag States relating to "jurisdiction and control in administrative, technical and social matters", and ensuring "safety of life at sea". States are required to regulate matters relating to manning, seaworthiness, collision prevention, construction and crew qualification in conformity with applicable international instruments and generally accepted international regulations, procedures and practices, including those relating to prevention, reduction and control of marine pollution.

Article 217 of the LOS Convention provides certain parameters to the concept of effective control, specifically within the context of pollution of the marine environment. States are obliged to ensure compliance by their vessels with applicable international rules and standards relating to the prevention, reduction and control of pollution of the marine environment and to go so far as to prohibit their vessels from sailing until such time as the vessel can do so in full compliance with these rules and standards. The international instruments and regulations referred to are predominantly those found in the various conventions, resolutions and recommendations adopted under the auspices of the International Maritime Organisation (IMO) and the International Labour Organisation (ILO).

In the fisheries context the general requirement in the LOS Convention on States to take either individually or in cooperation with other States "such measures for their respective nationals as may be necessary for the conservation of the living resources of the high seas"[36] is supplemented by specific obligations relating to effective control of fishing vessels found in the Compliance Agreement,[37] the Fish Stocks Agreement[38] and the constitutive treaties of and measures adopted by RFMOs. Within these instruments, a plethora of measures have been adopted to give content to the obligation of effective control.

For example, both the Compliance Agreement and the Fish Stocks Agreement oblige flag States to ensure, through various means such as vessel registers, fishing authorisations, and refusal of their flag to known IUU vessels, that their vessels do not engage in activities that undermine the effectiveness of international conservation and management measures including those

---

[36] LOS Convention, Article 117.

[37] Agreement to Promote Compliance with International Conservation and Measures of 24 November 1993 ((1994) 33 ILM 968).

[38] Agreement for the Implementation of the Provisions of the United Nations Convention on the Law of the Sea of 10 December 1982 Relating to the Conservation and Management of Straddling Fish Stocks and Highly Migratory Fish Stocks of 4 August 1995 ((1995) 34 ILM 1542).

adopted by RFMOs.[39] The Fish Stocks Agreement further obliges flag States to, *inter alia*: establish and enforce licensing schemes and regulations for high seas fishing; establish a national register of vessels authorised to fish on the high seas; establish requirements and verification programs for marking vessels and gear, recording and reporting vessel position, and verifying catch of target and non-target species; adopt monitoring, control and surveillance (MCS) measures including national, regional and global schemes, observer programs and the implementation of vessel monitoring systems (VMS); regulate high seas transhipment to ensure the effectiveness of conservation and management measures is not undermined; and regulate fishing activities to ensure compliance with regional, subregional and global measures. In addition, where a subregional, regional or global system of monitoring, control and surveillance exists, flag States must ensure that their measures are compatible with that system.[40]

The point of articulating these flag State responsibilities is to ensure that flag States are able to ensure compliance by their vessels with international obligations. The Compliance Agreement makes this point by requiring parties to take enforcement measures against any of their vessels which act in contravention of the Agreement. This requires making contravention of the Agreement an offence under national law with provision for sanctions of sufficient gravity to effect compliance and deprive offenders of the benefits accruing from their illegal activities. For serious offences, sanctions must include refusal, suspension, or withdrawal of the vessel's authorisation to fish on the high seas.[41]

The FSA seeks to ensure compliance not just with its own provisions but with measures adopted by RFMOs as well. Flag States are obliged to take enforcement action against their vessels for non-compliance with RFMO measures irrespective of where violations occur and must conduct immediate and full investigations of alleged violations and report on the progress and outcome of those investigations to the State alleging the violation and to the relevant RFMO. They must require their vessels to provide information on the vessel's fishing activities to the investigating authorities and, where sufficient evidence of a violation exists, flag States are obliged to refer the case to their authorities with a view to instituting proceedings without delay and to ensuring that further fishing activities are not carried out until any outstanding sanctions are complied with. Investigations and judicial proceedings are to be carried out expeditiously and sanctions imposed are to be adequate in severity to be effective in securing compliance and to discourage violations.

[39] Compliance Agreement, Articles III and IV; see also Fish Stocks Agreement, Article 18.
[40] Fish Stocks Agreement, Article 18.
[41] Compliance Agreement, Article II.

Sanctions shall also deprive offenders of the benefits accruing from their illegal activities. Flag States are obliged to ensure that masters and other officers of their fishing vessels risk refusal, withdrawal or suspension of their licences if they fail to comply with the flag State's obligations. In short, flag States are required to effectively enforce—and to enforce effectively.[42] Only then can a flag State be said to be exercising effective control over its fishing vessels.

Nevertheless, it is trite law that treaties are only binding on their parties. As will be immediately apparent, there is a complex patchwork of different levels of responsibility and differing obligations of effective control incumbent on each State as a result of their differing treaty relations. Unfortunately, this does little to advance the articulation and understanding of the substantive content of flag State responsibilities and the obligation of effective control. In particular, where a flag State is not party to all (or indeed any) of these international agreements, difficult questions arise as to the precise responsibilities incumbent on it. In other words, it is necessary to determine whether there are any flag State responsibilities which are binding on all States as a matter of customary international law.

In the high seas fisheries context, it is arguably uncontroversial to suggest that there are two fundamental customary flag State duties: the duty to cooperate in the conservation and management of marine living resources, and the duty to effectively control vessels flying your flag. The difficulty lies in defining the precise content of these customary rules.

With respect to the duty to cooperate, the LOS Convention requires all States whose nationals exploit the living resources of the high seas to negotiate with a view to take the measures necessary for the conservation of those resources, and to cooperate in the establishment, where appropriate, of sub-regional or regional fisheries organisations.[43] For parties to the Fish Stocks Agreement the duty to cooperate means not only the duty to establish RFMOs but also that only members of RFMOs or non-members who agree to abide by the conservation and management measures adopted by those RFMOs, can access the fishery concerned.[44] States that do not agree to abide by RFMO measures must refrain from fishing. If they do not they have breached their duty to cooperate. The difficult question here is whether the duty to *cooperate or refrain* can now be regarded as a rule of customary international law binding on *all* States.

[42] Fish Stocks Agreement, Article 19.
[43] LOS Convention, Article 118.
[44] Fish Stocks Agreement, Article 8.

With respect to the duty to effectively control vessels, the LOS Convention requirement to "effectively exercise jurisdiction and control"[45] includes the requirement for flag States to maintain a register of ships under their control. However, many States exempt fishing vessels from these requirements. Article 18 of the Fish Stocks Agreement makes clear that States shall only authorise their vessels to fish on the high seas where they can exercise flag State responsibilities effectively. As noted above, both the Compliance Agreement and the Fish Stocks Agreement provide more detail as to what this effective exercise of flag State responsibilities entails. For example, both agreements oblige flag States to ensure through various means such as vessel registers, fishing authorizations and refusal of their flag to known IUU vessels, that their vessels do not engage in activities that undermine the effectiveness of RFMO measures. The Fish Stocks Agreement goes further and obliges flag States to establish schemes for, *inter alia*: licensing, national registers of authorised vessels, vessel and gear marking, vessel reporting and recording, verification of catch data, MCS, regulation of transhipment, and ensuring compliance with RFMO measures.[46]

A comprehensive review of State practice and *opinio juris* to definitively ascertain the customary status of these obligations is beyond the scope of this paper. However, a cursory review of State practice by both members and non-members of RFMOs would seem to suggest that, at the very least, flag States might now be considered, as a matter of customary international law, to have a duty to maintain a vessel register the contents of which are publicly available. Registration requirements should involve, at a minimum, verification of provenance and ownership of the vessel in order to ensure that known IUU vessels or vessels operated by known IUU operators are not admitted to the register. Arguably too, all flag States are now obliged not to accept vessels onto their register if they are not willing and/or able to exercise effective control over them. This willingness should be evidenced by acceptance and implementation in the domestic law of the flag State of relevant internationally agreed conservation and management measures, the establishment of an effective licensing regime which issues authorisations to fish only upon verification of a vessel's aptitude to comply with relevant measures and the identification of the persons responsible for the vessel's operation, and the existence of a national regulatory framework for monitoring, control and enforcement (MCE). This MCE framework should include binding requirements on the reporting of fishing data by vessels, requirements to monitor vessels through the use of VMS and

---

[45] LOS Convention, Article 94.

[46] Fish Stocks Agreement, Articles 18–19.

observer programs, at-sea and in-port inspection, and regulation of transhipments. In addition, it should provide for a system of sanctions adequate in severity to act as an effective deterrent, including the revocation of authorizations to fish.[47]

A similar analysis can be made with respect to the rules relating to marine pollution. Take, for example, the case of high seas dumping. Dumping is defined, *inter alia*, as "any deliberate disposal of wastes or other matter from vessels, aircraft, platforms or other man-made structures at sea".[48] Article 210 of the LOS Convention requires all States to adopt national laws, regulations and other measures to prevent, reduce and control pollution of the marine environment by dumping. These laws, regulations and measures are to ensure that dumping is not carried out without the permission of the competent national authorities and, for dumping within the territorial sea, the exclusive economic zone (EEZ) or on the continental shelf (including the outer continental shelf), the express prior approval of the relevant coastal State. The national laws, regulations and measures adopted must be no less effective than internationally agreed global rules and standards, to prevent, reduce and control pollution from dumping.

These internationally agreed global rules and standards are found in a number of global and regional treaties, the most important of which for present purposes are the Convention for the Prevention of Marine Pollution by Dumping of Wastes and Other Matter, 1972 (London Convention),[49] and its Protocol to the Convention on the Prevention of Marine Pollution by Dumping of Wastes and Other Matter, 1996 (London Protocol).[50] Under the London Convention, dumping of certain wastes and other matter listed in two annexes (the 'black list' and the 'grey list') is either outright prohibited or requires a special prior permit. Dumping of all non-listed wastes and other matter requires a general prior permit. Under the Protocol, the dumping of all wastes or other matter except those specifically listed is prohibited and dumping of those listed substances is subject to stringent permitting and environmental assessment requirements.

---

[47] R. Rayfuse "To Our Children's Children's Children: From Promoting to Achieving Compliance in High Seas Fisheries" (2005) 20 (3–4) *International Journal of Marine and Coastal Law* 509–532 at 525–527.

[48] LOS Convention, Article 1(5).

[49] Convention for the Prevention of Marine Pollution by Dumping of Wastes and Other Matter of 29 December 1972 ((1976) UKTS 43).

[50] Protocol to the Convention on the Prevention of Marine Pollution by Dumping of Wastes and Other Matter of 29 December 1972 of 7 November 1996 ((2006) *Australian Treaty Series* 11).

Eighty-two States are party to the London Convention while 28 States are party to the London Protocol, which replaces the London Convention for States parties to both. *Prima facie*, only these States are bound by the respective treaty regimes. However, it has been argued that the London Convention and the London Protocol may both have much broader application. Article 210 of the LOS Convention requires States to adopt global rules and standards for the control of dumping, and to re-examine them from time to time. The ongoing revision of the London Convention and the adoption of the London Protocol might be said to fulfil this requirement such that, with the coming into force of the LOS Convention, all States parties to the LOS Convention are now bound by the obligations contained in the most recent document, the London Protocol, or at the very least by the provisions of the London Convention.[51] In addition, it has been asserted that:

> there is no evidence of any non-party [to the London Convention or the London Protocol] dumping significant wastes at sea, or asserting a freedom to do so beyond that implied in the LOS Convention and various global and regional instruments.[52]

Admittedly, neither States nor individuals would be likely to publicise any unregulated or unlawful dumping activities they engage in. However, if this is correct, then in the absence of any State practice evidencing an assertion of a right to the contrary, it is arguable that the prohibition exists as a matter of customary international law. The issue is not, however, entirely free from doubt.

Clearly, in developing the concept of flag State responsibilities and the content of the duty of effective control, the real challenge is to find a commonality of rules which are applicable to *all* States. In the absence of any authoritative articulation of the content of flag State responsibilities which are binding as a matter of customary international law, the best that can be said is that the precise content of these customary obligations remains vague and insufficiently developed to provide the basis for a clear and uncontroversial determination of rights and obligations.

---

[51] L.A. de La Fayette "The London Convention 1972: Preparing for the Future" (1998) 13(4) *International Journal of Marine and Coastal Law* 515–536 at 516.

[52] P. Birnie and A. Boyle *International Law and the Environment* 2nd (Oxford University Press, Oxford: 2002) at 421.

5. *Enforcing Effective Control*

However, even if the substantive gaps in the content of the duty of effective control are filled, application of the rules on nationality of ships and flag State jurisdiction continue to undermine the international community's ability to ensure that all flag States comply with these obligations. In the absence of globally applicable enforcement mechanisms which can be invoked by all States in situations of flag State inability or unwillingness to ensure compliance, effective protection, preservation, conservation and management of the high seas continues to be compromised and the objectives of the law of the sea continue to be undermined.

In recent years, a plethora of measures has been adopted by States designed to persuade flag States to ensure their vessels comply with international rules and to address the enforcement challenges posed by flag States which are unwilling or unable to do so. Admittedly, these measures are only binding on States parties to the relevant treaty regime. However, in their operation these measures are intended to—and often do—influence and affect the behaviour of non-party States as well. Port State measures, in particular, can exert a strong influence on the conduct of non-party flag States and their vessels, imposing *de facto*, even if not *de jure*, adherence to treaty standards as a condition of port entry. While these measures can not yet be described as a globally applicable enforcement mechanism available to all non-flag States, they demonstrate the resolve of the international community to continue to develop creative legal responses to overcome the shortcomings which have arisen from adherence to the principle of flag State jurisdiction in order to restore order and stability to the high seas regime.

The following discussion focuses primarily on measures adopted through RFMOs as illustrative of these creative legal developments and the challenges still faced in ensuring enforcement in situations where a flag State is unwilling or unable to do so.

A now commonly used method in a number of treaty bodies, including the IMO and RFMOs, is that of naming and shaming, particularly through the use of 'negative lists' of non-compliant vessels. Whether in the fisheries or the shipping context, being listed on a negative list can result in adverse consequences for listed vessels such as denial of flag or denial of port access. For example, under various RFMO schemes, member States are to take certain actions against listed vessels regardless of whether the vessel is flagged in a member or a non-member. These actions generally include: refusing to grant their flag to listed vessels; refusing to issue licences to fish in waters under national jurisdiction; refusing authorisation to land catch or to tranship in port; ensuring that fishing support vessels, cargo vessels and mother-ships flying their flag do not participate in any transhipment operations with listed vessels; and prohibiting chartering of listed vessels. Beyond this, States are to discourage their importers, transporters and other sectors to refrain from any transactions with, or transhipments from, listed vessels. Due process mechanisms have been adopted to allow States to explain, contest and thereby possibly avoid the inclusion of their vessels on the lists.

However, while these lists are useful in identifying individual offending vessels and in revealing patterns of flag State behaviour, they are subject to limitations. The tyranny of consensus decision-making in many RFMOs means that members (unlike non-members) can block the listing of their vessels, despite cogent evidence to the contrary. Procedural rules, possibly anathema to the principle of sovereign equality of States, are therefore required to ensure that member States cannot block consensus vis-à-vis their own vessels. In addition, listed vessels, once identified, may simply move into another RFMO area or change their name and register to avoid detection. RFMOs have therefore adopted the practice of making their lists publicly available and transmitting them to other RFMOs. In 2007 the five tuna RFMOs agreed to establish a common IUU list[53] while other RFMOs have agreed to reciprocal recognition of each other's lists.

RFMOs have also moved to adopt 'positive' lists, or registers of fishing vessels authorised to fish in a regulatory area. Unauthorised vessels are deemed to be IUU vessels. However, in some cases the requirement to authorise only applies to a specific gear type or to fishing vessels greater than 24 meters in length. Smaller vessels, still capable of fishing on the high seas, refrigerated transport vessels and other supply vessels may not be included and can therefore be used in the practice of laundering catch. In addition, authorisations are not necessarily linked to quotas. In other words, States are free to authorise vessels with capacity far in excess of that needed to take allocated quota. This lack of capacity-control does nothing to reduce the likelihood of overfishing. Moreover, as with negative lists, problems of consistency and application can arise as between the different lists adopted by different organisations. The FAO is currently examining the feasibility of, and *modus operandi* for, a global record of fishing vessels which will serve as a single record of all fishing, refrigerated transport, and supply vessels.[54] While the actual use to which the record will be put remains to be seen, the potential for controversy appears

---

[53] Report of the Joint Meeting of Tuna RFMOs (Tuna RFMOs, Kobe: 22–26 January 2007) (available at ⟨www.tuna-org.org⟩).

[54] See G. Lugten "The FAO Global Record of Fishing Vessels, Refrigerated Vessels and Fishing Support Vessels" (2008) 23(4) *International Journal of Marine and Coastal Law* 761–767.

great, particularly in view of the ongoing concerns as to the credibility and transparency of RFMOs in dealing with the issues of participation and allocation of quota to new entrants.[55]

Controls, and in some cases bans, on transhipments, either as between vessels of members or between vessels of members and non-members, are also increasingly frequent. Controls may include the requirement to establish a record of carrier vessels and conditions for at-sea transhipment such as flag State authorisation, notification procedures, and the use of on-board observers. However, monitoring and controlling at-sea transhipments is notoriously difficult and the regulations are easily circumvented, thereby allowing catch laundering. Even the presence of third-party observers may be insufficient deterrent if the observer's role is limited to catch-data recording for scientific purposes or if transhipment occurs beyond the jurisdictional area of the observer. Some RFMOs therefore now require transhipment to take place only within designated member ports after advance notification to the port State of the precise details of the catch to be transhipped, including total weight to be landed and the port and time of landing.

Port State measures have therefore also become increasingly popular. Under customary international law, port States are entitled to control access to their ports and persons and activities within their territory, subject only to exception in the case of *force majeure* or in cases specifically agreed to in treaties. However, a natural corollary of the right to control is the right not to control. To encourage adoption of port State controls, international agreements have been developed to provide an agreed minimum content to the rights of port States to act in support of internationally agreed measures, although nothing in these agreements prevents States from adopting more stringent measures should they desire to do so.[56]

Port State measures have the potential to be very effective, indeed, perhaps so much so that their introduction can lead vessels to seek ports in States which have not adopted the controls. The phenomenon of ports of convenience has been tackled in the shipping context by the introduction of regional

---

[55] See eg, E.J. Molenaar "Participation, Allocation and Unregulated Fishing: The Practice of Regional Fisheries Management Organisations" (2003) 18 (4) *International Journal of Marine and Coastal Law* 457–480 and R. Rayfuse "Regional Allocation Issues: Or Zen and the Art of Pie Cutting" (2006) Paper prepared for the *Sharing the Fish Conference 06: Allocation Issues in Fisheries Management*, Perth (available at ⟨http://www.fishallocation.com/papers/⟩).

[56] For detailed discussions of the development of port State controls in the shipping context see eg G.C. Kasoulides *Port State Control and Jurisdiction: Evolution of the Port States Regime* (Martinus Nijhoff Publishers, Dordrecht: 1993); E.J. Molenaar *Coastal State Jurisdiction over Vessel-Source Pollution* (Kluwer Law International, The Hague: 1998); and A. Tan *Vessel Source Marine Pollution, The Law and Politics of International Regulation* (Cambridge University Press, Cambridge: 2006).

memoranda of understanding (MOUs) on port State control which seek to harmonise the measures taken. As commercial shipping often follows common routes and uses common ports on a regular basis, monitoring in this way can be reasonably, albeit not wholly, effective in identifying and detaining substandard ships for the purpose of ensuring rectification of the deficiency before the ship continues on its voyage.[57]

Having originally found their application in the shipping context, measures requiring aspects of port State control are increasingly being adopted by a number of RFMOs. In the fisheries context, however, vessels may tranship at sea or off-load in ports of States not party to the relevant RFMO scheme. The banning of at-sea transhipment and the imposition of conditions on landing goes some way to alleviating this. Nevertheless, the existence of ports of convenience and the proliferation of inconsistent, un-harmonised RFMO port State control schemes poses a real threat to the efficacy of RFMO measures. For this reason efforts are underway to develop a global legally binding agreement on port State measures.[58] However, even when adopted, without global adherence, the phenomenon of ports of convenience will still persist.

Increasingly intertwined with port State measures, the use of trade-related measures such as catch documentation and certification schemes as well as export and import controls or prohibitions is becoming more widespread. The purpose of certification schemes is to create negative incentives to deter non-compliance with measures adopted by RFMOs. By removing competitive advantages arising from non-compliance these schemes create positive incentives to comply. They also provide information on the amount of fish in trade and which countries are involved in that trade thereby enabling more effective management and enforcement decisions to be taken. Catch certifications are issued at the point of harvesting and cover all fish to be landed or transhipped. They thus enable landings and trade flows to be monitored and make it possible to restrict access to markets for fish taken in contravention of RFMO measures. In some RFMOs these schemes are linked with port State control in that they require vessels to provide prior notification of landing, including a

---

[57] H.-S. Bang "Is Port State Control an Effective Means to Combat Vessel-Source Pollution? An Empirical Survey of the Practical Exercise by Port States of Their Powers of Control" (2008) 23 (4) *International Journal of Marine and Coastal Law* 715–759.

[58] E.J. Molenaar "Port State Jurisdiction: Towards Comprehensive, Mandatory and Global Coverage" (2007) 38 *Ocean Development and International Law* 225–257. The FAO Technical Consultation to draft a legally-binding instrument on port State measures to prevent, deter and eliminate illegal, unreported and unregulated fishing is expected to complete its work in 2009. See, FAO "Combating Illegal, Unreported and Unregulated Fishing, including Through a Legally Binding Instrument on Port States Measures and the Establishment of a Global Record of Fishing Vessels" (FAO, Rome: 2009) Doc. COFI/2009/6 (available at ⟨www.fao.org⟩).

declaration that the vessel has not been engaged in IUU fishing which must also be confirmed by the flag State. In such cases, failure to make the appropriate declaration will result in denial of port access and if there is evidence that the catch was taken in contravention of RFMO measures then the port State must not allow it to be landed or transhipped.[59]

Despite the apparent attractiveness of these certification schemes, their efficacy in combating IUU fishing has, however, been somewhat limited by their *inter partes* application and by their circumvention by landing in non-member ports. Additional technical shortcomings include double counting of catch, inadequate application to all catch and all species, and the ever present practice of fraudulent reporting. In general, catch documentation schemes have proven more effective than mere trade documentation schemes, and a number of RFMOs are considering replacing the latter with the former. To be truly effective, however, these schemes should apply to all sectors of the fleet regardless of size or gear, all forms of product (live, fresh, frozen, traded, for domestic consumption) and all stages of the catching, landing, transport, processing, trading and marketing chain. The introduction of electronic documentation will also reduce the potential for fraud, improve the speed at which information can be exchanged, and reduce the compliance burden on legitimate operators and regulatory authorities. However, there remains a need to harmonise the various RFMO schemes to make their application by port States more streamlined and therefore both more attractive and more effective.[60]

At-sea measures allowing for direct enforcement by one State against vessels of another State also exist.[61] The LOS Convention provides for non-flag State enforcement in cases of piracy, slave trading unauthorised broadcasting, and stateless vessels. Other treaty and customary regimes allow for non-flag enforcement in cases of illicit drug trafficking, self-defence, intervention in the case of accidents at sea, and in support of sanctions and blockades adopted pursuant to Chapter VII of the United Nations Charter. In the fisheries context, non-flag State boarding and inspection is provided for in a number of

[59] M. Lack "Catching on? Trade-related measures as a fisheries management tool" (Traffic International, Cambridge: 2007) (available at ⟨www.traffic.org/fisheries⟩).

[60] See eg C. Roheim and J.G. Sutinen "Trade and Marketplace Measures to Promote Sustainable Fishing Practices" in ICTSD Natural Resources *International Trade and Sustainable Development Series Issue Paper No 3* (International Centre for Trade and Sustainable Development and the High Seas Task Force, Geneva: 2006) (available at ⟨www.high-seas.org/⟩) and C. Roheim "Seafood Supply Chain Management: Methods to Prevent Illegally-Caught Product Entry into the Marketplace" (2008) Profish Law Enforcement, Corruption and Fisheries Work (available at ⟨www.illegal-fishing.info⟩).

[61] For a comprehensive discussion of these schemes see Rayfuse, note 19.

bilateral treaties[62] and RFMO schemes[63] as well as Articles 20–22 of the Fish Stocks Agreement. Admittedly, these schemes only operate *inter partes* or as against stateless vessels, although consent to boarding, inspection and arrest can always be given by a flag State in *ad hoc* cases. Nevertheless, there appears, as yet, to be no recognised general right of non-flag at-sea enforcement in the absence of flag State consent.

6. *Assessing Flag State Performance*

It will be immediately apparent that all of the measures described above relate to measures that are to be taken by a flag State or by another State either in respect of or against individual vessels or private persons (be they individual or corporate) in particular situations of non-compliance. However, the rights of high seas access and use are granted by the LOS Convention not to individuals, but to States. According to the 2008 Report of the UN Secretary-General on Oceans and Law of the Sea:

> there is now a prevailing view that fishing vessels on the high seas which are not effectively controlled by their flag States are liable to sanctions by other States, should they happen to contravene international conservation and measures.[64]

The task thus becomes one of establishing the criteria for assessing flag State performance.[65]

---

[62] See eg, U.S.-China Memorandum of Understanding on Effective Cooperation and Implementation of United Nations General Assembly Resolution 46/215 of December 20, 1991 (3 December 1993).

[63] See eg, Convention on the Conservation and Management of Pollock Resources in the Central Bering Sea (16 June 1994) (1994) 34 ILM 67, Article XI; Convention on the Conservation of Anadromous Stocks in the North Pacific Ocean (11 February 1992) (1992) 22 *Law of the Sea Bulletin* 21–29, Articles IV and V. See also, Convention on Future Multilateral Cooperation in the Northwest Atlantic Fisheries (24 October 1978) 1135 *UNTS* 369, Article XI(5); Convention on the Conservation of Antarctic Marine Living Resources (20 May 1980), 1329 UNTS 47, Article X; International Convention for the Conservation of Atlantic Tunas (14 May 1966) 673 UNTS 63 Article IX(3); Convention on the Conservation and Management of Highly Migratory Fish Stocks in the Western and Central Pacific Ocean (5 September 2001) (2001) 40(2) ILM 277, Articles 25 and 32; Convention on the Conservation and Management of Fishery Resources in the South East Atlantic (20 April 2001) (2002) 41(2) ILM 257, Article 16(3).

[64] Report of the Secretary General on Oceans and Law of the Sea (advanced and unedited text) (2008) UN Doc A/63/50, para. 249.

[65] In 2007 the United Nations General Assembly called upon the FAO to undertake this task. The FAO Committee on Fisheries has called on FAO to: (1) develop criteria for assessing the performance of flag States; and (2) identify actions that can be taken against vessels flying the flag of States not meeting these criteria. See FAO "Report of the 27th Meeting of the FAO Committee on Fisheries" in *FAO Fisheries Reports R830* (FAO, Rome: 2007) and UN General Assembly Resolution on Sustainable Fisheries (28 November 2007) UN Doc. A/62/L.24.

The purpose of establishing detailed criteria for assessing flag State performance is two-fold. As a matter of principle, the underlying objective must be to articulate the detailed content of flag State responsibilities, including the requirement of effective control, for the purposes of providing certainty, avoiding and minimising conflict, and enhancing the robustness of international governance and respect for the rule of law in the international order. As a practical matter, the purpose must be to establish the circumstances in which a State other than the flag State (a non-flag State) can take enforcement measures (non-flag enforcement) to protect either its interests or those of the international community in situations where a flag State has failed in the effective performance of its responsibilities.[66]

Prima facie, the content of flag State responsibilities against which performance will be assessed will depend on the treaty obligations to which a State has subscribed and the level and efficacy of its domestic implementation of the relevant treaty standards or obligations. By way of example, in its 2006 report, the High Seas Task Force (HSTF)[67] suggests a number of general criteria that should be addressed in determining whether a flag State is a responsible flag State in respect of its fisheries-related obligations. The first set of criteria relate to whether a State is a party to the global fisheries agreements, the LOS Convention, the Compliance Agreement and the Fish Stocks Agreement. Ratification of these treaties will provide *prima facie*, although not conclusive, evidence that a State is a responsible flag State. The presumption of responsibility will, however, be rebutted by instances of non-compliance.

The second set of criteria relate to whether a State implements the obligations contained in the global treaties to which it is party by ratifying relevant regional agreements which seek to implement the global agreements and by participating in RFMOs either as a member or as a cooperating non-member. Indeed, the Fish Stocks Agreement stipulates that in order to have access to a fishery any State with a real interest in that fishery *must* either be a member of the relevant RFMO or cooperate with it and comply with its measures or refrain from fishing. Without getting into the vexed question of what constitutes a real interest, for present purposes, suffice it to say that this would include any State whose vessels fish in any way or at any time in the relevant fishery. Also relevant will be whether the flag State requires its vessels to comply with the conservation and management measures of the RFMO and whether the

---

[66] R. Rayfuse "Non-Flag State Enforcement and Protection of the Marine Environment: Responding to IUU Fishing" in M.H. Nordquist, T.T.B. Koh and J. Norton Moore (eds) *Freedom of Seas, Passage Rights and the 1982 Law of the Sea Convention* (Martinus Nijhoff, Leiden/Boston: 2009) 573–600 at 575–576.

[67] High Seas Task Force *Closing the Net: Stopping Illegal Fishing on the High Seas* (Sadag SA, Bellegarde: 2006) 105–109 (available at ⟨http://www.high-seas.org⟩).

flag State itself complies with the obligations of membership or cooperation. A responsible flag State will do both. Whether a member of an RFMO or not, a flag State which does not ensure that its vessels comply with the regional conservation and management measures or which does not comply with its own obligations to implement the measures adopted, will *prima facie* be an irresponsible flag State.

The third set of criteria relate to whether the flag State has domestic measures in place which meet the internationally agreed minimum standards to ensure it exercises effective control over its vessels including measures to establish a register of fishing vessels, licensing and fishing authorisation requirements, vessel and gear marking standards, standards for verification of catch and effort data, and a working MCE regime. The absence of a formal regulatory system will be *prima facie* evidence of lack of responsibility, although this presumption will have to be rebuttable in the case of developing States which lack management and other capacities. In such cases it will be relevant to enquire whether technical or other assistance has been requested or not, requested and provided, requested but not provided, or offered and rejected. By the same token, the presence of a formal regulatory system will be *prima facie* evidence of responsibility. However, this, too, will be rebuttable in the case of a State which demonstrates a consistent pattern of failure to utilize its powers to control its vessels. In this respect, it will be necessary to go beyond the HSTF guidelines to investigate whether or not a flag State has in place a working and effective system to sanction wrongdoing by its vessels which provides for punishment sufficient to discourage future violations through, for example, withdrawal of fishing or seafaring authorisations. Positive inferences as to the efficacy of the system will be drawn where the measures have, in fact, discouraged violations. Adverse inferences will be available where the State's vessels continue to engage in IUU activities.

A similar analysis applies in respect of other activities in ABNJ. For example, in the shipping context it is first necessary to identify whether a State is party to the various ILO and IMO conventions on crewing, working and construction standards and those relating to protection of the marine environment from vessel source pollution. Participation in these agreements will be *prima facie* evidence that a flag State is a responsible flag State. However, the presumption that a flag State is responsible is a rebuttable one. While States may generally be taken to intend to fulfil their international obligations, the continuing incidence of problems relating to substandard shipping is testament to their inability or unwillingness to always do so. It is therefore necessary to examine the regulatory structures in place in the flag State to ensure compliance by its vessels with these internationally agreed standards and to assess the assiduousness of their implementation to determine their efficacy.

It could be argued that these criteria go no further than simply re-articulating the requirement that States should comply with their treaty obligations, and the logical consequence that failure to do so constitutes a breach of international law. Nevertheless, the purpose of articulating the primary rules binding upon flag States and assessing a flag State's performance therewith must, as a matter of logic, be to determine the consequences that attach to a failure to comply with those rules both in respect of individual vessels and also as against the State *qua* State. A flag State which effectively controls its vessels will be a responsible flag State. A flag State which fails to do so will have failed in its international duty to act responsibly vis-à-vis its vessels. It is in articulating the consequences of flag State 'irresponsibility' and the failure to exercise effective control that flag State responsibility takes on meaning as an effective mechanism for ensuring the LOS Convention objectives of promoting order on, and among uses and users of, the oceans.

7. The Wages of Sin: Bearing the Consequences of Irresponsibility

Turning, then, to the consequences of a failure to exercise effective control, or a failure of flag State responsibility, application of the general rules on State responsibility suggests that where a flag State has failed to ensure compliance by its vessel with its international obligations then any injured State may take action against that particular vessel. This would include coastal States whose rights in their EEZ have been adversely affected through, for example, pollution originating in the high seas or overfishing of straddling and highly migratory stocks. In the fisheries context this would also include members of an RFMO whose interests in the stocks regulated have been adversely affected by the activity in question. Port States, too, would be placed to take action in respect of activities that violate their sovereign right to control access to their ports as well as activities and persons within their territory.

What is not yet resolved, however, is the issue of standing of other non-specifically affected States to take action on the basis of protection of the interests of the international community as a whole. In the pollution context, Article 218 of the LOS Convention gives port States the right to institute proceedings against vessels voluntarily in their ports in respect of any discharge from such vessels which has taken place beyond their own maritime zones, although this right is subject to the right of flag-State pre-emption should a flag State intervene to take over the matter.[68] In the high seas fisheries context,

[68] LOS Convention, Article 228.

a new global agreement on port State measures may provide the jurisdictional entitlement for standing. However, until such agreement is concluded and has entered into force it can only be said that no similar jurisdictional entitlement appears yet to be recognised in the high seas fisheries context. Neither does there appear to be scope for its application in the case of environmental damage to the high seas water column and its resources occasioned by seabed activities either on the outer continental shelf or in the Area.

With respect to the broader question of a consistent pattern of failure by a flag State, it will be recalled that all States are under an obligation to exercise their high seas freedoms with due regard for the interests of other States. These interests include not only the rights of all States to access and use, but also the corollary rights to not access or use, as well as the interests of the international community as a whole in the protection and preservation of the marine environment and conservation and sustainable use of its resources. A consistent pattern of failure by a flag State to meet its responsibilities would arguably constitute a breach not only of those particular responsibilities but also a breach of the requirement of due regard articulated in Article 87 of the LOS Convention and an abuse of right contrary to Article 300 of the LOS Convention. In other words, while not entirely free from doubt, a consistent pattern of failure may be open to invocation by any and *all* States.

Regardless of which States have standing to invoke, the question remains as to the consequences for a flag State that flow from a consistent pattern of failure to effectively control its vessels. Certainly, the irresponsible flag State may be subject to public humiliation through naming and shaming and even diplomatic protests. Port States may close their ports to vessels of irresponsible flag States or otherwise deny port services. Other States may adopt non-discriminatory trade measures or other sanctions designed to persuade the recalcitrant flag State to see the error of its ways. RFMOs may remove vessels from the register of authorised fishing vessels or deny quota to member flag States who fail to effectively control their vessels. Each of these approaches has been taken in at least one RFMO or treaty body and could well be implemented in others.

More controversially, it is now being suggested that since States have the right to grant their flag and, by necessary implication, the right not to grant their flag, that they also have a correlative duty to decline to do so unless they are both willing and able to effectively control their vessels. Grant of flag, followed by a consistent pattern of failure to effectively control could therefore result in a denial of the right for that State's vessels to use the high seas. In other words, while a State would not lose its right to grant flag, the grant of flag by an irresponsible flag State or by a State which subsequently fails in its obligation to effectively control it vessels would not be opposable to other States and its vessels would not enjoy the protection of the flag State. In other words, the vessels would be assimilated to stateless—at least until such time as other States were satisfied that the flag State had taken steps to remedy its failings. There is no doubt that this is a serious consequence to be resorted to only in extreme circumstances. However, at some stage the logical consequence of developing the concept of legally binding flag State responsibilities must be admitted, and the rules on State responsibility regarding breaches of international obligations applied.

8. *Conclusion: Addressing the Enforcement Gaps in the Legal Regime for ABNJ*

At a general level, enforcement gaps in the legal regime for ABNJ can be identified as a lack of effective compliance and enforcement mechanisms and institutions and a lack of standing of States and international organisations to protect the interests of the international community as a whole. Despite the adoption of an increasing number of creative and complex enforcement measures, problems persist as a result of the inability or unwillingness of flag States to effectively control their vessels.

There are many who eschew the development of more law while others have expended considerable energy in analysing existing deficiencies and divining, designing and discussing new and ever more creative measures to deal with these enforcement gaps. Recent suggestions include a range of measures such as taxation, anti-corruption, labour standards, human rights standards and eco-labelling schemes that States could be required to adopt to control either their vessels or the interaction of their nationals with vessels flagged in other States.[69] Essentially these measures seek to deny individuals the economic advantages gained from the offending activity to reduce the incentive to engage in the activity and the likelihood of its recurrence.

There is no doubt that denying economic advantage can be a key element in controlling the activities of individuals, whether in the shipping, fishing or any other context. However, to ensure adequate protection of the legitimate interests of all States in ABNJ it may now be necessary to attach real consequences not just to the activity of individuals but to that of flag States as well. Indeed, as

[69] See eg note 67; M. Gianni and W. Simpson "The Changing Nature of High Seas Fishing: How Flags of Convenience Provide Cover for Illegal, Unreported and Unregulated Fishing" (Australian Department of Agriculture Fisheries and Forestry, International Transport Worker's Federation and WWF International: 2005); P. Bender and G. Lugten "Taxing Illegal Fishing: A Proposal for Using Taxation to Reduce Profiteering from IUU Fishing Offences" (2007) 22 (4) *International Journal of Marine and Coastal Law* 517–544.

discussed here, this appears to be precisely what States, through their practice, are doing. In the language of autopoietic theory, the claim that non-flag State action is permitted in situations where a flag State is unwilling or unable to effectively control its vessels is successfully being assimilated into the broader corpus of the law of the sea.

This is not to suggest that the precise parameters of non-flag State jurisdiction are yet fully articulated. Certainly, the development of globally applicable regimes for port State measures, a global register of vessels, global MCS frameworks, and criteria for assessing flag State performance are key indicators of its content and current limitations. In the end, however, it may require States brave enough to test the waters of international dispute settlement to clarify the current content of generally accepted international norms and the bounds of State responsibility in the sphere of the protection and preservation of the marine environment and the conservation and management of the marine living resources in ABNJ.

COMMENTARY: THE ANTHROPOCENE, AUTOPOIESIS AND THE DISINGENUOUSNESS OF THE GENUINE LINK: ADDRESSING ENFORCEMENT GAPS IN THE LEGAL REGIME FOR AREAS BEYOND NATIONAL JURISDICTION

RONÁN J. LONG*

1. *Introduction*

The Netherlands has a long and proud tradition of scholarship in the law of the sea that traces its roots back to Hugo de Groot. This tradition is exemplified by the work carried out over the last two decades by the Netherlands Institute for the Law of the Sea and the name of the institute is now synonymous with excellence in its field of research and learning. Against this background, I am privileged to participate at this year's J.H.W. Verzijl Memorial Symposium and delighted to comment upon Professor Rosemary Rayfuse's concise and thought-provoking paper which has an extraordinary title that draws inspiration from two scientific terms.

Perhaps it is appropriate to commence my contribution by making some brief observations about the title and to follow this with some general comments on the subject matter of compliance and enforcement of the law in areas beyond national jurisdiction (ABNJ). This includes a brief review of some of the reasons why the law of the sea is fragmented and why new approaches are required to improve compliance and enforcement at global, regional and national levels. My comments conclude by emphasising some positive features in the 1982 United Nations Convention on the Law of the Sea (LOS Convention)[1] which make it a solid normative basis for the adoption of new measures aimed at the conservation of marine biodiversity in ABNJ and managing its resources in a sustainable manner. The word 'measures' in this instance is chosen carefully as it signifies both coercive legally binding obligations backed by sanctions as well as a range of incentives aimed at inducing

* Jean Monnet Chair European Commercial Law, School of Law, National University of Ireland, Galway.

[1] Adopted on 10 December 1982; 1833 UNTS 296.

Alex G. Oude Elferink and Erik J. Molenaar (eds.), *The International Legal Regime of Areas beyond National Jurisdiction: Current and Future Developments*, pp. 191–204.

compliance by governments, industry and individuals. In other words, it is not limited to hard law options but also includes softer and more flexible instruments.

2. *Terminology*

Professor Rayfuse uses a number of very interesting scientific terms to give clarity and structure to the arguments she presents in her paper. As far as I can ascertain the term 'anthropocene' is attributed to Nobel Laureate Paul Crutzen who first used it as a term of art to describe the influence of human behaviour on the Earth since the industrial revolution which he identified as constituting a "new geological era of our own making".[2] There is little doubt that we are now firmly in this era and the future of the planet is irreversibly linked to how we manage the ocean as a source for food, minerals and new scientific discoveries, a medium for transport and communication, as well as a major provider of ecosystem services. In addition, the ocean has a major bearing on the world's climate and it are perhaps issues such as climate change and transnational uses of the marine environment such as carbon sequestration which will ultimately test whether the law of the sea can adapt to changing circumstances without leading to uncertainty and conflict about how the law is interpreted and applied in ABNJ.

This leads to a central theme in Professor Rayfuse's paper which revolves around the clever use of a second scientific term, 'autopoietic system', which was originally used by two Chilean biologists—Humberto Maturana and Francisco J. Varela—to describe the processes occurring at the level of the biological cell where cells regenerate within a closed system.[3] This theory has since been applied by sociologists and legal scholars to explain how social systems such as law self-perpetuate.[4] Significantly, the use of 'autopoiesis' to describe social systems has been criticised on the grounds that such systems arise as a result of the ongoing autopoiesis of the individual biological components of the systems, not as things that are themselves autopoietic.[5] Nevertheless, this term is clearly germane to the subject matter of Professor Rayfuse's paper as it allows her to emphasise that the law must change and adapt to new realities

[2] P.J. Crutzen and E.F. Stoermer "The 'Anthropocene'" (2000) *Global Change Newsletter* 41: 17–18.

[3] F. Varela, H. Maturana and R. Uribe (1974) "Autopoiesis: the Organization of Living systems, Its Characterization and a Model" 5 *Biosystems* 187–196.

[4] G. Teubner (ed.) *Autopoietic Law: A New Approach to Law and Society* (European University Institute: 1987) *passim*.

[5] T. Quick "A short Introductory Overview of Autopoesis" (available at ⟨www.cs.ucl.ac.uk⟩).

and new contexts, just as these realities and contexts must change and adapt to new laws. In the law enforcement context, this demands careful consideration of how the law protects the interests of the international community in ABNJ and how best to improve compliance with international treaty obligations.

One final point about terminology relates to the term 'areas beyond national jurisdiction' which for the purpose of this commentary is understood to refer to the Area and the high seas as defined under the LOS Convention.[6] This includes the air space over the high seas, as well as the high seas over the continental shelf where this extends more than 200 nautical miles (nm) from the baseline of the coastal State. The latter however is not entirely 'beyond national jurisdiction' *strictu sensu* as the coastal State has sovereign rights over certain resources of the shelf under international law where it extends beyond 200 nm.[7] Suffice to note here that activities in the water column which impinge on the resources of the extended continental shelf raise different compliance and enforcement issues and must therefore be distinguished very carefully from the high seas over the deep sea-bed which is more clearly beyond national jurisdiction.[8] In addition, it should also be borne in mind that the international legal regime governing the Area has very specific compliance and enforcement provisions including an enhanced enforcement role for the International Sea-Bed Authority (ISA) which is reviewed briefly below. For that reason, addressing compliance and enforcement gaps in ABNJ will often require careful consideration of the role and mandate of this organisation as is evident from the discussion in Judge Treves' paper, as well as the legal rights and duties of the coastal State over the extended continental shelf.[9]

3. *Compliance and Enforcement in ABNJ*

This session is concerned with addressing enforcement gaps in the legal regime for ABNJ. However, any discussion of law enforcement has to start with the subject of compliance which has been defined in the context of international environmental law as "the behaviour of a state, ascribed thereto by reason of and derived from the behaviour of its nationals, which conforms to a treaty's primary rules".[10] Compliance and enforcement are inextricably linked in so

---

[6] Articles 1(1)(1) and 86.

[7] Article 77.

[8] See paper by D. Owen in this volume at 27–31.

[9] See paper by T. Treves in this volume at 17.

[10] R.B. Mitchell "Compliance Theory: An Overview" in J. Cameron, J. Werksman and P. Roderick (ed.) *Improving Compliance with International Environmental Law* (Earthscan, London: 1996) 5–6.

far as compliance is rarely achieved without some degree of enforcement. In order to achieve compliance with its international obligations, a State must adopt national measures and ensure that these are complied with by those who are subject to its jurisdiction and control. The principal reason for studying compliance is to ensure that the law is working in practice and to determine whether State practice is leading to a new rule in customary international law.

In reviewing compliance with international law it is always a useful exercise to look at compliance with rights conferred on States parties by treaty and compliance with duties imposed thereunder.[11] Rights as a general rule are permissive in nature and are only effective if they are invoked in practice.[12] In contrast to rights, duties are by their very nature obligatory and will often entail States taking action at a national level. Rights and duties go hand-in-hand under the LOS Convention and this is emphasised by its article 300, which mandates good faith in the fulfilment of duties and proscribes the abuse of rights. In spite of the harmonious equilibrium between rights and duties under the LOS Convention, some States have shown a willingness to claim a right without discharging the correlative duties. This is most evident in high seas fisheries and the development of illegal, unreported and unregulated (IUU) fishing. Abuse of a right or failure by a State to comply with a duty undermines the efficacy of international law. Our knowledge of compliance is therefore crucial in assessing the efficacy of law and this in turn is very much dependent on national willingness to assume and report on the enforcement of international obligations through their domestic legal systems. In other words, there appears to be little value in any law enforcement model unless you can effectively monitor compliance with international obligations at a national level. Disappointingly, our knowledge of compliance with international regulation of ABNJ outside the domain of high seas fisheries is poor.[13] International law is not unique in this respect and it is pertinent to recall that knowledge of compliance with European Community law in the member States was described as a "black hole" nearly two decades ago.[14] One regional organisation which has gone a long way to closing both the knowledge and the compliance deficit is

[11] One authority makes the same argument regarding the implementation of the LOS Convention see R.R. Churchill "Levels of Implementation of the Law of the Sea Convention: An Overview" in D. Vidas and W. Østreng (eds) *Order for the Oceans at the Turn of the Century* (Kluwer Law International, The Hague/London/Boston: 1999) 317–323.

[12] For example the elaborate provisions on vessel source pollution in international law which are very much dependent on flag state, port state and coastal state enforcement jurisdiction.

[13] See paper by R. Rayfuse in this volume at 165–190.

[14] J. Weiler "The White Paper and the Application of Community Law" in R. Bieder, R. Dehousse, J. Pinder and J. Weiler (eds) *1992: One European Market?* (Nomos Verlagsgesellschaft, Baden-Baden: 1988).

the OSPAR Commission which has a formal role under the 1992 OSPAR Convention[15] in ensuring compliance by States parties with obligations to protect and preserve the marine environment and marine biodiversity of the North-East Atlantic. More specifically, the Commission must "assess" the compliance by States parties with the Convention on the basis of the reports they submit.[16] When appropriate the Commission may decide upon and call for steps to bring about full compliance with the Convention.[17] This is a potent measure for ensuring compliance even if it falls short of empowering the Commission to take enforcement proceedings in national courts or through international dispute settlement procedures. Importantly, the OSPAR maritime area extends beyond national jurisdiction and includes a large area of the North-East Atlantic and Arctic waters.[18]

The reasons for non-compliance with international obligations in ABNJ are numerous and may include a lack of resources, inadvertence and because the benefits of non-compliance may outweigh its costs.[19] Measures to achieve compliance with international obligations in ABNJ appear to fall into two categories: sanctions and incentives. Significantly, compliance can be improved through the process of 'naming and shaming' as is evident from a number of examples enumerated by Professor Rayfuse.[20] In light of this, there appears to be a strong case supporting the use of both methods to close enforcement gaps in the legal regime applicable to ABNJ. One of the principal reasons why both methods are required relates to the cost of compliance which rises sharply when regulatory standards get stricter and are enforced more vigorously. A similar trend is evident in environmental law where there is an increasing tendency for the law to focus on compliance incentives in response

[15] Convention for the Protection of the Marine Environment of the North-East Atlantic (the OSPAR Convention) of 22 September 1992 ((1993) 32 ILM 1072); Annex 5 of 23 September 1998 (amended and updated text available at www.ospar.org).

[16] OSPAR Convention, Article 23. For commentaries on the Convention, see, *inter alia*, E. Hey, T. IJlstra and A. Nollkaemper "The 1992 Paris Convention for the Protection of the Marine Environment of the North-East Atlantic: A Critical Analysis" (1993) 8 *International Journal of Marine and Coastal Law* 1–76; L. de La Fayette "The OSPAR Convention Comes into Force: Continuity and Progress" (1999) 14 *International Journal of Marine and Coastal Law* 247–297; W. Heintschel v. Heinegg "The Development of Environmental Standards for the North-East Atlantic, including the North Sea" in E. Mann-Borgese and R. Wolfrum (ed.) *Marine Issues* (Kluwer Law International, The Hague: 2002) 35–153. For a discussion of monitoring and compliance under the OSPAR framework see, R. Lagoni "Monitoring, Compliance and Enforcement of Compliance Through the OSPAR Commission" in *ibid.*, 155–163.

[17] Article 23(b) of the OSPAR Convention.

[18] Article 1(a) of the 1992 OSPAR Convention.

[19] For a discussion of why states often fail to comply with international environmental obligations see Mitchell, note 10 supra.

[20] Paper by R. Rayfuse in this volume at 179–189.

to greater awareness of environmental issues and the cost of compliance on the part of the public, environmental groups, green consumers and industry investors.[21]

Having noted the importance of compliance we can move to the topic of enforcement which for the purpose of this commentary is understood as the process of invoking and applying authoritative prescription.[22] The LOS Convention has a broad range of provisions that provide for flag State, port State, coastal State and universal enforcement jurisdiction in different circumstances.[23] The rules in the LOS Convention are also the basis for the allocation of enforcement jurisdiction in other agreements. Clearly, once an international measure has been implemented domestically then enforcement poses different challenges at sea and on land. At sea, the range of operations includes surveillance, stopping and boarding vessels, detention, and on land it also includes the formal application of the law by judicial or other means, including the imposition of sanctions.[24] From both a legal and practical perspective, law enforcement in ABNJ cannot be compared with enforcement in other maritime jurisdictional zones within national jurisdiction where the coastal State has considerable more scope under the LOS Convention to detect and penalise deviant behaviour. In ABNJ the traditional starting point of any discussion is the primacy of the high seas freedoms coupled with the rule of flag State jurisdiction. Professor Rayfuse gets straight to the crux of the problem when she argues that the most significant enforcement gap in the legal regime for the high seas is the rules on nationality of ships coupled with the rule of flag State jurisdiction. Simply stated, these rules are sometimes manipulated to gain advantage or avoid disadvantage under a given legal regime.[25] Indeed, one peculiarity about flag State jurisdiction is that States that comply assiduously with their international obligations very often do not monitor or enforce against others. Outside the domain of international trade law, few States have individual incentives to commence action for non-compliance and there has been a marked reluctance to empower other bodies such as treaty secretariats with enforcement powers. For that reason, if anything characterises the weakness of international law of the sea as it applies to ABNJ, it is the absence of an effective and centralised enforcement system. Several initiatives, some of which are

[21] S. Bell and D. McGillivray *Environmental Law* (Oxford University Press, Oxford: 2006) 40–42.

[22] W. Burke *The New International Law of Fisheries: UNCLOS 1982 and Beyond* (Clarendon Press, Oxford: 1994) 303.

[23] Articles 62(4)(k), 66(3)(d), 73, 217, 218, 219, 220, 224, 225, 233, 234 and 298(1)(b).

[24] See Burke, note 22 at 304.

[25] *Ibid.*, 335.

reviewed by Professor Rayfuse, have been taken at global and regional levels to address this shortcoming, including measures within the framework of, *inter alia*: regional high seas fishery agreements; agreements concerning co-operation in suppressing the smuggling of drugs; and agreements concerning unlawful acts which threaten the safety of ships and the security of their passengers and crews.[26] What is important in this context is that these initiatives indicate that law enforcement in ABNJ is evolving at global and regional levels and moving away from reliance on the flag State as the sole enforcer of international obligations.

The legal regime that applies in ABNJ is important for many reasons, including world security, international trade, international communications including the internet, overflight, scientific research, as well as for the exploration and exploitation of non-living resources of the seabed. Professor Rayfuse's paper focuses on high seas fishing and dumping at sea as a means to illustrate the matters under consideration and to test the efficacy of current measures. This is entirely correct in my view as international law has evolved considerably on these topics since the coming into force of the LOS Convention and we therefore stand to learn a great deal from her discussion and analysis. Moreover, fishing and dumping at sea are two areas where we face the greatest threats in protecting the marine environment in ABNJ and managing its resources.[27] In time, the lessons we learn about the enforcement of the law on high seas fishing and dumping at sea may well be applied to other activities that are currently unregulated in ABNJ.

Permit me to draw attention to one key issue which is highlighted in Professor Rayfuse's paper and this concerns the diffuse nature of the various legal and enforcement obligations that apply to ABNJ. In her words:

> the law of the sea regime is fragmented both sectorally and geographically, leaving a large range of [...] gaps which serve to limit its effectiveness in securing an orderly and sustainable future for the high seas and ocean in ABNJ.[28]

In responding to her call for the development of legal solutions to fill the gaps, it may be relevant to briefly consider the reasons why the law is fragmented and why new solutions are required to address the compliance and enforcement challenges we face in protecting the marine environment and its biodiversity in ABNJ and managing its resources in a sustainable manner. This is an important consideration as Judge Treves expresses the view in his paper that

---

[26] See paper by R. Rayfuse in this volume at 165–190.

[27] E.J. Molenaar "Managing Biodiversity in Areas Beyond National Jurisdiction" (2007) 22(1) *International Journal of Marine and Coastal Law* 89–123 at 90.

[28] R. Rayfuse at 169.

we must live with the "plurality of regimes" and that the best way forward is the development of separate regimes to solve specific problems and to regulate specific activities.[29]

4. *Fragmentation and the Need for New Approaches to Compliance and Enforcement*

The reasons for fragmentation in the law are numerous and may be traced back in some instances to a number of *lacunae* in the LOS Convention. Thus, for example, the LOS Convention did not adequately address the management of straddling and highly migratory fish stocks and this issue has since been addressed by means of an implementation agreement—the Fish Stocks Agreement[30]—which clarifies and elaborates upon the relevant provisions of the LOS Convention. Another reason for fragmentation is the exponential growth in our knowledge of the marine environment and its resources. Few of the participants at the Third United Nations Conference on the Law of the Sea (UNCLOS III) could have foreseen the importance of the exploration of the deep sea-bed for marine genetic resources, or the interest in carbon sequestration in the ocean. Therefore it is unsurprising that the precise legal regime applicable to these resources and to new issues under the LOS Convention is now the subject of controversy.[31] Similarly, it was not possible for the architects

[29] See the paper by T. Treves in this volume at pp. 20–21.

[30] Agreement for the implementation of the Provisions of the United Nations Convention on the Law of the Sea of 10 December 1982, Relating to the Conservation and Management of Straddling Fish Stocks and Highly Migratory Fish Stocks of 4 August 1995 ((1995) 24 ILM 1542).

[31] Paper by T. Scovazzi in this volume at pp. 53–60. Different views have been expressed on marine genetic resources in ABNJ at the United Nations, see UN Docs. A/59/122 of 1 July 2004 and A/61/65 of 20 March 2006. On the inapplicability of the common heritage of mankind see M.F. Hayes "Charismatic Microfauna: Marine Genetic Resources and the Law of the Sea" in M. Nordquist, R. Long, T. Heidar and J. Norton Moore (eds) *Law, Science and Ocean Management* (Martinus/Nijhoff, Boston/Leiden: 2007) 683–700. For a detailed articulation of this view see, *inter alia*, F.M. Armas Pfirter "The Management of Seabed Living Resources in 'the Area' under UNCLOS" (2006) 11 *Revista Electrónica de Estudios Internacionales*; F. Millicay "Legal Principles Applicable to the Biodiversity of the Area" in M. Nordquist, R. Long, T. Heidar and J. Norton Moore (eds) *Law, Science and Ocean Management* (Martinus/Nijhoff, Boston/Leiden: 2007) 739–850. At the Ad Hoc Open-ended Informal Working Group of the UN General Assembly which convened in February 2006 to study issues relating to the conservation and sustainable use of marine biodiversity beyond areas of national jurisdiction, the G-77/China argued that while the principle of the common heritage of mankind applies to all resources of the deep sea-bed, norms could be developed to implement access to, and benefit-sharing from, genetic resources beyond areas of national jurisdiction. This approach applies considerable emphasis on

of the LOS Convention to foresee the shift towards new concepts in resource management such as the precautionary principle, the ecosystem approach and the polluter-pays principle.[32] Managing complex marine ecosystems requires an integrated approach to the management of human activities in the marine environment and it is questionable whether the relatively simple jurisdictional model advanced by the LOS Convention—which allocates the rights and duties of States on a spatial basis—is adequate to a task which now demands integration at normative, ecological and institutional levels.[33] Again there is an obvious *lacuna* in the LOS Convention in relation to the protection of biodiversity in ABNJ.[34] Several attempts have been made in recent years to address this omission.[35] Indeed, the European Community has called for the negotiation of a new multilateral agreement addressing biodiversity in ABNJ. In parallel with these developments, new targets have been set by the World Summit on Sustainable Development to protect biodiversity including the call for the establishment of representative networks of marine protected areas (MPAs) by 2012 which extend to the high seas. All of these developments are testing the jurisdictional framework established by the LOS Convention and it is now apparent that the rules on nationality of ships coupled with the rule of flag State jurisdiction are no longer adequate under the changing structure of the international legal order. However, in considering this development we should not conceal the many positive aspects to the LOS Convention which make it a suitable normative framework for addressing enforcement gaps in the legal regime for ABNJ.

---

the role of the ISA and the contextual nature of the LOS Convention. The G-77/China also called for consideration of new or improved implementation mechanisms and options for institutional arrangements, including expanding the ISA's existing capacity.

[32] See, *inter alia*, D. Freestone "Modern Principles of High Seas Governance—The Legal Underpinnings" (2009) 39 (1) *Environmental Policy and Law* 44–49; D. Freestone, K.M. Gjerde, R. Rayfuse and D. VanderZwaag, "Workshop on High Seas Governance for the 21st Century" (2008) 23 *International Journal of Marine & Coastal Law* 359–363; R. Rayfuse and R. Warner "Securing a Sustainable Future for the Oceans Beyond National Jurisdiction: The Legal Basis for an Integrated Cross-Sectoral Regime for High Seas Governance for the 21st Century" (2008) 23(3) *International Journal of Marine and Coastal Law* 385–422.

[33] Y. Tanaka "Zonal and Integrated Management Approaches to Ocean Governance: Reflections on a Dual Approach in International Law of the Sea" (2004) 19 *International Journal of Marine and Coastal Law* 483–514.

[34] Articles 61 and 145.

[35] For an account see Molenaar, note 27 at 92–96.

5. *The Convention as a Normative Basis for Addressing Enforcement Gaps*

The first positive aspect of the LOS Convention is its almost universal acceptance by States as a normative basis for regulating current and future uses of the ocean. Although there are several claims to maritime jurisdiction by States which are clearly inconsistent with both the letter and the spirit of the LOS Convention, there is in general a high level of uniformity and consistency in the application of its provisions by States. Moreover, it is easy to understate the contribution the LOS Convention has made to the maintenance of international peace and security by replacing a plethora of conflicting claims by coastal States with agreed limits on those maritime areas that come within national jurisdiction and by setting down agreed rules regarding the delineation of ABNJ. Indeed, without the benefit of these rules it would be impossible to identify precisely the geographical areas where States may validly exercise legislative and enforcement jurisdiction in conformity with international law.

The second positive aspect of the Convention that is relevant to this discussion is that it is the outcome of a process which advances the consensus approach to international law-making by accommodating the competing interests of all States and the international community. This achievement is all the more impressive when one considers that the LOS Convention and the implementation agreements were negotiated over a period of 20 years and at a time when there was a serious crisis in international cooperation and a decline in the use of international machinery to resolve global problems.[36] This approach is important when one considers that some States have on occasion resorted to unilateral measures to address enforcement issues in ABNJ. A notable example was the detention of the Spanish fishing vessel *Estai* by the Canadian enforcement agencies in the NAFO Regulatory Area in 1994 and the subsequent influence of that action on the negotiation of the Fish Stocks Agreement.[37] Plainly, improving compliance with international regulation is

[36] Statement by Javier Pérez de Cuéllar, Secretary General of the UN "International Law is Irrevocably Transformed" (10 December 1982) after the LOS Convention was opened for signature.

[37] See *inter alia*: P. Curran and R. Long "Fishery Law, Unilateral Enforcement in International Waters: the case of the Estai" (1996) 5(2) *Irish Journal of European Law* 123–163; D.M. Kedziora "Gunboat Diplomacy in the Northwest Atlantic: The 1995 Canada-EU Fishing Dispute and the United Nations Agreement on Straddling and Highly Migratory Fish Stocks" (1996–1997) 17 *Northwestern Journal of International Law and Business* 1132–1162; C. Joyner and A. von Gustedt "The Turbot War of 1995: Lessons for the Law of the Sea" (1996) 11 *International Journal of Marine and Coastal Law* 425–458; D. Freestone "Canada and the EU Reach Agreement to Settle the *Estai* Dispute" (1995) 10 *International Journal of Marine and Coastal Law* 397–411.

best achieved in a multilateral setting and with a system of enforcement which is not dependent solely on the willingness of the flag State to implement and enforce international obligations.

The third aspect of the LOS Convention which is important to keep in mind is that one of the principal goals of UNCLOS III was to establish a stable legal framework for the mining of the deep sea-bed. This has largely been achieved by the LOS Convention and the 1994 Implementation Agreement[38] which provide a legal basis for the adoption of regulations applicable to the exploitation and exploration for minerals on the deep seabed. In time, these regulations will form the cornerstone of a comprehensive mining code covering all aspects of prospecting, exploration for and exploitation of sea-bed minerals, including polymetallic sulphides and cobalt-rich crusts. Although commercial seabed mining in the Area has not commenced, the ISA has issued exploration licences to 8 State-backed entities and received 2 new applications for exploration licenses from private-sector interests sponsored by developing States in 2008.[39] Most notably and despite the misgivings of many of those that participated at UNCLOS III, no State or private entity has attempted to mine the resources of the deep sea-bed in contravention with the provisions of the LOS Convention. One can therefore say that the LOS Convention supplemented by the 1994 Implementation Agreement has achieved one its principal objectives and prevented the unilateral exploitation of sea-bed minerals in the Area. This is of course subject to the caveat that mining the sea-bed for minerals has not been commercially feasible. For this reason, compliance and enforcement of the legal regime applicable to the Area has not posed any particular difficulty to date primarily because commercial mining of the deep-seabed is some way off. There is, however, general acceptance that the common heritage will be exploited for the benefit of mankind as a whole and through the procedures administered by the ISA. This reduces the possibilities for future conflict and removes any doubt regarding title over mineral resources in the Area. In the context of enforcement and compliance, what is significant is that States parties to the LOS Convention are responsible for ensuring that their activities, or the activities of their nationals or activities effectively controlled by them or their nationals, are carried out in conformity with Part XI of the LOS Convention as modified by the 1994 Implementation Agreement. States parties are subject to any rules that are adopted by the Authority concerning pollution and other hazards to the marine environment, as well as conservation of

[38] Agreement relating to the Implementation of Part XI of the United Nations Convention on the Law of the Sea of 10 December 1982 of 28 July 1994 ((1994) 33 ILM 1309).

[39] S. Nandan *The successes of the United Nations Convention on the Law of the Sea and some Future Challenges* (October 17–18, 2008, ABLOS Conference, Monaco).

natural resources.[40] The Council of the ISA is vested with considerable powers including the power to: "supervise and coordinate the implementation" of Part XI of the LOS Convention and "invite the attention of the Assembly to cases of non-compliance"; institute proceedings on behalf of the Authority before the Sea-Bed Dispute Chamber of the International Tribunal for the Law of the Sea (ITLOS); issue emergency orders "to prevent serious harm to the marine environment arising out of activities of the Area" and to direct and supervise inspectors to ensure compliance.[41] A Legal and Technical Commission is vested with powers to make recommendations to the Council on the institution of proceedings and measures to be taken following and decision by the Sea-Bed Dispute Chamber.[42] How these provisions will operate in practice will only become evident when deep sea-bed mining commences. At this point in time what is relevant to this discussion is that these provisions are entirely premised on a compliance and enforcement model which is not dependent on the exclusive remit of the flag State. Moreover, although Judge Treves concludes that the expansion or the adaptation of the Area regime may not be the most promising way to address the management of new activities in ABNJ, there is little doubt that any future measures will have to be reconciled with the elaborate arrangement and institutional structures that are already in place for the Area.

6. *Concluding Remarks*

In conclusion, I wish to congratulate Professor Rayfuse on her paper which conveys very clearly that the effectiveness of the law of the sea is very much dependent on the extent of compliance with the rules that are in place. This is a matter of increasing concern to the international community as is evident from the wide-ranging and innovative measures that are now in place for high seas fisheries. There is also evidence that new trends in the law of the sea such as the shift towards integrated management and the application of the ecosystem approach require a fundamental rethink about improving compliance and enforcement of the law in ABNJ. In particular, consideration needs to be given on how to improve domestic implementation of international legal obligations governing activities in ABNJ. States are clearly unwilling to take enforcement proceedings against other States for failure to implement international obliga-

[40] LOS Convention, Articles 139(1) and 145.
[41] *Ibid.*, Article 162(2)(a), (u), (v), (w) and (z).
[42] *Ibid.*, Article 165(2)(i) and (j).

tions with a number of notable exceptions.[43] There is nothing unusual in this when one considers that in 50 years of European Community (EC) law we have had only two cases of a member State taking enforcement proceedings against another member State for failure to implement an EC obligation.[44] One reason for this is the positive role played by the European Commission in taking enforcement proceedings against member States.[45] Indeed, the European Court of Justice (ECJ) has ruled in several hundred cases concerning member States failure to uphold their EC legal obligations as a result of legal proceedings initiated by the European Commission. Several of these cases concern a failure by member States to implement appropriate measures aimed at preserving and protecting the marine environment.[46] In many instances, the European Commission has received the initial information on non-compliance from non-governmental organizations (NGOs) or other public-interest groups. At the end of 2007, for example, the European Commission was investigating several hundred complaints from various interest groups concerning the failure of member States to implement their environmental obligations.[47] Many of these investigations were initiated on the basis of information obtained from diverse sources including petitions to the European Parliament, reports in the press, and as result of the work undertaken by NGOs. The European Commission has focused on identifying cases involving widespread and persistent breaches of EC law. In view of the European experience, there appears to be a strong case for strengthening the legal basis for the involvement of non-State

[43] There have been a number of proceedings at the ITLOS which have not reached the merits phase. This includes *The Mox Plant* case (Ireland v. United Kingdom) (2002) 41 ILM 405. For a detailed analysis of this case see R.R. Churchill and J. Scott "The Mox Plant Litigation: The First Half-Life" (2004) 53(3) *International and Comparative Law Quarterly* 643–676; M. Tanaka "Lessons from the Protracted Mox Plant Dispute: A Proposed Protocol on Environmental Impact Assessment to the United Nations Convention on the Law of the Sea" (2004) 25(2) *Michigan Journal of International Law* 337–428; Y. Shany "The first Mox Plant Award: the Need to Harmonise Competing Environmental Regimes and Dispute Settlement Procedures" (2004) 17(4) *Leiden Journal of International Law* 815–827; B. Kwiatkowska "The Ireland v. United Kingdom (Mox Plant) Case: Applying the Doctrine of Treaty Parallelism" (2003) 18(1) *The International Journal of Marine and Coastal Law* 1–58; D.J. Devine "Provisional measures ordered by the International Tribunal for the Law of the Sea in the Area of Pollution, the Mox Plant Case (Ireland v. United Kingdom) ITLOS Case No 10, 3 December 2001" (2003) 28 *South African Yearbook of International Law* 263–275; R. Nadelson "After Mox: The Contemporary Shipment of Radioactive Substances in the Law of the Sea" (2000) 15(2) *The International Journal of Marine and Coastal Law* 193–244.

[44] Case 141/78 *France v United Kingdom* [1979] ECR 2923; Case C-145/04 *Spain v United Kingdom* [2006] ECR I-7917.

[45] EC Treaty, Article 226.

[46] See, for example, Commission of the European Communities v. United Kingdom Case C-6/04 [2006] ECR [0000].

[47] European Commission *25th Annual Report from the Commission on Monitoring the Application of Community Law* (Brussels COM (2008) 777/9).

actors (such as NGOs and international bodies) in the law enforcement process and this may be one way to improve compliance with international regulation in ABNJ. At a European level, the European Commission can play a key role in ensuring member State compliance with their international obligations in ABNJ by resorting to enforcement proceedings in the ECJ. At an international level, however, emphasis must now be placed on enhancing the role of international organizations and NGOs in the enforcement process, as well as flag States, port States and the international community acting collectively.

THE ANTHROPOCENE, AUTOPOIESIS AND THE DISINGENUOUSNESS OF THE GENUINE LINK: ADDRESSING ENFORCEMENT GAPS IN THE LEGAL REGIME FOR AREAS BEYOND NATIONAL JURISDICTION—COMMENTARY ON ROSEMARY RAYFUSE

Louise A. de La Fayette*

Compliance and enforcement are critical issues as the oceans are being degraded, the fisheries depleted and biodiversity increasingly lost. The two issues should be distinguished. The term compliance is usually used to refer to the proper implementation by States of international obligations assumed under a treaty. In relation to the law of the sea, enforcement refers to measures taken by States to ensure that their nationals and vessels entitled to fly their flag act in accordance with regulations adopted by the State in implementation of its treaty obligations. In order to comply with a treaty, the State has first to implement the treaty in its national laws and administrative structures, and then to enforce those laws against persons and entities under its jurisdiction and control.

Professor Rayfuse has outlined the general issues involved in State compliance and enforcement of rules and regulations in areas beyond national jurisdiction (ABNJ), as well as the detailed measures in the field of international fisheries and to some extent ocean dumping. Because she has explained that she did not have time to delve into the situation regarding merchant shipping, I would like to describe the measures taken to promote compliance and enforcement in the regime relating to international shipping adopted in the context of the International Maritime Organization (IMO).

The regime applicable to international shipping with respect to safety, security and the protection of the marine environment in ABNJ is found in IMO instruments. Unless otherwise stated, IMO conventions, codes, guidelines and standards apply in all areas of the sea where there is freedom of navigation, that is, in the EEZ and on the high seas. In the territorial sea, coastal States may adopt their own laws for the protection of the marine environment, except with respect to design, construction, manning and equipment, as these

* Visiting Professor, Maritime Institute, University of Greenwich, London.

Alex G. Oude Elferink and Erik J. Molenaar (eds.), *The International Legal Regime of Areas beyond National Jurisdiction: Current and Future Developments*, pp. 205–214.

requirements must be the same wherever a ship navigates. According to the United Nations Convention on the Law of the Sea (LOS Convention)[1] and customary international law, flag States have exclusive enforcement jurisdiction on the high seas, unless otherwise provided.

Work of the United Nations on Flag State Implementation

Professor Rayfuse begins by referring to the issue of inadequate flag State control over their vessels and the pervasive problem of flags of convenience or of non-compliance. The attempt to eliminate flags of convenience by applying nationality rules for registration was abandoned years ago, in the wake of the failure to revive the 1986 Registration Convention[2] with respect to merchant shipping and the failure to eliminate re-flagging to flags of non-compliance with respect to fishing in the 1993 FAO Compliance Agreement.[3] The issue of the 'genuine link' in relation to flags of convenience was raised at the United Nations several years ago and has figured in several UN General Assembly resolutions, and two comprehensive reports.

After the marine pollution disaster occasioned by the sinking of the tanker *Prestige*, three non-governmental organisations wrote to the United Nations Secretary-General expressing concern over the problems caused by 'flags of convenience' that did not fulfil their responsibilities under the law of the sea to ensure that vessels flying their flag were seaworthy and did not pose a threat to the marine environment. They suggested that the elaboration of an implementation agreement to the LOS Convention might resolve the issues.

The Legal Counsel at the time decided to pursue the matter and the Division for Ocean Affairs and the Law of the Sea (DOALOS) convened a meeting of interested international organisations to discuss the issue of how to ensure that flag States fulfil their international obligations in respect of vessels flying their flag. The Inter-Agency Consultative Group produced a report, which was presented to the United Nations General Assembly. It contains contributions by each organisation setting out the measures taken to address inadequate flag state compliance, plus a list of flag state obligations in the relevant instruments. Before the completion of the report, IMO sent a letter to the General Assembly stating that there was no further need for the Consultative Group to meet and that the issue of flag State implementation was within its exclusive mandate.

---

[1] Adopted on 10 December 1982; 1833 UNTS 396.

[2] United Nations Convention on Conditions for the Registration of Ships of 7 February 1986 ((1987) 26 ILM 1229).

[3] FAO Agreement to Promote Compliance with International Conservation and Management Measures by Fishing Vessels on the High Seas of 24 November 1993 ((1994) 33 ILM 969).

Displeased at this position, in 2003, the General Assembly invited IMO:

> to examine and clarify the role of the 'genuine link' in relation to the duty of flag States to exercise effective control over ships flying their flag, including fishing vessels, and the potential consequences of non-compliance with duties and obligations of flag States described in relevant international instruments.[4]

In 2004, the General Assembly requested DOALOS to report on the outcome of its invitation to IMO.

In July 2005, IMO convened another meeting of the Consultative Group. A second report was issued, containing an update of the information in the first report.[5] On the issue of the 'genuine link', the Consultative Group referred to and relied upon the judgment of the International Tribunal on the Law of the Sea (ITLOS) in the *M/V Saiga No. 2* case.[6] Regarding the potential consequences of non-compliance by flag States, the Tribunal had stated that non-recognition of nationality was not an option. The Consultative Group commented that all the usual rules of international law applied and that it was possible for affected States to use the customary means of settlement of disputes, including third party settlement, where applicable. However, it was recognized that States were usually reluctant to go to third party settlement because of the trouble and the cost. In its annual resolution on oceans and the law of the sea in 2006, the General Assembly welcomed the report, as well as certain initiatives that IMO had taken to improve flag State implementation.[7]

IMO Measures to improve Flag State Implementation

In recent years, IMO has redoubled its efforts to try to ensure that flag States fulfill their international legal obligations and conform to the very extensive set of IMO conventions and regulations. Many of these efforts have been undertaken in the context of the Sub-Committee on Flag State Implementation (FSI), established in 1992 to identify and develop the measures needed to ensure effective and consistent implementation of global instruments, including consideration of the special difficulties of developing countries. FSI has produced

---

4 UNGA resolutions 58/14 of 24 November 2003 (Doc. A/RES/58/14 of 21 January 2004) and 58/240 of 23 December 2003 (Doc. A/RES/58/240 of 5 March 2004).

5 Annexed to a letter from the secretary-general of the IMO to the Secretary-General dated 23 June 2006 (Doc. A/61/160 of 17 July 2006).

6 *The M/V "SAIGA" (No. 2) Case* (Saint Vincent and the Grenadines v. Guinea) case No. 2 [1999] ITLOS Reports 10.

7 UNGA resolution 61/222 of 20 December 2006 (Doc. A/RES/61/222 of 16 March 2007) paras 71–73.

a number of important guidelines and recommendations, some of which have been adopted as resolutions by various IMO bodies, while others have been published as circulars.

The Voluntary IMO Member State Audit Scheme

The Voluntary IMO Member State Audit Scheme is the flagship IMO measure designed to ensure member State compliance with IMO instruments. In December 2005, the 24th session of the IMO Assembly adopted resolution A.974(24) on the Framework and Procedures for the Voluntary IMO Member State Audit Scheme. The goal of the Audit Scheme is to provide an independent and objective assessment of the performance of a member State in meeting its obligations and responsibilities contained in the relevant IMO mandatory instruments. Because of the comprehensive scope of the audit, its results should assist the audited State to address any shortcomings in a holistic and systematic manner. Furthermore, the results from the audits revealed in the consolidated reports should assist other States in examining their performance, as well as suggesting to IMO any necessary improvements in its regulatory regime.

The audits are based upon the Code for the implementation of mandatory IMO instruments.[8] The Code sets out basic requirements for all States, flag States, coastal States and port States in narrative form, followed by annexes listing in tabular form the obligations in the various IMO instruments. It notes that the effectiveness of any instrument depends, *inter alia*, upon all States:

a. becoming a party to all instruments related to maritime safety, security and pollution prevention and control;
b. implementing and enforcing such instruments fully and effectively;
c. reporting to the Organization, as required.

The resolution recognises that the enactment of appropriate legislation and its implementation and enforcement are the three key issues on which a member State's performance can be measured. By the end of 2008, around 25 % of IMO member States had volunteered to be audited. The Secretary-General proposed to the IMO Council that the Audit Scheme be made mandatory, and the Council agreed to this proposal in June 2009.

---

[8] Adopted by IMO Assembly in resolution A.996(25) of 29 November 2007 (Doc. A 25/Res. 996 of 15 January 2008).

The STCW

The International Convention on Standards of Training, Certification and Watchkeeping for Seafarers (STCW)[9] implemented IMO's first effort in evaluating member States' implementation of their treaty obligations. The Convention was completely revised by amendments adopted in 1995.[10] The revised STCW gives IMO the authority to assess the performance of member States, the first time this has been done. Parties are required to provide detailed information to IMO concerning administrative measures taken to ensure compliance with the Convention. The information is reviewed by panels of competent persons, which report to the IMO Secretary-General, who, in turn, reports to the Maritime Safety Committee (MSC) on the parties that fully comply. After examining the reports, the MSC produces a list of parties in compliance with the 1995 amendments, referred to as the "White List" of compliant States parties. Although there is no black list, by inference, those States that are not on the White List may be suspected of not having complied with their obligations under the STCW. In addition, revised Chapter I includes enhanced procedures to allow Port State intervention in the case of deficiencies deemed to pose a danger to persons, property or the environment.

PSC

Port State Control (PSC) is the inspection of foreign ships in ports in order to verify that the condition of the ship and its equipment comply with the requirements of international regulations and that the ship is manned and operated in compliance with these rules. While the primary responsibility for ships' maintaining standards rests with the flag State, PSC provides a means of ensuring that substandard ships are identified and the defects remedied, where flag States are unable or unwilling to properly supervise the operation of their ships.

---

9 The International Convention on Standards of Training, Certification and Watchkeeping for Seafarers of 7 July 1978 (1361 UNTS 2).

10 Amendment to the International Convention on Standards of Training, Certification and Watchkeeping for Seafarers of 7 July 1995 ((1997) UKTS 61). Entry into force: 1 February 1997.

The main IMO conventions for safety (SOLAS),[11] pollution prevention (MARPOL)[12] and manning (STCW) contain provisions for ships to be inspected when they visit foreign ports to ensure that they meet IMO requirements. Other IMO conventions and an ILO convention are also subject to PSC. Any deficiencies found are reported to the flag State and have to be rectified. In the case of a serious deficiency, the ship must be detained until a repair ensures that the ship is seaworthy and does not present a hazard to the marine environment. The application of the principle of "no more favourable treatment" means that ships of non-parties are inspected in the same way and against the same standards as parties to the relevant conventions. IMO has encouraged the development of Memoranda of Understanding (MOUs) on PSC and the establishment of regional PSC organizations. There are currently nine MOUs on PSC covering most of the world's oceans.

GISIS

The MOUs are considering providing information to IMO in electronic form for publication on the Global Integrated Shipping Information System (GISIS), which is an integrated database managed by IMO containing 17 modules, with four under development, for the collection, processing and sharing of shipping-related data in order to generate reports, to provide information about shipping to the public, and to assist IMO member States in fulfilling their duties. A broad range of information is already available and modules are in preparation including lists of mandatory and non-mandatory instruments, with the facility for member States to upload their national implementing legislation. FSI is considering the possibility of States using GISIS to fulfil their reporting requirements under IMO Conventions. Thus, GISIS could provide easily accessible information on how IMO member States are fulfilling their obligations. This transparency could result in a 'naming and shaming' effect.

---

[11] International Convention for the Safety of Life at Sea of 1 November 1974 (1184 UNTS 2). SOLAS is amended (updated) almost every year. Updated versions are published and sold by IMO on a regular basis.

[12] International Convention for the Prevention of Pollution from Ships of 2 November 1973 ((1973) 12 ILM 1319) as amended by the Protocol of 1978 ((1978) 17 ILM 511). MARPOL is amended (updated) almost every year. Updated versions are published and sold by IMO on a regular basis.

IMO Rules are Applicable to All States

The LOS Convention contains numerous provisions requiring States to "take account of" "conform to", "give effect to" or "implement" the relevant international rules and standards developed by or through "the competent international organisation", which in the case of shipping is understood to be IMO. The rules and standards that States must apply are variously referred to as for instance "generally accepted international rules and standards" or "applicable international rules and standards". The degree to which these rules or instruments must be applied depends upon the specific wording of the provision, from "take account of" to "implement".

By virtue of these provisions, generally accepted rules, regulations, etc. must be applied by all States parties to the LOS Convention, even if they are not parties to IMO instruments. Because the LOS Convention is generally considered to reflect customary international law, IMO instruments must also be applied by non-parties. Thus, IMO's rules on safety, navigation and environmental protection are applicable by all States under both the LOS Convention and customary international law. The UN and IMO secretariats and most IMO member States have agreed on this analysis, with the proviso that the rules etc. must be generally accepted.[13] The criterion of "generally accepted" is easily fulfilled, as IMO has 169 member States and three associate members, a majority of the international community, and its conventions and other instruments are normally adopted by consensus. Furthermore, most conventions cover 95–99 % of world shipping tonnage.

As to the issue of jurisdiction regarding pollution on the high seas, under the LOS Convention Article 218, a port State may take enforcement action against a foreign vessel in respect of pollution on the high seas. Under Article 228, although a port State must suspend proceedings against a foreign vessel for a violation beyond its territorial sea if the flag State begins proceedings on the same charges, it does not have to do so if the ship has caused major damage to the coastal State or if the flag State "has repeatedly disregarded its obligation to enforce effectively the applicable international rules and standards in respect of violations committed by its vessels." These provisions indicate that flag State jurisdiction over its vessels is qualified, not absolute, even on the high seas and that the international community has an interest in ensuring that all ships

[13] See IMO document "Implication of the United Nations Convention on the Law of the Sea for the International Maritime Organization" (IMO Doc. LEG/MISC.6 of 10 September 2008). The same reasoning applies to the London Convention (Convention for the Prevention of Marine Pollution by Dumping of Wastes and Other Matter of 29 December 1972 (1976) UKTS 43) and the London Protocol (Protocol to the Convention for the Prevention of Marine Pollution by Dumping of Wastes and Other Matter of 29 December 1972, 7 November 1996, 35 ILM (1996) 1415).

meet international standards and conform to international rules and regulations. Furthermore, under Article 228, enforcement jurisdiction depends upon a flag State's willingness and ability to exercise the necessary supervision and control. This provision could form the basis for the further development of the law in a new agreement.

State Responsibility

According to the Preamble to the LOS Convention, any matters not regulated by the Convention continue to be governed by the rules and principles of general international law. These rules and principles include those relating to State responsibility and the settlement of disputes. Flag States not fulfilling their international obligations under the LOS Convention or IMO conventions are responsible to the other States parties to the conventions, and arguably, to all States, since the main obligations of flag State control over their vessels and of implementation and enforcement of international rules and regulations are part of general international law.

Furthermore, States that are responsible for not having fulfilled their obligations are subject to the rules concerning settlement of disputes under Part XV of the LOS Convention for States parties, under other agreements or under general international law for non-parties. Aggrieved States may approach a flag State, which they consider has violated international law by not controlling its ships, and request negotiation, mediation, conciliation or third party settlement. Third party settlement may include proceedings before an ad-hoc tribunal, the ITLOS, or the International Court of Justice (ICJ). If all else fails and compulsory third party settlement is not available, then aggrieved States may apply the rules of State responsibility and use counter-measures.

However, States are very reluctant to litigate, because litigation is expensive, time-consuming and troublesome and may be perceived as an 'unfriendly act', having undesirable political repercussions. On the other hand, sometimes litigation can help resolve a difficult domestic political issue. Likewise, with some exceptions, States are usually reluctant to use counter-measures, because that involves using an otherwise illegal act to counter another illegal act in the hope of inducing the State responsible for the original illegality to cease. Under the rules for counter-measures, the counter-measure would not be illegal if it fulfilled certain conditions. However, some States still do not accept the legitimacy of counter-measures and counter-measures may be difficult to defend, especially if the illegality of the initial act is uncertain. More positively, a unilateral act, even if illegal, may prompt other States to address a problem that they had been reluctant to resolve, and may even result in a new and better law.

A good example of these issues in the case of over-fishing and the failure of a flag State to control its vessels is that of the Spanish fishing vessel *Estai*. In March 1995, when Spanish vessels were fishing over the quota set by Northwest Atlantic Fisheries Organization (NAFO) for Greenland halibut, a Canadian fisheries patrol vessel arrested the Spanish fishing vessel *Estai* on the high seas and brought it into port in Newfoundland.[14] Spain protested that this was a violation of its sovereignty and exclusive jurisdiction under the law of the sea and instituted proceedings against Canada at the ICJ.[15] The Canadian Prime Minister had decided to avoid litigation by means of a reservation to Canada's acceptance of the compulsory jurisdiction of the ICJ. The Court upheld the reservation. However, if the objection to jurisdiction had failed, Canada could have relied on the work of the International Law Commission in relation to counter-measures to justify its action.

In any event, far from provoking a disaster, as feared by some, the arrest of the *Estai* led to three beneficial results. First, within a month, Canada and the EC had negotiated an agreement on new, more stringent conservation and enforcement measures in the NAFO Regulatory Area. Second, these measures were adopted officially by NAFO as a whole at its meeting in September 2005. Third, in the interim, afraid of the possible world-wide emulation of such unilateral measures, the EC and other participants finally concluded negotiations at the UN Conference on Straddling Fish Stocks and Highly Migratory Fish Stocks with the adoption of the UN Fish Stocks Agreement, an outcome they had resisted for several years. Thus, unilateral acts can provoke positive legal developments.

Concluding Remarks

States that do not control their vessels on the high seas and that do not enforce international rules and regulations are responsible to other States. They can be sued in court and, where necessary, can be stopped by the use of carefully crafted and timed counter-measures. However, the problems regarding substandard merchant vessels and errant fishing boats are so complex that

---

[14] The Spanish catch had soared from only 13 tonnes in 1989 to over 40,000 tonnes in 1994. At the request of Canada, NAFO decided to regulate fishing for Greenland halibut. Because most other fish stocks in the Regulatory Area of the NAFO had been placed under moratorium, Spanish and Portuguese fishers had begun taking unsustainable amounts of Greenland halibut from a stock that straddled the Canadian EEZ and the NAFO Regulatory Area. The EU objected to its quota of 3,400 tonnes, and set itself a much higher quota of 18,630 tonnes. This amount would have undermined conservation measures and depleted the stock.

[15] *Fisheries Jurisdiction Case* (Spain v. Canada) [1995] ICJ Reports 97.

litigation may not be the best response. The measures now being taken to deal with both problems could be effective in time. Despite some high-profile disasters, in recent years, pollution from vessels has been reduced. On the other hand, in the case of fisheries, by the time all the current and planned measures become effective, most of the world's fish stocks could collapse.[16] The real underlying problem is political will. Political will is currently present to a considerable degree at the IMO, but in relation to fisheries, is still sadly lacking.

[16] Some scientists estimate that if present trends continue, all commercial fish stocks could collapse by 2050. B. Worm et al. "Impacts of Biodiversity Loss on Ocean Ecosystem Services" (2006) 314(5800) *Science* 787–790.

LUNCHEON SPEECH

THE CONTRIBUTION OF THE INTERNATIONAL TRIBUNAL FOR THE LAW OF THE SEA TO INTERNATIONAL LAW

HELMUT TUERK*

Ladies and Gentlemen,

It is a distinct honour and high privilege indeed to have been asked to speak before such a distinguished audience of international lawyers and renowned experts on the law of the sea on the contribution of the International Tribunal for the Law of the Sea (ITLOS) to international law at this Fourth J.H.W. Verzijl Memorial Symposium. Let me express my particular gratitude and appreciation to the Director of the Netherlands Institute for the Law of the Sea, Professor A.H.A. Soons, to Dr. A.G. Oude Elferink and to Dr. E.J. Molenaar for having invited me to this important and highly interesting Symposium.

As time is limited I will endeavour to concentrate on the most important points of my topic and first give you an overview regarding the jurisdiction, composition and structure of the ITLOS, and then briefly deal with its jurisprudence. I am also aware of the fact that much, if not most, of what I am going to say is already well-known to you.

The United Nations Convention on the Law of the Sea[1] (LOS Convention) of 10 December 1982 which entered into force on 16 November 1994 after eight years of protracted and particularly difficult negotiations—to which all of us who participated in them can bear witness—is certainly one of the most important treaties ever elaborated under the auspices of the United Nations. At present, 158 States and the European Community are parties to it. The Convention is thus slowly moving towards universal adherence and there is even some optimism in Washington that the United States might finally adhere to it.

Since its entry into force the LOS Convention has undoubtedly played a major role in bringing order to the oceans and eliminating the causes for many maritime disputes between States. Although the Convention provides a comprehensive regime for the seas, regulating all ocean space, its uses and its resources, there are nevertheless bound to be gaps—partly addressed by

* Vice-President of the International Tribunal for the Law of the Sea.

[1] Adopted on 10 December 1982; 1833 UNTS 296.

Alex G. Oude Elferink and Erik J. Molenaar (eds.), *The International Legal Regime of Areas beyond National Jurisdiction: Current and Future Developments*, pp. 217–230.

this Symposium—as in any multilateral convention which is also a framework treaty. These gaps have been and will continue to be filled in by implementing instruments and to a certain extent by jurisprudence. The latter is facilitated by the fact that the Convention contains quite an innovative system for the settlement of disputes. It has been observed that it is one of the most far-reaching and complex systems of dispute settlement to be found anywhere in international law. There can be no doubt that the underlying rationale for the creation of such a system was the wish to safeguard the many delicate compromises enshrined in the Convention and to secure its uniform interpretation and application.

Part XV of the Convention deals with the settlement of disputes. It imposes an obligation on States Parties to settle disputes by peaceful means and, in particular, also provides for compulsory procedures with binding decisions. Annex VI of the Convention contains the Statute of the ITLOS which is one of the four means for the settlement of disputes entailing such decisions. The other alternative means are the International Court of Justice (ICJ), an arbitral tribunal constituted in accordance with Annex VII of the Convention and a special arbitral tribunal under Annex VIII for certain categories of disputes—fisheries, protection and preservation of the marine environment, marine scientific research, or navigation, including pollution from vessels and dumping.

The ITLOS, which became operational on 1 October 1996, is the specialized international judicial body established for the settlement of disputes concerning the interpretation or application of the LOS Convention, and for rendering advisory opinions. The jurisdiction of the Tribunal, in principle, includes any dispute relating to the law of the sea, such as disputes relating to maritime boundaries, fisheries, sea pollution or marine scientific research. Its jurisdiction is, however, subject to limitations spelled out in Article 297 of the Convention which relates to the exercise of certain discretionary powers by the coastal State, in particular, disputes relating to its sovereign rights in respect of fisheries in the exclusive economic zone (EEZ). Furthermore, according to Article 298 exceptions to the compulsory procedures may also be made for matters concerning sea boundary delimitations, historic bays or titles, or military activities by virtue of written declarations. To date 29 States have made such declarations. In two instances the Tribunal has compulsory jurisdiction, that is, Article 290(5), regarding provisional measures, and Article 292 concerning the prompt release of vessels and/or crews.

It is important to note that a State Party is supposed to have accepted compulsory procedure by the mere fact of having ratified or adhered to the Convention in respect of any dispute arising thereunder, unless it expressly excludes the application of this type of procedure. There is thus no need to make a separate declaration to accept the compulsory procedure, a declaration being required only to exclude such procedure. This is a significant innovation with respect to the traditional compulsory jurisdiction system, which requires separate consent, as is the case with Article 36, paragraph 2, of the Statute of the ICJ.

Article 287 of the Convention outlines various procedures available to parties to settle their disputes peacefully through the compulsory mechanisms established by it. That Article provides that a State party, when signing, ratifying or acceding to the Convention or at any time thereupon, is free to choose one or more of the four means for the settlement of disputes already mentioned, by submission of a written declaration to the Secretary-General of the United Nations. So far only 41 States have made such a declaration—and a mere 24 of those have accepted the Tribunal's compulsory jurisdiction. In the absence of such a declaration or if the parties have not accepted the same procedure under Article 287, parties are deemed to have accepted arbitration under Annex VII of the Convention.

Arbitration is, in practice, turning out to be rather the general rule. It may seem somewhat doubtful whether this development was really anticipated at the time of the negotiations on the Convention, or whether it was believed that arbitration—although the default procedure—would turn out to be a rather subsidiary means for the settlement of disputes. So far, six cases, including two maritime boundary delimitation cases, have been referred to arbitral tribunals constituted in accordance with Annex VII.

The jurisdiction of the Tribunal may also derive from relevant clauses included in international agreements relating to the law of the sea. At present, there are nine international agreements containing provisions making specific reference to the dispute settlement procedures of Part XV of the Convention and conferring therewith jurisdiction on the Tribunal. Let me just mention the Fish Stocks Agreement[2] of 1995, the UNESCO Convention on the Protection of the Underwater Cultural Heritage[3] of 2001 and as most recent example the Nairobi International Convention on the Removal of Wrecks.[4] With respect to these agreements, the procedures of Part XV apply, whether a party to the agreement is a State Party to the LOS Convention.

In this connection it has to be borne in mind that the ICJ is referred to as the dispute settlement mechanism in more than 300 international agreements,

[2] Agreement for the Implementation of the Provisions of the United Nations Convention on the Law of the Sea of 10 December 1982 Relating to the Conservation and Management of Straddling Fish Stocks and Highly Migratory Fish Stocks of 4 August 1995 ((1995) 34 ILM 1542).

[3] Convention on the Protection of the Underwater Cultural Heritage of 2 November 2001 ((2002) 41 ILM 40).

[4] International Convention on the Removal of Wrecks of 18 May 2007 ((2007) 46 ILM 694).

most of which have been concluded long before the establishment of the ITLOS. This is undoubtedly an important reason why the Court is being used more often for the settling of maritime disputes than the Tribunal.

Finally, Article 22 of the Statute allows the Tribunal to exercise jurisdiction over disputes relating to the interpretation or application of treaties which are already in force, and concern the subject-matter covered by the Convention, provided that all the parties to that treaty so agree.

The Convention does not contain any provision conferring advisory jurisdiction on the Tribunal as such, which may, however, on the basis of Article 21 of its Statute give an advisory opinion on a legal question if this is provided for by an international agreement related to the purposes of the Convention conferring jurisdiction on it. Thus far, no use has been made of that interesting option in any international instrument.

The law to be applied by the Tribunal comprises the Convention, and other rules of international law not incompatible with it. This does not, however, preclude the Tribunal from holding jurisdiction to determine a matter *ex aequo et bono*, if the parties so agree. Decisions are final and the parties to the dispute are required to comply with them. The decisions, however, have no binding force beyond the parties to the dispute, although they may be quite significant for the development of the law of the sea in general, and may, in addition, influence the future interpretation of this body of law.

The Tribunal is, at present, the largest world-wide judicial body, being composed of 21 judges elected by the States Parties to the Convention for a term of nine years. The composition of the Tribunal must ensure adequate representation of the principal legal systems of the world and an equitable geographical distribution. The States Parties—which hold annual meetings in New York—have agreed to elect five judges each from Africa and Asia, four each from Latin American and Caribbean States, as well as Western European and Other States, and three from the Group of Eastern European States. This distribution of seats is now being challenged by the African and the Asian Groups which demand that the Western European and Other States Group surrender one seat in their favour.

The composition of the Tribunal clearly shows that added weight has been given to developing countries in comparison with the ICJ, where, in practice, judges from the five permanent members of the Security Council occupy one third of the 15 seats. If the Tribunal does not include upon the bench a judge of the nationality of a party to a dispute, that party may designate a person of its choice to sit as a judge *ad hoc*.

The Tribunal is open to States Parties to the Convention, other States, as well as other entities, such as international organizations and natural or legal persons in any case expressly provided for in Part XI of the Convention—regarding exploration and exploitation of the International Seabed Area—or in any case submitted pursuant to any other agreement conferring jurisdiction on the Tribunal which is accepted by all the parties to the case.

The jurisdiction of the ITLOS is not as broad *ratione materiae* as that of the ICJ, being confined to matters provided for in the Convention and related instruments. However, it is certainly more comprehensive *ratione personae*, as in cases before the Court only States may be parties. Access is probably the most significant difference between the Tribunal and the ICJ.

The Statute of the Tribunal makes provision for the establishment of the Seabed Disputes Chamber as well as special chambers for dealing with particular disputes or categories of disputes. The Seabed Disputes Chamber, which is a 'tribunal within a tribunal', consists of eleven judges selected every three years. We have the privilege of having the once again elected President of that Chamber, Judge Tullio Treves, in our midst today. The Conference on the Law of the Sea had originally envisioned the establishment of a Seabed Tribunal as one of the principal organs of the International Seabed Authority (ISA) to deal exclusively with seabed disputes. This approach was, however, abandoned in favour of establishing a fully-fledged Tribunal as an autonomous international organ with a Seabed Disputes Chamber.

That Chamber—the jurisdiction of which is compulsory—has not yet heard a single case, mainly because deep seabed mining is not yet commercially viable, and may not be anytime soon, if at all. It may also give advisory opinions at the request of the Assembly or the Council of the ISA on legal questions arising within the scope of their activities. Thus far, these organs of the Authority have not made use of that possibility.

Following a similar system of the ICJ, the Tribunal established several special chambers: the Chamber of Summary Procedure, the Chamber for Fisheries Disputes, the Chamber for Marine Environment Disputes and the Chamber for Maritime Delimitation. More important in practice, however, seems to be the possibility to form an *ad hoc* special chamber consisting of at least three members, who may be chosen from among the members of the Tribunal; the Parties may also designate *ad hoc* judges. That system should be of particular interest to parties considering arbitration, since, as in arbitration, parties are given substantial freedom to choose the judges who are to sit in such a chamber, and may even propose modifications to the Tribunal's rules of procedure for the chamber to apply. Thus, the parties can enjoy all the benefits of arbitration, without being required to bear the expenses of the chamber. It is important to note that recourse to the Tribunal as such involves no cost for the States Parties to the Convention.

Let me now turn to the jurisprudence of the Tribunal:

Since the commencement of its activities, 15 cases have been submitted to the Tribunal, mainly on the basis of its compulsory jurisdiction. That jurisdiction encompasses cases in which it is alleged that by detaining a vessel flying the flag of another State and/or its crew for certain offences—for instance in respect of illegal fishing or pollution—a State has violated the provisions of the Convention for the prompt release of the vessel and/or its crew upon the posting of a reasonable bond or other financial security. It is important to point out that the Convention permits coastal States to exercise enforcement jurisdiction through the seizure of vessels and crews in certain limited circumstances. The coastal States are entitled to board and inspect any vessel within their 200 nautical mile EEZs—where around 90 % of commercial fishing takes place—in order to enforce their laws and regulations in respect of the living resources of that area.

Whenever it is alleged that the detaining State has not complied with its duty under the Convention of prompt release of vessels and crew, the flag State of the vessel is entitled under Article 292—a provision which constitutes a counterpart to the rights granted to coastal States—to request the release of the vessel before the Tribunal. The question of release may be submitted not only by the flag State, but also 'on its behalf'. This permits States either once and for all, or on a case-by-case basis, to entrust the interested ship-owners, or for instance, associations of such ship-owners with the power to act on their behalf. In this way, in practice even though not in principle, private parties may be allowed to further their interests directly before the Tribunal.

In prompt release proceedings, the Tribunal may, however, deal only with the question of the release of the vessel without prejudice to the merits of any case before the appropriate domestic forum in respect of the vessel, its owner or its crew. In its jurisprudence, the Tribunal has strictly applied this requirement of the Convention.

The prompt release procedure before the Tribunal is also characterised by its swiftness. The Tribunal, according to its Rules, shall give priority to applications for the release of vessels or crews over all other proceedings. The hearing must take place within a period of 15 days commencing with the first working day following the date on which the application is received and the judgment must not be read later than 14 days after the closure of the hearing. In its practice, the Tribunal has acted in prompt release proceedings with remarkable efficiency and speed, having delivered its decisions within the timeframe of approximately one month. The urgency of these proceedings is justified in view of the financial burden resulting from the detention of a vessel as well as humanitarian considerations regarding detained crews.

The Tribunal has so far been seized of applications for prompt release in nine cases, nearly all of them connected with fisheries. In the course of this presentation I will only briefly outline the last two of these cases:

The *Hoshinmaru* case[5] concerned a dispute submitted by Japan on 6 July 2007 regarding the detention of that fishing vessel by the authorities of the Russian Federation for the alleged infringement of national fisheries legislation in its EEZ. On 13 July—more than five weeks after the detention of the vessel—Russia set a bond of 25,000,000 roubles—approximately US$ 980,000—and claimed that the application was therefore inadmissible. Japan maintained that the amount of the bond was unreasonable and did not meet the requirements of Article 292 of the Convention. Both parties further disagreed as to whether the crew and the Master were being detained along with the vessel.

In its judgment of 6 August 2007 the Tribunal confirmed its previous jurisprudence regarding the reasonableness of a bond or other financial security and, *inter alia*, stated that the amount of the bond should be proportionate to the gravity of the alleged offences. It thus considered the amount of the bond fixed by the Russian Federation not to be reasonable and decided that the *Hoshinmaru* including its catch on board should be promptly released upon the posting of a bond or other security as determined by the Tribunal—10,000,000 roubles, approximately US$ 390,000—and that the Master and the crew should be free to leave without any conditions. On 16 August 2007 the bond was received by the Russian Federation and the vessel and crew were released on the same day. This is an excellent example as to the efficiency of the prompt release procedure provided for in the Convention.

The *Tomimaru* case[6] was submitted by Japan on the same day as the *Hoshinmaru* case and also concerned the detention of that fishing vessel by the authorities of the Russian Federation for the alleged infringement of national fisheries legislation in its EEZ. In that case the Tribunal had to deal with the thorny issue of the effects of the confiscation of a fishing vessel—a measure that many States have in their legislation with respect to the conservation and management of natural resources. The *Tomimaru* had already been detained on 31 October 2006 and the crew had been allowed to leave the Russian Federation long before the application was submitted by Japan. The competent Russian courts had decided to confiscate the vessel and Russia thus maintained that the application by Japan had been rendered without object.

In its judgment of 6 August 2007 the Tribunal expressed the view that the decision to confiscate eliminates the provisional character of the detention of the vessel rendering the procedure for its prompt release without object. It,

[5] *Hoshinmaru Case* (Japan vs. Russian Federation) case No. 14 [2007] ITLOS.

[6] *Tomimaru* case (Japan v. Russian Federation) (2007) 46 ILM 1183.

however, also observed that such a decision should not be taken in such a way as to prevent the ship owner from having recourse to available domestic judicial remedies, or as to prevent the flag State from resorting to the prompt release procedure set forth in the Convention. The Tribunal further underscored that a decision to confiscate the vessel did not prevent it from considering an application for prompt release while proceedings are still before the domestic courts of the detaining State. Note was taken of the fact that the decision of the Supreme Court of the Russian Federation—which confirmed the decision of the lower courts to confiscate the *Tomimaru*— had brought to an end the procedures before the domestic courts. The Tribunal thus found that the application of Japan no longer had any object and that it was therefore not called upon to give a decision thereon.

In respect of the six cases in which the Tribunal ordered the release of the vessel and/or its crew upon the posting of a reasonable bond, it can fairly be said that it has developed a coherent jurisprudence, particularly as regards the relevant factors for determining the reasonableness of bonds or other financial security. These factors—which by no means constitute a complete list—include the gravity of the alleged offences, the penalties imposed or imposable under the laws of the detaining State, the value of the detained vessel and of the cargo seized, the amount of the bond imposed by the detaining State and its form. The assessment of the relevant factors by the Tribunal is an objective one, taking into account all information provided by the parties and having regard to all the circumstances of the particular case.

The procedure for the prompt release of vessels and crews, with the possibility for private parties, if properly authorized by the flag State, to appear before the Tribunal, is certainly a significant innovation provided by the Convention, if not the most important novel feature of its entire dispute settlement mechanism. This procedure constitutes an appropriate and cost-effective mechanism for parties faced with the arrest of vessels and crews. It seems, however, that the possibility to institute such proceedings is not yet known well enough neither by ship owners nor by flag States. It has not without some reason been said that the existence of the ITLOS is one of the better-guarded secrets of the United Nations system. Flag States may also sometimes hesitate to have recourse to the Tribunal. In this context, it has been suggested that owners who register their ships with flag States should, in the negotiations prior to registration, obtain the right to act on behalf of the flag State in the event of a dispute with a coastal State regarding prompt release of vessels and crew.

As regards provisional measures, the Tribunal may be requested to prescribe these in two situations: first where a dispute on the merits has been submitted to it, and second when a dispute on the merits has been submitted to an arbitral tribunal, pending its constitution.

When provisional measures have been requested by a party to a dispute that has been submitted to an arbitral tribunal, the Tribunal is empowered, pursuant to Article 290(5), of the Convention, to grant such measures pending the constitution of the arbitral tribunal, unless the parties have agreed to seize another court or tribunal within two weeks from the date of the request for provisional measures. Thus, the Tribunal may, at the request of a State Party, prescribe provisional measures against another State Party pending the final decision to be given not by the Tribunal itself, but by an arbitral tribunal that is yet to be constituted. In order to prescribe provisional measures, the Tribunal must consider that the measures are required by the urgency of the situation and that, *prima facie*, the arbitral tribunal to be constituted would have jurisdiction.

As regards disputes in relation to activities in the International Seabed Area, an arbitral tribunal dealing with a commercial dispute shall according to Article 188(2), refer any question of the interpretation of Part XI of the Convention and the annexes relating thereto to the Seabed Disputes Chamber for a ruling, either at the request of any party to the dispute, or *proprio motu*.

It is interesting to note in this regard important innovations introduced by the Convention. First, the measures prescribed by the Tribunal are binding upon the parties to the dispute. Second, the Tribunal may prescribe provisional measures not only to preserve the respective rights of the parties to the dispute, but also to "prevent serious harm to the marine environment". In addition, the Tribunal may follow up the measures it has prescribed by requesting the parties to submit reports on compliance. The Tribunal has so far once made use of this possibility.

The Tribunal's power to prescribe provisional measures has already been invoked in four cases dealing with the protection of the marine environment:

In the *Southern Bluefin Tuna* cases,[7] the applicants, Australia and New Zealand, sought relief from the Tribunal in relation to Japan's unilateral decision to conduct an experimental fishing program, which was planned for a duration of three years. The Tribunal was requested to prescribe provisional measures to the effect that Japan immediately cease its unilateral experimental fishing of southern bluefin tuna, restrict its catch to the national quotum as last agreed, and require all parties to act consistently with the precautionary principle—caution and vigilance—in fishing for southern bluefin tuna pending final settlement of the dispute. Japan contended that the Tribunal had no jurisdiction, and that even if it did, the prescription of provisional measures would not be appropriate, since there was no risk of irreparable damage to the fish stock in question.

---

[7] *Southern Bluefin Tuna* (New Zealand v. Japan; Australia v. Japan) (1999) 38 ILM 1624; (2000) 39 ILM 1359.

In its Order of 27 August 1999, the Tribunal considered that the conservation of the living resources of the sea is an element in the protection and preservation of the marine environment. The parties should, in the circumstances, act with "prudence and caution" to ensure that effective conservation measures were taken to prevent serious harm to stock of southern bluefin tuna. The Tribunal also ordered, *inter alia*, that the parties should resume negotiations without delay, with a view to reaching agreement on measures for the conservation and management of these fish stocks, and that the parties should restrict their catches. Although there is no express reference in the Order to the precautionary principle itself, the Tribunal nevertheless prescribed de facto precautionary measures and seems at least implicitly to have relied on that principle.

It has been observed that the Tribunal's intervention at the stage of provisional measures played a very significant role in bringing the parties—Australia, New Zealand and Japan—back to negotiations with each other, with the eventual result that the Southern Bluefin Tuna Commission was revitalized and is now functioning well.

In the *MOX Plant* case,[8] the Tribunal heard a dispute between Ireland and the United Kingdom regarding the potentially harmful impact on the marine environment of the operation of a MOX plant situated at Sellafield, United Kingdom, on the coast of the Irish Sea. Such a plant recycles material from nuclear reactors and converts it into a new fuel called MOX—mixed oxide fuel—intended for use as an energy source in nuclear power stations. Ireland requested that the dispute be submitted to an arbitral tribunal to be established under Annex VII of the Convention, and furthermore submitted a request for the prescription of provisional measures, pending the constitution of the arbitral tribunal.

In its Order of 3 December 2001, the Tribunal found that the urgency of the situation did not, in the short period before the constitution of the Annex VII arbitral tribunal, require the prescription of provisional measures as requested by Ireland. However, the Tribunal did consider that the duty to co-operate is a fundamental principle in the prevention of pollution of the marine environment under Part XII of the Convention, as well as under general international law, and that rights arise therefrom which it may consider appropriate to conserve under Article 290 of the Convention. The Tribunal therefore ordered the litigants—pending a decision by the arbitral tribunal—to co-operate and enter into consultations in order to exchange further information regarding the possible consequences for the Irish Sea arising from the commissioning of

[8] *The MOX Plant Case* (Ireland v. United Kingdom) (2002) 41 ILM 405.

the MOX plant, and to devise, as appropriate, measures to prevent pollution of the marine environment which might result from the plant's operation.

The Order itself contains no reference to the precautionary principle, except to note that Ireland had argued its application in the case. The reason therefore may have been that in the opinion of the Tribunal, provisional measures should not anticipate a judgment on the merits.

Let me, however, also mention that the Court of Justice of the European Communities, in its judgment of 30 May 2006, in the case *Commission of the European Communities versus Ireland*,[9] stated that it had exclusive jurisdiction to rule on disputes concerning the interpretation and application of provisions of the LOS Convention which form part of the Community legal order. By bringing proceedings under the dispute settlement procedure laid down in the Convention, Ireland had failed to comply with its duty of cooperation under the European Community and Euratom Treaties, and accordingly was in breach of Community Law. This judgment clearly cannot please the Tribunal. For, the position taken by the Court of Justice of the European Communities may seriously affect the future possibility of Member States of the European Union to make use of the dispute settlement mechanism of the Convention on the Law of the Sea in cases of disputes among them.

The case of *Land Reclamation by Singapore in and around the Straits of Johor*[10] concerned a dispute between Malaysia and Singapore relating to land reclamation activities carried out by Singapore which, according to Malaysia, impinged upon its rights in and around the Straits of Johor, the body of water separating Malaysia from the island of Singapore. Malaysia claimed that Singapore's actions were in breach of its duties under international law, including, *inter alia*, its duties to preserve and protect the marine environment.

In its Order of 8 October 2003, the Tribunal prescribed provisional measures, pending a decision by an Annex VII arbitral tribunal, requiring Malaysia and Singapore to cooperate and enter into consultation to establish promptly a group of independent experts to study the effects of Singapore's land reclamation. Singapore was, furthermore, directed not to conduct its land reclamation in ways that might cause irreparable prejudice to the rights of Malaysia or serious harm to the marine environment. The Order also stated that "prudence and caution" require Malaysia and Singapore to establish mechanisms for exchanging information, assessing risks of the reclamation projects, and devising mechanisms to deal with it.

---

[9] *Commission of the European Communities v. Ireland* C-459/03 [2006] European Court of Justice, Official Journal of the European Union 2006/C 165/04.

[10] *Land Reclamation by Singapore in and around the Straits of Johor* (Malaysia v. Singapore) case No. 12 [2003] ITLOS 10.

It should further be mentioned that Malaysia and Singapore settled their dispute by signing an agreement to this effect. A final arbitral award was made in the case on 1 September 2005 in accordance with the terms specified in that agreement. The provisional measures ordered by the Tribunal in 2003 were obviously instrumental in bringing the parties together and providing a successful diplomatic solution to the dispute.

The record of the Tribunal on environmental disputes is thus a positive one, despite the absence of any opportunity to decide such a case on the merits. The aforementioned cases have enabled the Tribunal to contribute to the development of international environmental law, in particular by emphasizing the duty of cooperation, the notion of prudence and caution, and the importance of procedural rights, as essential components of environmental obligations. In its orders for provisional measures, the Tribunal followed the line of adopting a pragmatic approach and prescribing measures which, in its view, would assist the parties to find a solution.

The parties may also submit a particular dispute to the Tribunal at any time by means of a special agreement, which has to date been done on two occasions. In the *M/V "SAIGA" (No. 2)* case,[11] Saint Vincent and the Grenadines and Guinea agreed to submit to the Tribunal the merits of the dispute relating to the arrest and detention of the vessel *M/V Saiga*. This has been the only case which the Tribunal has so far decided on the merits. The other case, also relating to the merits and still on the docket concerns a dispute between Chile and the European Community[12] regarding the conservation and sustainable exploitation of swordfish stocks in the South-Eastern Pacific Ocean.

In the *M/V "SAIGA" (No. 2) Case*, the Tribunal had to deal with both the merits and the request for the prescription of provisional measures. That vessel and its crew continued to be held by Guinea even after the Tribunal had prescribed their prompt release. Guinea had not only arrested the tanker *M/V Saiga*, but also its master for providing fishing vessels with gasoil—bunkering—off the coast of Guinea, which it alleged was an offence under its customs laws. Saint Vincent and the Grenadines claimed, however, that the bunkering of vessels is within the freedom of navigation in the EEZ. The arrest of the *Saiga* had taken place at a point outside Guinea's EEZ, with Guinea claiming that the arrest followed its right of "hot pursuit".

On 11 March 1998, the Tribunal delivered its Order regarding the prescription of provisional measures, stating that Guinea should refrain from taking or

---

[11] *The M/V "SAIGA" (No. 2) Case* (Saint Vincent and the Grenadines v. Guinea) case No. 2 [1999] ITLOS Reports 10.

[12] *Case concerning the Conservation and Sustainable Exploitation of Swordfish Stocks in the South-Eastern Pacific Ocean* (Chile v. European Community) (2001) 40 ILM 474.

enforcing any judicial or administrative measures against the *Saiga*, its master and the other members of the crew, its owners or operators, in connection with the incidents leading to the arrest and detention of the vessel and to the subsequent prosecution and conviction of the master. The vessel, its captain and its crew had in fact already been released shortly before in compliance by Guinea with a previous judgment of the Tribunal.

On 1 July 1999, the Tribunal delivered its judgment on the merits declaring that Guinea had violated the rights of Saint Vincent and the Grenadines in arresting the *Saiga*, and awarded Saint Vincent and the Grenadines US$ 2,123,357 with interest as compensation. In that judgment, the Tribunal made several important pronouncements concerning issues such as freedom of navigation, enforcement of customs laws, nationality of claims, reparation, use of force in law enforcement activities, hot pursuit and the question of the genuine link between the vessel and its flag State, thereby making an important contribution to the development of international law regarding these aspects.

In the *Case concerning the Conservation and Sustainable Exploitation of Swordfish Stocks in the South-Eastern Pacific Ocean*, the Tribunal, at the request of Chile and the European Community, on 20 December 2000 formed a special chamber to deal with the dispute, consisting of four judges of the Tribunal and one judge *ad hoc*. This has so far been the only case where one of the parties to the dispute is an international organization, namely the European Community. The case, *inter alia*, concerns whether the European Community has complied with its obligations under the Convention to ensure the conservation of swordfish in the fishing activities undertaken by vessels flying the flag of its Member States in the high seas adjacent to Chile's EEZ. At the request of the parties, the time limits for the proceedings continue to be suspended until 1 January 2010, with both parties maintaining their right to revive them at any time.

The ITLOS has already established a reputation for the expeditious and efficient management of cases, and has made a substantial contribution to the development of international law. According to the LOS Convention it has the competence and means to deal with a wide range of disputes, and is well equipped to discharge its functions speedily, efficiently and cost-effectively. The continued and significant contribution to the peaceful settlement of disputes in accordance with Part XV of the Convention is regularly being noted with satisfaction by the United Nations General Assembly.

The total of fifteen cases—of which twelve were fisheries related and thirteen were introduced on the basis of the Tribunal's compulsory jurisdiction, may not appear particularly impressive. This record, however, does not compare unfavourably to that of other international judicial bodies in the initial stages of their existence. It should be borne in mind that the Tribunal is a relatively new judicial body which is yet to fulfil its potential as the specialized judicial organ of the international community for the settlement of disputes relating to the law of the sea. There is, for instance, no doubt that the Tribunal is competent to deal with environmental matters, as evidenced by the numerous provisions of the Convention relating to the protection of the marine environment. So far, however, it has dealt with marine environment issues only in the context of provisional-measures proceedings.

The creation of the ITLOS has from the very beginning been subject to a certain degree of criticism as being unnecessary and risking a fragmentation of international law. It is certainly true that States, under the LOS Convention, have a wide choice of forum for the settlement of disputes, which has been significantly expanded by the creation of the Tribunal. The evidence so far nevertheless suggests that a choice of forum is more beneficial than harmful and that the danger of conflicting jurisdiction has been widely overestimated. Fragmentation of the law of the sea has thus far not occurred, and the Tribunal also makes every effort to keep abreast of the developments that take place in other international judicial fora, in particular the ICJ. In spring 2008, an official exchange of views between the Court and the Tribunal has taken place which will be continued in the future.

The relative paucity of cases brought before the Tribunal, and the fact that it is thus underutilized is certainly a matter of concern for the judges, but one over which they have little or no control. It could, however, also be said that the relatively few cases of litigation among the States Parties to the United Nations Convention on the Law of the Sea is a compliment to the work of the negotiators of the Convention. I nevertheless hope that in the future the International Tribunal for the Law of the Sea will be given a more active role in the settlement of international maritime disputes.

Thank you very much for your kind attention.[13]

[13] This speech is based on an article on this topic, H. Tuerk "The Contribution of the International Tribunal for the Law of the Sea to International Law" (2007) 26(2) *Penn State International Law Review* 289–316.

BIBLIOGRAPHY

Ackerman, B.A. *Private property and the constitution* (Yale University Press, New Haven: 1977)

Alchian, A.A. "Some Economics of Property Rights" (1961) *Rand Paper No 2316*

Anderson, L.G. *The Economics of Fisheries Management* (John Hopkins University Press, Baltimore: 1977)

Annala, J.H. "New Zealand's ITQ System: Have the First Eight Years Been a Success or a Failure?" (1996) 6 *Reviews in Fish Biology and Fisheries* 43–62

Applebaum, R. "The Straddling Stocks Problem: The Northwest Atlantic Situation, International Law, and Options for Coastal State Action" in A.H.A. Soons (ed.) *Implementation of the Law of the Sea Convention through International Organizations: Proceedings of the 23rd Annual Conference of the Law of the Sea Institute, June 12–15, 1989, Noordwijk aan Zee, The Netherlands* (Honolulu, Law of the Sea Institute, University of Hawaii: 1990) 282–317

Aqorau, T. "Moving Towards a Rights-Based Fisheries Management Regime for the Tuna Fisheries in the Western and Central Pacific Ocean" (2007) 22 (1) *International Journal of Marine and Coastal Law* 125–142

Ardron, J. and K. Gjerde, S. Pullen and V. Tilot "Marine Spatial Planning in the High Seas" (2008) 32 *Marine Policy* 832–839

Arico, S. and C. Salpin *Bioprospecting of Genetic Resources in the Deep Seabed: Scientific, Legal and Policy Aspects* (United Nations Institute of Advanced Studies, Yokohama: 2005)

Armas Pfirter, F. "The Management of Seabed Living Resources in 'the Area' under UNCLOS" (2006) 11 *Revista Electrónica de Estudios Internacionales*

Arnason, R. "Ocean fisheries management: recent developments" (1993) 17 *Marine Policy* 334–339

Arnason, R. "On Catch Discarding in Fisheries" (1994) 9 *Marine Resource Economics* 189–207

Arrow, D. "Seabeds, Sovereignty and Objective Regimes" (1984) 7 *Fordham Journal of International Law* 169–243

Balton, D.A. "Strengthening the Law of the Sea: The New Agreement on Straddling Fish Stocks and Highly Migratory Fish Stocks" (1996) 27 *Ocean Development and International Law* 125–151

Bang, H.-S. "Is Port State Control an Effective Means to Combat Vessel-Source Pollution? An Empirical Survey of the Practical Exercise by Port States of Their Powers of Control" (2008) 23 (4) *International Journal of Marine and Coastal Law* 715–759

Barkenbus, J. *Deep Seabed Resources* (Free Press, New York: 1979)

Barnes, R. "Objective Regimes Revisited" (2000) 9 *Asian Yearbook of International Law* 97–145

Barnes, R. *Property Rights and Natural Resources* (Hart, Oxford: 2009)

Barzel, Y. *Economic Analysis of Property Rights* (Cambridge University Press, Cambridge: 1989)

Batstone, C.J. and B.M.H. Sharp "New Zealand's quota management system: The first ten years" (1999) 23 *Marine Policy* 177–190

Baxter, H. "Autopoiesis and the 'Relative Autonomy' of Law" (1998) 19 *Cardozo Law Review* 2087–2190

Becker, L.C. *Property Rights* (Routledge and Kegan Paul, London: 1977)

Bell, S. and D. McGillivray *Environmental Law* (Oxford, Oxford University Press: 2006)

Bender, P. and G. Lugten "Taxing Illegal Fishing (A Proposal for Using Taxation to Reduce Profiteering from IUU Fishing Offences)" (2007) 22 (4) *International Journal of Marine and Coastal Law* 517–544

Bensaler, F.P., P.M. Hejl and W.K. Kock (eds) *Autopoiesis, communication and Society: The Theory of Autopoietic Systems in the Social Sciences* (Campus Verlag, Frankfurt: 1980)

Bentham, J. "Principles of the Civil Code" in C.K. Ogden (ed.) *Jeremy Bentham: The Theory of Legislation* (Kegan Paul, London: 1931)

Birnie, P. and A. Boyle *International Law and the Environment* 2nd (Oxford University Press, Oxford: 2002)

Boczek "The Soviet Union and the Antarctic Regime" (1984) 78 *American Journal of International Law* 834–858

Briggs, A. *The Conflict of Laws* (Clarendon Press, Oxford: 2002)

Brilmayer, L. and N. Klein "Land and Sea: Two Sovereignty Regimes in Search of a Common Denominator" (2001) 33 *New York University Journal of International Law and Politics* 703–768

Brownlie, I. "Legal Status of Natural Resources" (1979-I) 162 *Recueil des Cours* 245–318

Brownlie, I. *Principles of Public International Law* 6th ed. (Oxford University Press, Oxford: 1998)

Burke, W.T. *The New International Law of Fisheries: UNCLOS 1982 and Beyond* (Clarendon Press, Oxford: 1994)

Butterworth, D.S. and A.J. Penney "Allocation in high seas fisheries: avoiding meltdown" in A. Payne, C. O'Brien and S. Rogers (eds) *Management of Shared Fish Stocks* (Blackwell Publishing Ltd, Oxford: 2003) 165–189

Buzan, B. "Negotiating by Consensus: developments in technique at the United Nations Conference on the Law of the Sea" (1981) 75 *American Journal of International Law* 324–348

Caron, D.D. and H.N. Scheiber "Bringing New Law to Ocean Waters" in D.D. Caron and H.N. Scheiber (eds) *Bringing New Law to Ocean Waters* (Martinus Nijhoff Publishers, Leiden/Boston: 2004) 3–14

Chinkin, C. *Third Parties in International Law* (Clarendon Press, Oxford: 1993)

Christie, D. "The Conservation and Management of Stocks Located Solely Within the Exclusive Economic Zone" in E. Hey (ed.) *Developments in International Fisheries Law* (Kluwer Law, The Hague: 1999)

Christman, J. *The Myth of Property* (Oxford University Press, New York: 1994)

Christy, F.T. and A. Scott *The Common Wealth in Ocean Fisheries* (John Hopkins Press, Baltimore: 1965)

Christy, F.T., Jr. "Fisheries Goals and the Rights of Property" (1969) 2 *Transactions of the American Fisheries Society* 369–378

Christy, F.T. "The Death Rattle of Open Access and the Advent of Property Rights Regimes in Fisheries" (1996) 11 *Marine Resource Economics* 287–304

Churchill, R.R. and A.V. Lowe *The Law of the Sea*, 3rd ed. (Manchester University Press, Manchester: 1999)

Churchill, R.R. "Levels of Implementation of the Law of the Sea Convention: An Overview" in D. Vidas and W. Østreng (eds) *Order for the Oceans at the Turn of the Century* (Kluwer Law International, The Hague/London/Boston: 1999) 317–323

Churchill, R.R. and J. Scott "The Mox Plant Litigation: The First Half-Life" (2004) 53(3) *International and Comparative Law Quarterly* 643–676

Connor, R. "Trends in Fishing Capacity and Aggregation of Fishing Rights in New Zealand Under Individual Transferable Quota" in Shotton, R. (ed.) *Use of Property Rights in Fisheries Management* (FAO, Rome: 2000)

Copes, P. "A Critical Review of Individual Quotas as a Device in Fisheries Management" (1986) 62 *Land Economics* 278–291

Crothers, G.T. and L. Nelson "High Seas Fisheries Governance: A Framework for the Future?" (2006) 21 *Marine Resource Economics* 341–354

Crowley, B.L. (ed.) *Taking Ownership. Property Rights and Fishery Management on the Atlantic Coast* (AIMS, Halifax: 1996)

Crowley, R.W. and H. Palsson "Rights based fisheries management in Canada" (1992) 7 *Marine Resource Economics* 1–21

Crutzen, P.J. and E.F. Stoermer "The 'Anthropocene'" (2000) *Global Change Newsletter* 41: 17–18

Cunningham, S. "The Increasing Importance of Economics in Fisheries Regulation" (1983) 34 *Journal of Agricultural Economics* 69–78

Curran, P. and R. Long "Fishery Law, Unilateral Enforcement in International Waters: the case of the Estai" (1996) 5(2) *Irish Journal of European Law* 123–163

D'Amato, A. "International Law as an Autopoietic System" in R. Wolfrum and V. Röben (eds) *Developments of International Law in Treaty Making* (Springer: 2005) 335–399

Davidson, J.S. "The Rights of Indigenous Peoples in Early International Law" (1994) 5 *Canterbury Law Review* 391–423

Davies, P.G.G. and C. Redgwell "The International Regulation of Straddling Fish Stocks" (1996) 67 *British Yearbook of International Law* 199–274

de Klemm, C. and C. Shine *Biological Diversity Conservation and the Law: Legal Mechanisms for Conserving Species and Ecosystems* (IUCN, Gland: 1993)

de La Fayette, L.A. "The London Convention 1972: Preparing for the Future" (1998) 13(4) *International Journal of Marine and Coastal Law* 515–536

de La Fayette, L. "The OSPAR Convention Comes into Force: Continuity and Progress" (1999) 14 *International Journal of Marine and Coastal Law* 247–297

de La Fayette, L.A. "A New Regime for the Conservation and Sustainable Use of Marine Biodiversity and Genetic Resources beyond the Limits of National Jurisdiction", 24 (2009) *International Journal of Marine and Coastal Law* pp. 221–280

de Lone, E. "Improving the Management of the Atlantic Tuna: The Duty to Strengthen the ICCAT in Light of the 1995 Straddling Stocks Agreement" (1998) 6 *New York University Environmental Law Journal* 656–673

Demetz, H. "Toward a Theory of Property Rights" (1967) 57 (2) *American Economic Review* 347–359

de Vattel, E. *Le Droit des Gens* (1758) trans. Fenwick (Clarendon Press, Oxford: 1916)

Devine, D.J. "Provisional measures ordered by the International Tribunal for the Law of the Sea in the Area of Pollution, the Mox Plant Case (Ireland v. United

Kingdom) ITLOS Case No 10, 3 December 2001" (2003) 28 *South African Yearbook of International Law* 263–275

de Vitoria, F. *De Indis et de Iure Belli Relectiones* (1557) trans. E. Nys (Carnegie Institute, Washington: 1917)

Dolman, A.J. "The Common Heritage of Mankind and Global Reform" in A.J. Dolman (ed) *Resources, Regimes, World Order* (Pergamon Press, New York: 1981)

Dross, M. and F. Wolff "Do We Need a New Access and Benefit sharing Instrument?" (2004) 15 *Yearbook of International Environmental Law* 95–118

Dupuy, R.J. "The Area as the Common Heritage of Mankind" in R.J. Dupuy and D. Vignes (ed.) *A Handbook on the New Law of the Sea* (Martinus Nijhoff Publishers, Dordrecht: 1991)

Ederington, L.B. "Property as a Natural Institution. The Separation of Property from Sovereignty in International Law" (1997) 13 *American University International Law Review* 263–332

Fabra, A. and V. Gascón "The Convention on the Conservation of Antarctic Marine Living Resources (CCAMLR) and the Ecosystem Approach" (2008) 23 *International Journal of Marine and Coastal Law* 567–598

Falloon, R. (with the assistance of T.M. Berthold) "Individual Transferable Quotas: the New Zealand Case" in OECD *The Use of Individual Quotas in Fisheries Management* (OECD, Paris: 1993) 43–62

Fitzgerald, P.J. *Salmond on Jurisprudence* (Sweet and Maxwell, London: 1966)

Frakes, J. "The Common Heritage of Mankind Principle and the Deep Seabed, Outer Space, and Antarctica: Will Developed and Developing Nations Reach a Compromise?" (2003) 21 *Wisconsin International Law Journal* 409–434

Francioni, F. "Genetic Resources, Biotechnology and Human Rights: The International Legal Framework" in F. Francioni (ed.) *Biotechnologies and International Human Rights* (Oxford: 2007)

Franck, T.M. *Fairness in International Law and Institutions* (Clarendon, Oxford: 1995)

Franckx, E. *Pacta Tertiis and the Agreement for the Implementation of the Provisions of the United Nations Convention on the Law of the Sea of 10 December 1982 relating to the Conservation & Management of Straddling Fish Stocks and Highly Migratory Fish Stocks* (FAO Legal Papers Online #8, Rome: July 2000)

Freestone, D. "Canada and the EU Reach Agreement to Settle the *Estai* Dispute" (1995) 10 *International Journal of Marine and Coastal Law* 397–411

Freestone, D. and Z. Makuch "The New International Environmental Law of Fisheries: The 1995 United Nations Straddling Stocks Agreement" (1996) 7 *Yearbook of International Environmental Law* 3–51

Freestone, D. and A.G. Oude Elferink "Flexibility and Innovation in the Law of the Sea: Will the LOS Convention Amendment Procedures Ever be Used?" in A.G. Oude Elferink (ed.) *Stabilty and Change in the Law of the Sea: the Role of the LOS Convention* (Martinus Nijhoff, Leiden/Boston: 2005) 169–221

Freestone, D., K.M. Gjerde, R. Rayfuse and D. VanderZwaag, "Workshop on High Seas Governance for the 21st Century" (2008) 23 *International Journal of Marine & Coastal Law* 359–363

Freestone, D. "Modern Principles of High Seas Governance—The Legal Underpinnings" (2009) 39 (1) *Environmental Policy and Law* 44–49

Gianni, M. and W. Simpson "The Changing Nature of High Seas Fishing: How Flags of Convenience Provide Cover for Illegal, Unreported and Unregulated Fishing" (Aus-

tralian Department of Agriculture Fisheries and Forestry, International Transport Worker's Federation and WWF International: 2005)
Gillespie, A. *International Environmental Law, Policy and Ethics* (Oxford University Press, Oxford: 1997)
Gissurarson, H.H. *Overfishing: The Icelandic Solution* (IEA, London: 2000)
Gjerde, K. "High Seas Fisheries Management under the LOSC" in D. Freestone, R. Barnes and D. Ong (eds) *Law of the Sea. Progress and Prospects* (Oxford University Press, Oxford: 2006)
Gjerde, K. *et al. An Analysis of the Regulatory and Governance Gaps in the International Regime for the Conservation and Sustainable Use of Marine Biodiversity in Areas beyond National Jurisdiction* IUCN Marine Law and Policy Paper No 1 (IUCN, Gland: 2008)
Gjerde K. *et al. Options for Addressing Regulatory and Governance Gaps in the International Regime for the Conservation and Sustainable Use of Marine Biodiversity in Areas beyond National Jurisdiction* IUCN Marine Law and Policy Paper No 2 (IUCN, Gland: 2008)
Glowka, L. "The Deepest of Ironies: Genetic Resources, Marine Scientific Research and the International Deep Sea-bed Area" (1996) 12 *Ocean Yearbook* 154–178
Goldie, L.F.E. "A General International Law Doctrine for Seabed Regimes" (1973) 7 *International Lawyer* 796–824
Goldie, L.F.E. "Title and Use (Usufruct)—An Ancient Distinction Oft Forgot" (1985) 79 *American Journal of International Law* 689–714
Gordon, H.S. "The Economic Theory of a Common Property Resource: The Fishery" (1954) 62 *Journal of Political Economy* 124–142
Gray, K. "Property in Thin Air" (1991) 50 *Cambridge Law Journal* 252–307
Grotius, H. *Mare Liberum* (1608) trans. R.V.D. Magoffin (Oxford University Press, Oxford: 1916)
Grotius, H. *De Jure Belli ac Pacis Libri Tres* (1625) trans. F.W. Kelsey (Oxford University Press, Oxford: 1925)
Guggenheim, P. *Traité de Droit International Public* (Georg, Geneva: 1954)
Gulland, J. "Letter to the editor: How much of the world's fisheries lies within EEZs?" (1984) 8 *Marine Policy* 359
Gulland, J.A. "The Antarctic Treaty system as a resource management mechanism" in G.D. Triggs (ed.) *The Antarctic Treaty Regime. Law Environment and Resources* (Cambridge University Press, Cambridge: 1987)
Guntrip, E. "The Common Heritage of Mankind: An Adequate Regime for Managing the Deep Seabed?" (2003) 4 *Melbourne Journal of International Law* 376–405
Hackworth, G.H. 1 *Digest of International Law* (U.S. Government Printing Office, Washington, D.C.: 1927)
Hannesian, J. "The Antarctic Treaty 1959" (1960) 9 *International and Comparative Law Quarterly* 436–480
Hannesson, R. *The Privatization of the Oceans* (MIT Press, Cambridge, Mass: 2004)
Hardin, G. "Tragedy of the Commons" (1968) 162 *Science* 1243–1248
Hatcher, A. *et al.* "Future Options for UK Fish Quota Management" (University of Portsmouth, Portsmouth 1992)
Hayashi, M. "The 1995 Agreement on the conservation and management of straddling and highly migratory fish stocks: significance for the Law of the Sea Convention" (1995) 29 *Ocean and Coastal Management* 51–69

Hayashi, M. "Three Decades' Progress in High Seas Fisheries Governance: Towards a Common Heritage Regime?" in M.H. Nordquist, J. Norton Moore and S. Mahmoudi (eds) *The Stockholm Declaration and Law of the Marine Environment* (Martinus Nijhoff Publishers, The Hague, London and New York: 2003) 375–398

Hayes, M.F. "Charismatic Microfauna: Marine Genetic Resources and the Law of the Sea" in M.H. Nordquist, R. Long, T.H. Heidar, J.N. Moore (eds) *Law, Science and Ocean Management* (M. Nijhoff, Leiden/Boston: 2007) 683–700

Hayton, R.D. "The Antarctic Settlement of 1959" (1960) 54 *American Journal of International Law* 349–371

Heintschel von Heinegg, W. "The Development of Environmental Standards for the North-East Atlantic, including the North Sea" in E. Mann-Borgese and R. Wolfrum (eds) *Marine Issues* (Kluwer Law International, The Hague: 2002) 35–153

Henriksen, T., G. Hønneland and A. Sydnes *Law and Politics in Ocean Governance. The UN Fish Stocks Agreement and Regional Fisheries Management Regimes* (Martinus Nijhoff, Leiden: 2005)

Hey, E., T. IJlstra and A. Nollkaemper "The 1992 Paris Convention for the Protection of the Marine Environment of the North-East Atlantic: A Critical Analysis" (1993) 8 *International Journal of Marine and Coastal Law* 1–76

High Seas Task Force *Closing the Net: Stopping Illegal Fishing on the High Seas* (Sadag SA, Bellegarde: 2006) 105–109 (available at ⟨http://www.high-seas.org⟩)

Hobbes, T. *Leviathan* J.C.A. Gaskin (ed.) (OUP, New York: 1996)

Hoel, A.H. and I. Kvalvik "The allocation of scarce natural resources: The case of fisheries" (2006) 30 *Marine Policy* 347–356

Honoré, A.M. "Ownership" in A.G. Guest (ed.) *Oxford Essays in Jurisprudence* (Oxford University Press, London: 1961)

Howard, M. "The Convention on the Conservation of Antarctic Marine Living Resources: A Five-Year Review" (1989) 38 *International and Comparative Law Quarterly* 104–150

Hume, D. *Treatise of Human Nature* (ed.) Selby-Bigge (Clarendon Press, Oxford: 1955)

Jennings, R.Y. *The Acquisition of Territory in International Law* (Manchester University Press, Manchester: 1963)

Joyner, C.J. and E.R. Theis "The United States and Antarctica: Rethinking the Interplay of Law and Interests" (1987) *Cornell International Law Journal* 65–102

Joyner, C. and A. von Gustedt "The Turbot War of 1995: Lessons for the Law of the Sea" (1996) 11 *International Journal of Marine and Coastal Law* 425–458

Kaitala, V. and G.R. Munro "The Management of High Seas Fisheries" (1993) 8 *Marine Resource Economics* 313–329

Kasoulides, G.C. *Port State Control and Jurisdiction: Evolution of the Port States Regime* (Martinus Nijhoff Publishers, Dordrecht: 1993)

Kearney, R.E. "Fisheries Property Rights and Recreational/Commercial Conflict: The Implications of Policy Development in Australia and New Zealand" (2001) 25 *Marine Policy* 49–59

Kedziora, D.M. "Gunboat Diplomacy in the Northwest Atlantic: The 1995 Canada-EU Fishing Dispute and the United Nations Agreement on Straddling and Highly Migratory Fish Stocks" (1996–1997) 17 *Northwestern Journal of International Law and Business* 1132–1162

Klein, E. *Staatsvertäge im Völkerrecht* (Springer, Berlin: 1980)

Koers, A.W. *International Regulation of Marine Fisheries: A Study of Regional Fisheries Organizations* (Fishing News Books Ltd, West Byfleet and London: 1973) 253–258

Koh, T. "A Constitution for the Oceans" *The Law of the Sea—Official Text of the United Nations Convention on the Law of the Sea with Annexes and Index* (United Nations, New York: 1983)

König, D. "Genetic Resources of the Deep Sea—How Can They Be Preserved?" in D. König, P.T. Stoll, V. Röben and N. Matz-Lück (eds) *International Law Today: New Challenges and the Need for Reform?* (Springer, Berlin: 2008) 141–163

Knight, H.G. *Managing the Sea's Living Resources: Legal and Political Aspects of High Seas Fisheries* (Lexington Books, Lexington MA and Toronto: 1977)

Kunz, J. "Austria's Permanent Neutrality" (1956) 50 *American Journal of International Law* 418–425

Kwiatkowska, B. "The Ireland v. United Kingdom (Mox Plant) Case: Applying the Doctrine of Treaty Parallelism" (2003) 18(1) *The International Journal of Marine and Coastal Law* 1–58

Lack, M. "Catching on? Trade-related measures as a fisheries management tool" (Traffic International, Cambridge: 2007) (available at ⟨www.traffic.org⟩)

Lagoni, R. "Monitoring, Compliance and Enforcement of Compliance Through the OSPAR Commission" in *Marine Issues* (E. Mann-Borgese and R. Wolfrum ed., Kluwer Law International, The Hague: 2002) 155–163

Lansing, R. "A Unique International Problem" (1917) 11 *American Journal of International Law* 763–771

Lauterpacht, H. *Private Law Sources and Analogies of International Law* (Longmans, Green & Co, London: 1927)

Lauterpacht, H. *Oppenheim's International Law* 6th ed. (Longmans, London: 1947)

Lauterpacht, H. *Oppenheim's International Law* 8th ed. (Longman, Green & Co., London: 1955)

Leary, D.K. *International Law and Genetic Resources of the Deep Sea* (Martinus Nijhoff, Leiden: 2006)

Leary, D.K. "Bioprospecting and the Genetic Resources of Hydrothermal Vents on the High Seas: What is the Existing Legal Position, Where are we Heading and What are our Options?" (2004) 1 *Maquairie Journal of Comparative and Environmental Law* 137–178

Lindley, M.F. *The Acquisition and Government of Backward Territory in International Law* (Longmans, Green and Co., London: 1926)

Livingstone, I. *Between Science and Literature: An Introduction to Autopoietics* (University of Illinois Press, Illinois: 2006)

Locke, J. *Two Treatises of Government* (1690) P. Laslett (ed.) (Cambridge University Press, Cambridge: 1960)

Lodge, M.W. and S.N. Nandan "Some Suggestions Towards Better Implementation of the United Nations Agreement on Straddling Fish Stocks and Highly Migratory Fish Stocks of 1995" (2005) 20 *International Journal of Marine and Coastal Law* 345–380

Lugten, G. "The FAO Global Record of Fishing Vessels, Refrigerated Vessels and Fishing Support Vessels" (2008) 23(4) *International Journal of Marine and Coastal Law* 761–767

Luhmann, N. "The Coding of the Legal System" in G. Teubner and A. Febbrajo (eds) *State, Law and Economy as Autopoietic Systems: Regulation and Autonomy in a New Perspective* (Dott. A. Giuffrè Editore, Milan: 1992)

Luhmann, N. "The Autopoiesis of Social Systems" in F. Geyer and J. van der Zouwen (eds) *Sociocybernetics Complexity, Autopoiesis and Observation of Social Systems* (Greenwood Publishing Group, Westport: 2001)

Mann Borgese, E. "Introduction" in A. Pardo *The Common Heritage—Selected Papers on Oceans and World Order* (International Ocean Institute, Valletta: 1975)

Maturana, H.R., R. Uribe and F.J. Varela "Auotpoiesis: the organisation of living systems, its characterisation and a model" (1974) 5 *Biosystems* 187–196

Maturana, H.R. and F. Varela "Autopoiesis and Cognition: Realisation of the Living" in R.S. Cohen and M.W. Wartofsky (eds) *Boston Studies in the Philosophy of Science* (D. Reidel Publishing Co, Dordrecht: 1980)

McDougal, M.S., W.T. Burke and I.S. Vlasic "The Maintenance of Public Order at Sea and the Nationality of Ships" (1960) 59 *American Journal of International Law*

McDougal, M.S. and W.T. Burke *The Public Order of the Oceans: A Contemporary International Law of the Sea* (Brill Academic Publishers, Leiden/Boston: 1987)

McNair, A.C. *Law of Treaties* (Clarendon, Oxford: 1961)

Mgbeoji, I. "Beyond Rhetoric: State Sovereignty, Common Concern, and the Inapplicability of the Common Heritage Concept to Plant Genetic Resources" (2003) 16 *Leiden Journal of International Law* 821–837

Millicay, F. "A Legal Regime for the Biodiversity of the Area" in M.H. Nordquist, R. Long, T.H. Heidar, J.N. Moore (eds) *Law, Science and Ocean Management* (Martinus Nijhoff, Leiden/Boston: 2007) 739–850

Mingers J. *Self-Producing Systems: Implications and Applications of Autopoiesis* (Springer, Berlin: 1994)

Mitchell, R.B. "Compliance Theory: An Overview" in J. Cameron, J. Werksman and P. Roderick (eds) *Improving Compliance with International Environmental Law* (Earthscan, London: 1996) 5–6

Morgan, G.R. "Optimal fisheries quota allocation under a transferable quota management system" (1995) 19 *Marine Policy* 379–390

Molenaar, E.J. *Coastal State Jurisdiction over Vessel-Source Pollution* (Kluwer Law International, The Hague: 1998)

Molenaar, E.J. "The Concept of 'Real Interest' and Other Aspects of Co-operation through Regional Fisheries Management Mechanisms" (2000) 15 *International Journal of Marine and Coastal Law* 475–532

Molenaar, E.J. "Participation, Allocation and Unregulated Fishing: The Practice of Regional Fisheries Management Organisations" (2003) 18 (4) *International Journal of Marine and Coastal Law* 457–480

Molenaar, E.J. "Addressing Regulatory Gaps in High Seas Fisheries" (2005) 20(3–4) *International Journal of Marine and Coastal Law* 533–570

Molenaar, E.J. "Managing Biodiversity in Areas Beyond National Jurisdiction" (2007) 22(1) *International Journal of Marine and Coastal Law* 89–124

Molenaar, E.J. "Managing Biodiversity in Areas Beyond National Jurisdiction" in M.H. Nordquist, R. Long, T.H. Heidar, J.N. Moore (eds) *Law, Science and Ocean Management* (Martinus Nijhoff, Leiden/Boston: 2007) 625–681

Molenaar, E.J. "Port State Jurisdiction: Towards Comprehensive, Mandatory and Global Coverage" (2007) 38 *Ocean Development and International Law* 225–257

Moore, J.B. *A Digest of International Law* vol. 1 (Government printing, Washington: 1906)

Mosler, H. "The International Society as a Legal Community" (1974-IV) 150 *Recueil des Cours* 11

Mouton, M.W. "The International Regime of the Polar Regions" (1962-III) 107 *Recueil des Cours* 174

Munro, G., A. van Houtte and R. Willmann "The Conservation and Management of Shared Fish Stocks: Legal and Economic Aspects" (2004) 465 *FAO Fisheries Technical Paper*

Munzer, S. *A Theory of Property* (Cambridge University Press, New York: 1990)

Muse, B. and K. Schelle *Individual Fishermen's Quotas: A Preliminary Review of Some Recent Programs* (CFEC, Alaska: 1989).

Nadelson, R. "After Mox: The Contemporary Shipment of Radioactive Substances in the Law of the Sea" (2000) 15(2) *The International Journal of Marine and Coastal Law* 193–244

Nandan, S. *The successes of the United Nations Convention on the Law of the Sea and some Future Challenges* (October 17–18, 2008, ABLOS Conference, Monaco)

National Research Council *Sharing the Fish. Towards a National Policy on Individual Fishing Quotas* (National Academy Press, Washington: 1999)

Nellemann, C., S. Hain and J. Alder (eds) *In Dead Water—Merging of Climate Change with Pollution, Over-Harvest, and Infestations on the World's Fishing Grounds* (United Nations Environmental Programme, GRID-Arendal, Norway: 2008)

Nelson, L.D.M. "The New Deep Sea-Bed Mining Regime" (1995) 10 *International Journal of Marine and Coastal Law* 189–203

Nielsen, F.K. "The Solution of the Spitsbergen Question" (1920) 14 *American Journal of International Law* 232–235

Oda, S. *International Control of Sea Resources* (A.W. Sijthoff, Leiden: 1963)

Oda, S. "Distribution of Fish Resources of the High Seas: Free Competition or Artificial Quota?" in L.M. Alexander (ed.) *The Law of the Sea: The Future of the Sea's Resources: Proceedings of the Second Annual Conference of the Law of the Sea Institute* (University of Rhode Island, Kingston: 1968)

Oda, S. "Fisheries under the United Nations Convention on the Law of the Sea" (1983) 77 *AJIL* 739–755

OECD *Towards Sustainable Fisheries: Economic Aspects of the Management of Living Resources* (OECD, Paris: 1997)

Orrego Vicuña, F. *Antarctic mineral exploitation. The emerging legal framework* (Cambridge University Press, Cambridge: 1988)

Orrego Vicuña, F. *The Changing International Law of High Seas Fisheries*, (Cambridge University Press, Cambridge: 1999)

Ostrom, E., R. Gardner and J. Walker *Rules, Games and Common-Pool Resources* (University of Michigan Press, Ann Arbor: 1994)

Oude Elferink, A.G. (ed) *Stability and Change in the Law of the Sea: The Role of the LOS Convention* (Martinus Nijhoff Publishers, Leiden: 2005)

Oude Elferink, A.G. "The Regime of the Area: Delineating the Scope of Application of the Common Heritage Principle and Freedom of the High Seas" (2007) 22 *International Journal of Marine and Coastal Law* 143–176

Oxman, B. "Law of the Sea Forum: The 1994 Agreement on the Implementation of the Seabed Provisions of the Convention on the Law of the Sea. The 1994 Agreement and the Convention" (1994) 88 *American Journal of International Law* 687–696

Oxman, B.H. "Tools for Change: the Amendment Procedure" in *Proceedings of the Twentieth Anniversary Commemoration of the Opening for Signature of the United Nations Convention on the Law of the Sea, New York, 9 and 10 December 2002* (United Nations, New York: 2003) 195–207

Pardo, A. *The Common Heritage—Selected Papers on Oceans and World Order* (International Ocean Institute, Valletta: 1975)

Pearse, P.H. "Fishing rights, regulations and revenues" (1981) 15 *Marine Policy* 135–146

Pearse, P.H. "From Open Access to Private Property: Recent Innovations in Fishing Rights as Instruments of Fisheries Policy" (1992) 23 *Ocean Development and International Law* 71–83

Penner, J. *The Idea of Property in Law* (Clarendon Press, Oxford: 1997)

Pinto, M.C.W. "'Common Heritage of Mankind': From Metaphor to Myth, and the Consequences of Constructive Ambiguity" in J. Makarczyk (ed.) *Theory of International Law at the Threshold of the 21st Century* (Kluwer, The Hague *et al.*: 1999) 249–268

Pinto, D. *et. al.* "Summary of the Eighth Round of Informal Consultations of States Parties to the United Nations Fish Stocks Agreement (ICSP-8): 16 to 19 March 2009" (2009) 7 *Earth Negotiations Bulletin of the International Institute for Sustainable Development* No. 64

Pontecorvo, G. "The economics of the resources of Antarctica" in J.I. Charney (ed.) *The New Nationalism and Use of Common Spaces* (ASIL, Allanheld Osmun: 1982) 155–166

Pontecorvo, G. "The Enclosure of the Marine Commons: Adjustment and Redistribution in World Fisheries" (1988) 12 *Marine Policy* 361–372

Post, H.H.G. (ed.) *International Economic Law and Armed Conflict* (Martinus Nijhoff Publishers, Dordrecht: 1994)

Proelss, A. "Marine Genetic Resources under UNCLOS and the CBD" (2009) 51 *German Yearbook of International Law* 417–446

Puffendorf, S. *De Jure Naturae et Gentium Libri Octo* (1688) trans. Oldfather (Clarendon Press, Oxford: 1934)

Quentin Grafton, R. *et al.* "The Economics of Allocation in Tuna Regional Fisheries Management Organisations" (2006) *ANU Economics and Environment Network Working Paper* EEN0612

Rayfuse, R. *Non-Flag State Enforcement in High Seas Fisheries* (Martinus Nijhoff Publishers, Leiden/Boston: 2004) 24–38

Rayfuse, R. "To Our Children's Children's Children: From Promoting to Achieving Compliance in High Seas Fisheries" (2005) 20 (3–4) *International Journal of Marine and Coastal Law* 509–532

Rayfuse, R. "Regional Allocation Issues or Zen and the Art of Pie Cutting" (2007) *University of New South Wales Faculty of Law Research Paper Series* 10

Rayfuse, R. and R. Warner "Securing a Sustainable Future for the Oceans Beyond National Jurisdiction: The Legal Basis for an Integrated Cross-Sectoral Regime for High Seas Governance for the 21st Century" (2008) 23(3) *International Journal of Marine and Coastal Law* 399–422

Rayfuse, R. "Non-Flag State Enforcement and Protection of the Marine Environment: Responding to IUU Fishing" in M.H. Nordquist, T.T.B. Koh and J. Norton Moore (eds) *Freedom of Seas, Passage Rights and the 1982 Law of the Sea*

Convention (Martinus Nijhoff, Leiden Boston: 2009) 573–600

Redgwell, C. *Intergenerational trusts and environmental protection* (Manchester University Press, Manchester: 1999)

Redgwell, C. "Protection of Ecosystems under International Law: Lessons from Antarctica" in A. Boyle and D. Freestone (eds) *International Law and Sustainable Development* (Oxford University Press, Oxford: 1999) 205–224

Rich, R. "A Minerals Regime for Antarctica" (1982) 31 *International and Comparative Law Quarterly* 709–725

Robb, F.F. "Accounting—A Virtual Autopoietic System?" (1991) 4(3) *Systems Practice* 215–235

Roelofsen C.G. *Jan Hendrik Willem Verzijl 1888–1987* (T.M.C. Asser Instituut, The Hague: 1993)

Roheim, C. and J.G. Sutinen "Trade and Marketplace Measures to Promote Sustainable Fishing Practices" in ICTSD Natural Resources *International Trade and Sustainable Development Series Issue Paper No 3* (International Centre for Trade and Sustainable Development and the High Seas Task Force, Geneva: 2006)

Roheim, C. "Seafood Supply Chain Management: Methods to Prevent Illegally-Caught Product Entry into the Marketplace" (2008) Profish Law Enforcement, Corruption and Fisheries Work (available at www.illegal-fishing.info⟩)

Rose, C.M. *Property and Persuasion: Essays on the History, Theory and Rhetoric of Ownership* (Westview Press, Boulder: 1994)

Rousseau, J.-J. *The Social Contract and Discourse on the Origin of Inequality* L.G. Crocker (ed.) (Washington Square Press, New York: 1967)

Roxburgh, R. *International Conventions and Third States* (Longmans, Green & Co., London: 1917)

Saguirian, A.A. "Excision of the Deep Seabed Mining Provisions from the 1982 Law of the Convention: Reappraising the Principle of a Treaty's Integrity under the New Realities" in J.M. van Dyke, D. Zaelke and G. Hewison (eds) *Freedom of the Seas for the 21st Century* (Island Press, Washington: 1983) 375–387

Schachter, O. *Sharing the World's Resources* (Columbia University Press, New York: 1977)

Scheiber, H.N. "From Science to Law to Politics: An Historical View of the Ecosystem Idea and its Effect on Resource Management" (1997) 24 *Ecology Law Quarterly* 631–651

Schrijver, N. *Sovereignty over Natural Resources* (Cambridge University Press, Cambridge: 1997)

Scott, A.D. "The Fishery: The Objectives of Sole Ownership" (1955) 63 *Journal of Political Economy* 116–124

Scott, A.D. "Conceptual Origins of Rights Based Fishing" in P. Neher *et al.* (eds) *Right Based Fishing* (Kluwer, Dordrecht: 1988)

Scovazzi, T. The Evolution of International Law of the Sea: New Issues, New Challenges *Hague Academy of International Law*, 286 *Recueil des Cours* (2001) 39–52

Scovazzi, T. "Mining, Protection of the Environment, Scientific Research and Bioprospecting: Some Considerations on the Role of the International Sea-Bed Authority" (2004) 19 *International Journal of Marine and Coastal Law* 383–409

Serdy, A. "Trading of Fishery Commission Quota under International Law" (2007) 21 *Ocean Yearbook* 265–288

Shany, Y. "The first Mox Plant Award: the Need to Harmonise Competing Environmental Regimes and Dispute Settlement Procedures" (2004) 17(4) *Leiden Journal of International Law* 815–827

Sharp, B.M.H. "New Zealand's quota management system: The first ten years" (1999) 23 *Marine Policy* 177

Shotton, R. (ed.) *Use of Property Rights in Fisheries Management* (FAO, Rome: 2000)

Sinclair, I. *The Vienna Convention on the Law of Treaties*, 2nd ed. (Manchester University Press, Manchester, 1984)

Singer, J.W. "Sovereignty and Property" (1991) *Northwestern University Law Review* 1–56

Sissenwine, M.P. and J.E. Kirkley "Fishery management techniques: Practical aspects and limitations" (1982) 6 (1) *Marine Policy* 43–57

Snape, W.J. *Biodiversity and the Law* (Island Press, Washington: 1996)

Soons, A.H.A. (ed.) *International Arbitration: Past and Prospects* (Martinus Nijhoff Publishers, Dordrecht: 1990)

Steffen, W.L. *et al. Global Change and the Earth System: A Planet Under Pressure* (IGBP Global Change Series) (Springer-Verlag, Berlin/Heidelberg/New York: 2004)

Stewart, C. *Legislating for Property Rights in Fisheries* (FAO, Rome: 2004)

Subedi, S.P. "The Doctrine of Objective Regimes in International Law and the Competence of the United Nations to Impose Territorial or Peace Settlements on States" (1994) 37 *German Yearbook of International Law* 162–205

Tan, A. *Vessel Source Marine Pollution, The Law and Politics of International Regulation* (Cambridge University Press, Cambridge: 2006)

Tanaka, Y. "Zonal and Integrated Management Approaches to Ocean Governance: Reflections on a Dual Approach in International Law of the Sea" (2004) 19 *International Journal of Marine and Coastal Law* 483–514

Tanaka, M. "Lessons from the Protracted Mox Plant Dispute: A Proposed Protocol on Environmental Impact Assessment to the United Nations Convention on the Law of the Sea" (2004) 25(2) *Michigan Journal of International Law* 337–428

Teubner, G. (ed.) *Autopoietic Law: A New Approach to Law and Society* (European University Institute: 1987)

Teubner, G. *Law as an Autopoietic System* (Blackwell, Oxford: 1993)

Tladi, D. "Genetic Resources, Benefit Sharing, and the Law of the Sea: the Need for Clarity" (2007) 13 *Journal of International Maritime Law* 183–193

Treves, T. "Les lectures nationales de la convention de Montego Bay" in *Ministère de la Défense, Colloque "Droits maritimes et défense"* (Ecole militaire, Paris: 1996)

Treves, T. "Le role du droit international de l'environnement dans l'élaboration du droit interne de l'environnement: quelques réflexions" M. Prieur and C. Lambrecht (eds) *Les hommes et l'Environnement, Etudes en homage à Alexandre Kiss* (Frison Roche, Paris: 1998) 345–349

Treves, T. "The Settlement of Disputes According to the Straddling Stocks Agreement of 1995" in A. Boyle, D. Freestone (eds) *International Law and Sustainable Development* (Oxford University Press, Oxford: 1999) 252–269

Treves, T. "Flags of Convenience Before the Law of the Sea Tribunal" (2004–2005) 6 *San Diego International Law Journal* 179–189

Treves, T. "Fragmentation of International Law: The Judicial Perspective" (2007) 23 *Comunicazioni e Studi* 821–875

Treves, T. "Dispute-Settlement in the Law of the Sea: Disorder or System?" in M.G.

Kohen (ed.) *Promoting Justice, Human Rights and Conflicts Resolution through International Law, Liber Amicorum Lucius Caflisch* (Martinus Nijhoff, Leiden: 2007) 927–949
Triggs, G.D. "The Antarctic Treaty System: some jurisdictional problems" in G.D. Triggs (ed.) *The Antarctic Treaty Regime. Law Environment and Resources* (Cambridge University Press, Cambridge: 1987)
Tsuru, Y. "Rethinking the Principle of Abstention: The North Pacific and Beyond" (2004) 28 *Marine Policy* 541–552
Tuerk, H. "The Contribution of the International Tribunal for the Law of the Sea to International Law" (2007) 26(2) *Penn State International Law Review* 289–316
Turner, R.K. *et al.* "Valuing Nature: Lessons Learned and Future Directions" (2003) 46 *Ecological Economics* 493–510
Underkuffler, L. *The Idea of Property: Its Meaning and Power* (Oxford University Press, Oxford: 2003)
Van Krieken, R. "From *Milirrpum* to *Mabo*: The High Court, *Terra nullius* and Moral Entrepreneurship" (2000) 23 *University of New South Wales Law Journal* 63–77
Varela, F., H. Maturana and R. Uribe (1974) "Autopoiesis: the Organization of Living systems, Its Characterization and a Model" 5 *Biosystems* 187–196
Vascianne, S. "Part XI of the Law of the Sea Convention and Third States: Some General Observations" (1989) 48 *Cambridge Law Review* 85–97
Waldron, J. *The Right to Private Property* (Clarendon Press, Oxford: 1990)
Watts, A.D. "Antarctic Mineral Resources: Negotiations for a Mineral Resources Regime" in G.D. Triggs (ed.) *The Antarctic Treaty Regime. Law Environment and Resources* (Cambridge University Press, Cambridge: 1987)
Watts, A.D. *International Law and the Antarctic Treaty System* (Grotius, Cambridge: 1992)
Weiler, J. "The White Paper and the Application of Community Law" in R. Bieder, R. Dehousse, J. Pinder and J. Weiler (eds) *1992: One European Market?* (Nomos Verlagsgesellschaft, Baden-Baden: 1988)
Wesney, D. "Applied Fisheries Management Plans: Individual Transferable Quotas and Input Control" in P. Neher *et al.* (eds) *Right Based Fishing* (Kluwer, Dordrecht: 1988)
Westlake, J. *Chapters on the Principles of International Law* (Cambridge University Press, Cambridge: 1894)
Wolff, C. *Jus Gentium Methodo Scientifica Pertractatum* trans. Drake (Clarendon Press, Oxford: 1934)
Wolfrum, R. "The Principle of the Common Heritage of Mankind" (1983) 43 *Heidelberg Journal of International Law* 312–337
Wolfrum, R. "Hohe See und Tiefseeboden" in Wolfgang Graf Vitzthum (ed.) *Handbuch des Seerechts* (C.H. Beck, München: 2006) 287–345
Wolfrum, R. and N. Matz "The Interplay of the United Nations Convention on the Law of the Sea and the Convention on Biological Diversity" (2000) *Max-Planck Yearbook of United Nations Law* 445–480
Wolfrum, R. and N. Matz, *Conflicts in International Environmental Law* (Springer, Berlin: 2003)
Worm, B. *et al.* "Impacts of Biodiversity Loss on Ocean Ecosystem Services" (2006) 314(5800) *Science* 787–790
Zeleny, M. (ed.) *Autopoiesis: A Theory of Living Organisation* (Elsevier, New York: 1981)

INDEX

Alex G. Oude Elferink and Erik J. Molenaar (eds.), *The International Legal Regime of Areas beyond National Jurisdiction: Current and Future Developments*, pp. 245–251.

www.ingramcontent.com/pod-product-compliance
Lightning Source LLC
LaVergne TN
LVHW012051011026
849162LV00017B/133